Cognitive Psychology
in Question

Cognitive Psychology in Question

Editors

ALAN COSTALL
Lecturer in Psychology
University of Southampton

ARTHUR STILL
Senior Lecturer in Psychology
University of Durham

ST. MARTIN'S PRESS
New York

First published in the United States of America in 1987

Printed in Great Britain

ISBN 0-312-00378-1

Library of Congress Cataloging in Publication Data

Cognitive psychology in question.

Includes bibliographies and index.
1. Cognition—Philosophy. I. Costall, Alan.
II. Still, Arthur. (DNLM: 1. Cognition. 2. Psychology.
BF 311 C67843)
BF311.C55185   1987   153   86-24877
ISBN 0-312-00378-1

600 85476

Contents

List of Contributors

NEIL BOLTON Division and Institute of Education, Sheffield University, England.

ALAN COSTALL Department of Psychology, University of Southampton, England.

HUBERT DREYFUS Department of Philosophy, University of California, Berkeley, USA.

STUART DREYFUS Department of Mathematics, University of California, Berkeley, USA.

MICHAEL GHISELIN Department of Invertebrate Zoology, California Academy of Sciences, California, USA.

STUART KATZ Department of Psychology, University of Georgia, Georgia, USA.

IVANA MARKOVÁ Department of Psychology, University of Stirling, Scotland.

DON MIXON Department of Psychology, University of Wollongong, New South Wales, Australia.

WILLIAM NOBLE Department of Psychology, University of New England, Armidale, New South Wales, Australia.

ANTHONY PALMER Department of Philosophy, University of Southampton, England.

EDWARD S. REED Department of Humanities and Communications, Drexel University, Pennsylvania, USA.

JOHN SHOTTER Department of Psychology, University of Nottingham, England.

NOEL W. SMITH Department of Psychology, State University of New York, Plattsburg, New York, USA.

ARTHUR STILL Department of Psychology, University of Durham, England.

Acknowledgements

It has been a pleasure working with the contributors to this volume, and we appreciate their support and suggestions. We would also like to acknowledge the encouragement and help of George Butterworth, Jim Good, Ann Richards, and the many students whose interest has helped keep alive our own.

An earlier version of Chapter 2 was read at a conference sponsored by the Society for Philosophy and Technology in New York, September 1983. It is reprinted with the permission of their journal, *Research in Philosophy and Technology*.

Chapter 5 is based, in part, on material published in S. Torrance (ed.), *The Mind and the Machine: Philosophical aspects of Artificial Intelligence* (Chichester, Sussex: Ellis Horwood, 1985). We are grateful to Stephen Torrance and Ellis Horwood for their permission to use this material.

1

Introduction:
In Place of Cognitivism

Arthur Still and Alan Costall

Cognitivism draws upon the imagery of political struggle to explain its origins. 'A revolution', we are told, 'occurred in the 1950s which might crudely be summarized as the overthrow of Behaviourism by Information Processing' (Johnson-Laird and Wason, 1977, p. ix). As a scientific movement, it is hardly unique in this kind of talk. However, setting aside the question of whether this overthrow was quite as heroic and radical as we have been led to believe, cognitivism does pose a curious puzzle. For cognitivists still manage to present themselves as the *avant-garde* a quarter of a century after their celebrated victory, and at a stage when even some in their number have noticed that theirs is now the 'establishment view' (Fodor and Pylyshyn, 1981). This continued posture as a radical movement is beginning to seem forced and unconvincing. The revolution has become complacent and restrictive.

It is not that cognitivism fails to acknowledge at least some of its many fundamental problems. Its complacency derives, rather, from the conviction that its was *the* revolution—the one to end all others. Repeatedly we are assured that 'it's the only game in town', the only alternative to the old regime: *anything* must be better than behaviourism, and *nothing* could be better than cognitivism. Behaviourism (despite its existence) continues to be reinvented by cognitivism to sustain its own curious status as a revolutionary orthodoxy. Dissenters, no matter how original their views, are persistently dismissed as unreformed reactionaries, behaviourists who 'do not seem to have realised that [the revolution] has occurred' (Johnson-Laird and Wason, 1977, p. ix).

1

But why do we claim that cognitivism is restrictive, as well as complacent? What objection could we have to a research programme devoted to the study of human knowledge and representational practices? Well none, unless such a programme were mistaken for the entire domain of psychological inquiry. However, as many before us have insisted (e.g. Atherton, 1978; Lundh, 1983; Monk, 1978; de Gelder, 1985), a distinction must be made between cognitivism as a field of research (i.e. the psychology *of* cognition) and cognitivism as a dogma: the presumption that all psychological explanation must be framed in terms of internal, mental representations, and processes (or rules) by which these representations are manipulated and transformed. It is this dogma which our book seeks to disturb, by means of criticism, and also, more positively, by the presentation and discussion of real alternatives.

It would not surprise us if psychologists were to find the following chapters too diverse in style and content to be gathered together in a single volume. Certainly they appear to range widely, and one might be hard-pressed to discover even a chain of family resemblances, let alone a common, defining property, to link the four sections. Is any resemblance merely in the name anti-cognitivism, the whole collection just a pile of bricks to hurl at the Establishment? Can we afford nowadays to take such risks with the good name of academic psychology?

Not only would we not be surprised by such questions, we would be disappointed to find psychologists detecting too easily a positive common theme, as though this were a book on dreams, or the amygdala. For although we believe there *is* a theme which holds the chapters together quite tightly, it is one that has been obscured and scattered by the rise of cognitivism. One purpose of the book is to bring this theme to light again, and its relative concealment is the assumption upon which we began; our efforts would be superfluous if it were already so familiar to our readers, that the coherence of the chapters turned out to be obvious.

To claim that there exists a theme does not mean we can demonstrate a common property or set of family resemblances linking the chapters, at least at a superficial level. They may resemble each other like members of a family, with different members being more or less similar in a host of different features, no one feature running through all the instances. But members of a *family* are connected by more than resemblance, since they belong together in the first place because of parentage, not likeness. They are, one might say, part of a common history, and it is history, not resemblance, that gives us a coherent theme for this book. The point we are making is similar to the one made by Ghiselin (Chapter 6) about classification in general, based on his earlier demonstrations that Darwinian species should be regarded, logically speaking, as individuals rather than classes (Ghiselin, 1974). Unlike classes, species are historical entities, with a beginning and an end, and over an evolutionary timescale they interact causally with environments and each other. As individuals (it is argued), they cannot be defined except ostensively. In particular, they cannot be defined in terms of some underlying essence or natural kind, nor in terms of resemblance; yet they are real entities, and not just held together by our habits of naming. Postulated traditions are less clearcut than species and more provisional, since the classification of traditions changes more rapidly with changes in intellectual fashion than classification of species. Nevertheless, since traditions are historical and evolving, it may be helpful to think of them also as individuals, rather than to search for defining characteristics. (Marková, discussing Hegel in Chapter 13, makes a similar point about universals.) But even if we do treat traditions as individuals, we are still bound to describe them in terms of characteristics, since such descriptions are the only means for ostensive definition. Just as with species, we cannot actually see the beginnings, the ramifications, the decline and eventual extinction of traditions, as though speeded up and played through in a matter of minutes, to enable us to point out the one of interest. To do this would require seeing as a whole all the discourses, those embodied in apparatus and practices, as well as those written and spoken, that make up the tradition. Like a grossly inadequate fossil record, we must make do with parts here and there, always mixed in with other traditions and subject to misinterpretation. Our chapters, therefore, touch on a few scattered parts, in the hope that they will define for the reader the shape of the whole to which they belong.

The theme, of which the chapters of this book form a very small part, is thus a tradition, and its coherence depends on what Danziger (1983) has referred to as a 'generative schema'. Adapting this idea for our own purposes, we suppose that over many years a number of writers, who may not be connected in any other obvious way, start from a common stock of assumptions which serve to distinguish them from other thinkers in the same field. The assumptions may not be dwelt upon in what they write, whose content can therefore vary widely, and share little in common save the underlying assumptions which have generated the family of theories.

ANTI-DUALISM

In the present case, one shared assumption is that the mind is not a substance distinct from matter, but nor is it merely matter complexly organised. Instead, mind can only be understood through its place in nature, conceived in Darwinian terms, though not as a useful appendage to an automaton. It is clear that most of the chapters are anti-dualist in this sense, although they do not make an issue of it, except for Chapters 11 and 12 on behaviourist theories, especially that by Smith on Kantor; and Chapter 5 by Palmer, who analyses cognitivist failures to evade the infinite regress of homunculi inherent in dualist theories that aim for completeness. Shelving intentionality by reducing it to *stupid* homunculi, fares no better than Descartes' attempt to evoke the pineal gland as *deus ex machina*.

At the turn of the century, traditional assumptions about the nature of mind and consciousness were subjected to a profound *questioning* led by Husserl and William James. The failure on the part of modern cognitive science to benefit from these anti-dualist critiques of consciousness by pragmatists and phenomenologists probably has many explanations but one of them concerns their usual scapegoat, behaviourism. For behaviourism was itself a part of the anti-dualist movement, and the part that managed for a time to establish itself as an institution within psychology. And part of this part, namely stimulus-response, mechanistic behaviourism, became the inadequate champion of the whole movement. This champion, and therefore the movement falsely identified with it, proved easy to overturn, and to replace with its metaphysical predecessor, dualism.

The shared name 'behaviourism' made it easy to blur the difference between mechanistic and non-mechanistic forms, and to ignore the powerful critique of dualism from which behaviourism stemmed. Important residues from this critique continued within behaviourism, and are discussed in Chapters 11 and 12. But even S-R versions remained avowedly anti-dualist, whatever they might have led to in practice (see Chapter 11). Since 'anti-dualism' is also a label which covers all mind-body identity theories, it includes too much that would not be endorsed by our writers, to qualify as a unifying assumption for the chapters of this book.

MUTUALISM

There is a more subtle shared assumption than anti-dualism, and it is one that comes to light when we try to *replace* the dualist ontology that is suggested by our language of mind and body. The mind, we may say, cannot be understood independently of its world, or the organism independently of its environment. These seem to be ways of expressing a form of anti-dualism, but they are ways that are apt to undermine themselves, since the use of distinct terms, such as 'organism' and 'environment', hint at the very separation the theory is concerned to deny. Dewey, Mead and more lately J.J. Gibson have been aware of this linguistic difficulty, and in grappling with it developed a set of ideas that may usefully be called 'mutualism'.

The tradition of mutualism has not been celebrated like that of laboratory psychology, whose chief chronicler, E.G. Boring, continues to determine the historical priorities, even of his critics. Thus William James, whose attempts to develop an alternative to dualism opened the way to mutualism, is treated in psychology textbooks as a somewhat diffuse thinker, worth reading more for his literary style than to extract a viewpoint that is of any relevance to us today. It is left to phenomenologists (Wild, 1970) and philosophers (Rorty, 1982) to recognise

James' importance as precursor of a non-dualist, non-reductionist psychology. Similarly Dewey often seems regarded as primarily a philosopher and educationalist rather than a psychologist, and his only contribution familiar to psychologists, the 1986 paper on 'The reflex arc concept in psychology', is apt to be interpreted in isolation as little more than a critique of simple-minded reflexology (e.g. Miller *et al*, 1960). But as part of a mutualist tradition it is clearly directed at *any* form of input-output mechanism as a suitable biological framework for psychology. Finally Mead has been an influence on sociology rather than psychology, although currently the details of his psychology are receiving attention (e.g. Lewis, 1981).

This theme or assumption of mutualism is one that appears in many chapters of the present book, especially in Katz's and other chapters in section IIA on Ecological Psychology, and in the chapters on Hegel, Tolman and Kantor (Chapter 12, by Smith) in the final section, IIB. It is implicit in Mixon's chapter on Dewey, as well as Bolton's on phenomenology, and is assumed, we would argue, in all the others. But there is a still deeper level of assumption from which these chapters are generated, deeper in that it assumes, but is not assumed by, mutualism. This deeper level concerns the problem of abstraction.

THE QUESTIONING OF ABSTRACTION

As long ago as 1971, Dreyfus traced the history of the search for the 'rules of thought', which began with Plato and which, so cognitivists might argue, has achieved its scientific legitimation in artificial intelligence and cognitive science. But AI claims to do more than lay down the rules of thought. It has extended its domain to perception and all skilled activity, and Longuet-Higgins has even proposed that it should be renamed 'theoretical psychology'. Thus, as cognitive science, psychology in general attempts to abstract rules in the form of 'effective procedures' (Johnson-Laird, 1983). In this way, as Shotter points out in Chapter 4, it has taken on the mantle of Taylorism, which attempted to reduce skills to rules, and whose success paved the way for replacing humans with machines. For it *is* successful, and so is AI, at abstracting from human activity to mechanical rules. And while we may lament the social and economic consequences, this is scarcely to impugn its scientific qualities. After all, physics abstracted laws from observed regularities against a chaotic background, and these laws were eventually harnessed to technology, and have effected remarkable changes in the conditions of life. Some have thought these changes undesirable, but no one would deny physics its success as science. Likewise, we may regret the unemployment and alienation that results from automation, but this regret itself bears witness to the success of the underlying science.

But is an *adequate psychology* part of that underlying science? Or have we taken certain routine activities that happen to be of great importance to the economic success of industrial societies, and then generalised to see these as representative of all human activity? Such routines involve operating machines, responding to meter readings, carrying out repetitive conveyor-belt tasks, etc. It is not difficult to see that these are mirrored in the apparatus of the traditional cognitive psychology laboratory. The assumption *here* is that the rather mechanical activities that go on in such laboratories are a valid abstraction from the world of everyday human activities, from walking to talking and the most specialised skills. This assumption is questioned directly in the chapters of the first section of the book. In Chapter 2, Dreyfus and Dreyfus argue that expertise does not involve classifying situations and then mechanically applying rules, but 'the capacity. . . to recognise tens of thousands of paradigmatic situations and to see the present situation as similar to one of these'. In Chapter 3 Mixon writes about Dewey's attempt to revive the traditional sense of 'habit' as 'manner of conducting oneself in the external relations of life', in order to reverse the tendency to reduce the *minutiae* of everyday activities to the mechanical exercise of a stimulus-response bond (or a TOTE unit; Miller *et al*, 1960). To do so is to abstract a mechanism from behaviour, and to ignore the extent to which 'habits' (of posture, speech, etc.) determine character, rather than the other way round. In Chapter 6, Ghiselin points out that classification is itself an act of abstraction that demands to be understood in evolutionary terms—to which we may add that there is another infinite regress if all activities are construed as controlled by abstract rules based on appropriate classification.

This questioning of abstraction is the deepest assumption holding the chapters of this book together. It includes anti-dualism, since mind-body dualism abstracts a reasoning or intellectual component from activity. Conversely, anti-dualism, as we have seen, does not preclude the use of abstract mechanisms, since stimulus-response theories are ostensibly anti-dualist, but abstraction is embodied in their experiments and their apparatus as well as in their theoretical models. Mutualism entails a questioning of abstraction, since it denies the validity of separating (abstracting) organism and environment. But this denial itself is compatible with abstraction of a different kind, the mechanical abstraction of cybernetic models linking organism and environment (Miller *et al*, 1960; McFarland, 1971). Perhaps these should not be regarded as mutualist theories, but this could only be because of their abstract and mechanical nature, and therefore the questioning of abstraction remains the source of the critique of cognitivism.

It is not abstractions *per se* that are questionable, or even abstractions from lived experience to mechanisms, but abstractions that lead a life independent of the field from which they are drawn. After all, are not all scientific descriptions and theories abstractions, in so far as they select from experience? In spite of its impressive mathematical tractability and computability, and the readiness with which its hypotheses can be tested through laboratory investigation, cognitivism is nevertheless an abstraction that *fails* to return to the world to throw light on our experience there (see Chapter 14, by Bolton, for a phenomenological account of these shortcomings). It is not simply that it is self-validating, testing its hypotheses in a laboratory world of its own making; nor that, like many well-entrenched academic institutions, it is sole judge of its own products and finds no need to evaluate its abstractions against the fullness of experience (William James' *Principles of Psychology* discusses many examples of this failure). Rather it is the very project of cognitivism to provide the blueprint of a machine (Haugeland, 1978), and this *requires* that its abstractions should be isolable and self-contained.

This problem is not novel, but stems from the traditional notion of perception as based upon a passively received input, forming part of a causal chain culminating in experience (Hatfield and Epstein, 1979). This notion is exemplified in the classical analogy between eye and camera. Such inputs are manifestly inadequate to account for our most basic experience of a 3-D world of solid objects, and therefore internal (cognitive) mechanisms and representations are called for. Prior knowledge and memory, it is said, *must* be involved, and cognitivism is thereby launched. But that is only true if we insist on starting with this abstraction of static perception and causal contact as the epitome of knowledge-getting, and bundle up the continuous flow of activity into a succession of snapshots. Unfortunately, this way of thinking is deeply ingrained, and not to be shaken off lightly. As the 'metaphysics of presence' (Fuchs, 1976) and the 'logic of the steady gaze' (Bryson, 1983), it has been much criticised, especially by phenomenologists (e.g. Merleau-Ponty, 1962). But if such criticisms are to have an impact upon empirically minded psychologists, alternative paradigms must be provided.

The alternatives of Part II of the book all set out to avoid a linear causal framework of the stimulus-response or input-output kind. Causality operates, but the world is not funnelled through the narrow filters of perceptual instants and 2-D retinal images. Instead, there is a more direct link between structures of the world and experience, and it is this directness that renders cognitive construction unnecessary, except perhaps in a very secondary capacity. Both Tolman (Chapter 11) and Kantor (Chapter 12), assumed such directness, at least in some of their writings; but they were unable to give a convincing account of how knowledge of the world is actually gained, to replace the traditional causal contact paradigm. Of current theories, only J.J. Gibson's has the potential to do this, and it is discussed in the four chapters of Section IIA.

Gibson's key insight was to replace the static conception of input, by a law of specificity connecting informational structures in the ambient array (of light in the case of vision), to the surrounding surfaces, events, etc. Animals pick up this information through active exploration, rather than through passive observation. The information in the case of vision is not mediated through a 2-D array as input, but is contained within transformations that specify persistence and change in the animal's world. Thus, as Reed shows in Chapter 7, Gibson was able to develop a new *ontology* of persistence and change, to replace the traditional ontology of sensation and perception. Since information in the ambient array specifies its sources, the self as well as the surrounding surfaces, there is no need to appeal to cognitive construction and representations to account for our experience of the world. The abstractions involved, information pick-up, affordances, etc. are *parts* of activity. Instead of having to move from static perception, through cognitive processes, to rules for activity, and finally activity itself, Gibson's theory makes perception a part of activity from the beginning, and the return from abstractions to the concrete is not problematic.

Gibson's ecological psychology should not be taken as a mere theory of perception to which 'cognition', traditionally conceived, must be appended. His account of perception was intended as a preliminary to a psychology of human cognition, framed in terms of what Reed (Chapter 10) calls 'representational systems'. Through a study of such systems and the activities which give rise to them, we may come to understand our use of such words as 'memory' and 'representation'. And we may find, following the argument of Marková in Chapter 13, that these words do not refer to timeless universals, but are to be understood historically as the concepts of a particular culture at a particular time. If these points seem distant from the current practice of cognitive psychology, it is due as much as anything to cognitivism's search for ultimate abstractions in its attempt 'to locate a world beyond the social and the historical' (Volosinov, 1976, p. 14). It is our hope that this book will encourage psychologists to question the fruitfulness of such a quest, and return again to the world in which people actually live.

REFERENCES

Atherton, M., 'The scope of cognition', *Behavioral and Brain Sciences*, 1978, *2*, 228-9.

Bryson, N., *Vision and Painting* (London: Macmillan, 1983).

Danziger, K., 'Origins of the schema of stimulated motion: Towards a pre-history of modern psychology', *History of Science*, 1983, *21*, 183-210.

Dewey, J., 'The reflex arc concept in psychology', *Psychological Review*, 1986, *3*, 357-70.

Dreyfus, H.L., *What Computers Can't Do: A critique of artificial reason* (New York: Harper & Row, 1971).

Fodor, J.A. and Pylyshyn, Z., 'How direct is visual perception? Some reflections on Gibson's "Ecological Approach"', *Cognition*, 1981, *10*, 139-96.

Fuchs, W.F., *Phenomenology and the Metaphysics of Presence* (North-Holland: Martinus Nijhoff, 1976).

de Gelder, B., 'The cognitivist conjuring trick or how development vanished', in C.J. Bailey and R. Harris, (eds.), *Developmental Mechanisms of Language* (London: Pergamon Press, 1985), p. 149-66.

Ghiselin, M.T., 'A radical solution to the species problem', *Systematic Zoology*, 1974, *23*, 536-54.

Hatfield, G.C. and Epstein, W., 'The sensory core and the medieval foundations of early modern perceptual theory', *Isis*, 1979, *70*, 363-84.

Haugeland, J., 'The nature and plausibility of cognitivism', *Behavioural and Brain Sciences*, 1978, *2*, 215-260.

Johnson-Laird, P.N., *Mental Models: Towards a Cognitive Science of Language, Inference, and Consciousness* (Cambridge: Cambridge University Press, 1983).

Johnson-Laird, P.N. and Wason, P.C., *Thinking: Readings in Cognitive Science* (Cambridge: Cambridge University Press, 1977).

Lewis, J.D., 'G.H. Mead's contact theory of reality: The manipulatory phase of the act in the constitution of mundane, scientific, aesthetic, and evaluative objects', *Symbolic Interaction*, 1981, *4*, 129-41.

Longuet-Higgins, H.C., 'Artificial Intelligence—a new theoretical psychology?', *Cognition*, 1981, *10*, 197-200.

Lundh, L.-G., 'Mind and meaning: Towards a theory of the human mind considered as a system of meaning structures', *Acta Universitatis Upsaliensis: Studia Psychologica Upsaliensia*, No 10, 1983.

McFarland, D., *Feedback Mechanisms in Animal Behaviour* (London: Academic Press, 1971).

Merleau-Ponty, M., *Phenomenology of Perception* (London: Routledge & Kegan Paul, 1962).

Miller, G.A., Galanter, E. and Pribram, K.H., *Plans and the Structure of Behavior* (New York: Holt, Rinehart and Winston, 1960).

Monk, R., 'Cognitivism and cognitive psychology', *Behavioral and Brain Sciences,* 1978, *2*, 242-3.

Rorty, R., *Consequences of Pragmatism* (Brighton: Harvester, 1982).

Volosinov, V.N., *Freudianism: A Marxist Critique* (London: Academic Press, 1976).

Wild, J., *The Radical Empiricism of William James* (New York: Doubleday, 1970).

PART I

Against Cognitivism

Section IA
Skills and Action

Cognitivism is the attempt to explain human and even animal cognition in terms of internal representations and rules. The theory of perception has, for many years, been premised upon the assumption that the perceiver must construct a mental representation of the physical environment (see Part II, section A). However, technological developments such as cybernetics, information theory, signal detection theory and, most recently, computer science, have encouraged a similar approach to the topic of 'skills'. This has led to a research programme directed towards the discovery of the rules underlying skilled activity. The three chapters in this section all question the validity of this goal of reducing skills (and, more generally, actions) to rules.

One obvious problem of the rule-following model is why long experience and practice is necessary for the development of skills—why not just feed in the rules in the form of instructions, as one might for a computer controlling a robot? The answer given by Dreyfus and Dreyfus (Chapter 2) is that skill simply is not a matter of mechanically applying rules, except perhaps in the case of a complete novice. The expert *sees* what to do, in the light of detailed experiences of a vast number of particular cases. This process of 'involved immersion', they argue, is distorted and in no way explained by trying to abstract rules.

The current emphasis within cognitive psychology upon abstract, decontextualised rules is also rejected by Mixon (Chapter 3). Following Dewey, Mixon examines how our everyday bodily activities, our 'habits' of posture, movement, speech, etc. can constitute our 'selves', and must be taken into account if we are to understand human action. Shotter, (Chapter 4) argues that the attempt to abstract rules underlying skilled practice is not merely absurd but dangerous. He points out the political and economic motivation in reducing the expertise of the skilled worker to rules. He shows how, in this respect, cognitive science is in the tradition of Taylorism, which had the avowed aim of mechanising human skills and substituting machines.

2

The Mistaken Psychological Assumptions Underlying Belief In Expert Systems

Hubert L. Dreyfus and Stuart E. Dreyfus

For the past quarter of a century researchers in a new field called artificial intelligence have been trying without success to write programs which will enable computers to exhibit general intelligence like Hal in '2001'. Now out of this work has recently emerged a new field called knowledge engineering which by limiting its goals has applied this research in a way which actually works in the real world. The result is the so-called expert system which has been the subject of recent cover stories in *Businessweek* and *Newsweek* and a book, *The Fifth Generation: Artificial intelligence and Japan's computer challenge to the world* (Feigenbaum and McCorduck, 1983). The occasion for this new interest is no specific new accomplishment but rather a much publicised competition with Japan to build a new generation of computers, with built-in expertise. This is the so-called fifth generation. (The first four generations were computers whose components were vacuum tubes, transistors, chips and large-scale integrated chips.) According to a *Newsweek* headline: 'Japan and the United States are rushing to produce a new generation of machines that can very nearly think.' Edward Feigenbaum, one of the original developers of expert systems, spells out this goal:

> In the kind of intelligent systems envisioned by the designers of the Fifth Generation, speed and processing power will be increased dramatically; but more importantly, the machines will have reasoning power: they will automatically engineer vast amounts of knowledge to serve whatever purpose humans propose, from medical diagnosis to product design, from management decisions to education. (Feigenbaum and McCorduck, 1983, p. 56)

17

What the knowledge engineers claim to have discovered is that in areas which are cut off from everyday common sense and social intercourse, all a machine needs in order to behave like an expert are some general rules and lots of very specific knowledge. As Feigenbaum puts it:

> The first group of artificial intelligence researchers. . . was persuaded that certain great, underlying principles characterized all intelligent behavior . . .
> In part, they were correct. . . [Such strategies] include searching for a solution (and using 'rules of good guessing' to cut down the search space); generating and testing (does this work? no; try something else); reasoning backward from a desired goal; and the like.
> These strategies are necessary, but not sufficient, for intelligent behavior. The other ingredient is knowledge—specialized knowledge, and lots of it . . . . No matter how natively bright you are, you cannot be a credible medical diagnostician without a great deal of specific knowledge about diseases, their manifestations, and the human body. (ibid., p. 38)

This specialised knowledge is of two types:

> The first type is the *facts* of the domain—the widely shared knowledge . . . that is written in textbooks and journals of the field, or that forms the basis of a professor's lectures in the classroom. Equally important to the practice of the field is the second type of knowledge called *heuristic knowledge*, which is the knowledge of good practice and good judgement in a field. It is experiential knowledge, the 'art of good guessing' that a human expert acquires over years of work. (ibid., pp. 76-7)

Using all three kinds of knowledge Feigenbaum developed a program called DENDRAL which is an expert in the specific and isolated domain of spectrograph analysis. It takes a pattern of lines which show up in the spectrum produced by the light of a chemical heated to incandescence, and, like a human expert, deduces from these lines the molecular structure of the chemical that gave out the light. Another program, MYCIN, takes the results of blood tests such as the number of red cells, white cells, sugar in the blood, etc. and comes up with a diagnosis of which blood disease is responsible for this condition. It even gives an estimate of the reliability of its own diagnosis. Such programs are as good as most experts in their domain.

And is not this success just what one would expect? If we

agree with Feigenbaum that 'almost all the thinking that professionals do is done by reasoning, not calculating' (ibid., p. 18), we can see that once computers are used for reasoning and not just computation they should be as good or better than we are at following rules for deducing conclusions from a lot of facts. So we would expect that if the rules which an expert has acquired from years of experience could be abstracted and programmed the resulting program would exhibit expertise. Again Feigenbaum puts the point very clearly:

> [The] matters that set experts apart from beginners, are symbolic, inferential, and rooted in experiential knowledge. Human experts have acquired their expertise not only from explicit knowledge found in textbooks and lectures, but also from experience: by doing things again and again, failing, succeeding . . . getting a feel for a problem, learning when to go by the book and when to break the rules. They therefore build up a repertory of working rules of thumb, or 'heuristics,' that, combined with book knowledge, make them expert practitioners. (ibid., p. 64)

Since each expert already has a repertory of rules in his or her mind, all the expert system-builder need do is get the rules out and program them into a computer.

This view is not new. In fact, it goes back to the beginning of western culture when the first philosopher, Socrates, stalked around Athens looking for experts in order to draw out and test rules. In one of his earliest dialogues, *The Euthyphro*, Plato tells us of such an encounter between Socrates and Euthyphro, a religious prophet, and so an expert on pious behaviour. Socrates asks Euthyphro to tell him how to recognise piety: 'I want to know what is characteristic of piety . . . to use as a standard whereby to judge your actions and those of other men.' But instead of giving Socrates his piety-recognising heuristic, Euthyphro does just what every expert does when cornered by Socrates. He gives him examples from his field of expertise; in this case, situations in the past in which men and gods have done things which everyone considers pious. Socrates persists throughout the dialogue in demanding that Euthyphro tell him his rules, but although Euthyphro claims he knows how to tell pious acts from impious ones, he will not give Socrates the rules which generate his judgements.

Plato admired Socrates and sympathised with his problem.

So he developed an account of what caused the difficulty. Experts had once known the rules they use, Plato said, but then they had forgotten them. The role of the philosopher was to help people remember the principles on which they act. Knowledge engineers would now say that the rules the experts use have been put in a part of their mental computers where they work automatically:

> When we learned how to tie our shoes, we had to think very hard about the steps involved. . . . Now that we've tied many shoes over our lifetime, that knowledge is 'compiled', to use the computing term for it; it no longer needs our conscious attention. (ibid., p. 55)

On this view, the rules are there functioning in the expert's mind whether they are conscious or not. How else could we account for the fact that he or she has learned to perform the task?

Now 2000 years later, thanks to Feigenbaum and his colleagues, we have a new name for what Socrates was doing: '[We] are able to be more precise about the problem of machine learning, and with this increased precision has come a new term, *knowledge acquisition research*' (ibid., p. 79). But although philosophers and even the man in the street have become convinced that expertise consists in applying sophisticated heuristics to masses of facts, there are few available rules. As Feigenbaum explains: '[An] expert's knowledge is often ill-specified or incomplete because the expert himself doesn't always know exactly what it is he knows about his domain' (ibid., p. 85). '[The expert's] knowledge is currently acquired in a very painstaking way; individual computer scientists work with individual experts to explicate the expert's heuristics—to mine those jewels of knowledge out of their heads one by one . . . the problem of knowledge acquisition is the critical bottleneck in artificial intelligence' (ibid., pp. 79-80). When Feigenbaum suggests to an expert the rules the expert seems to be using he gets a Euthyphro-like response. 'That's true, but if you see enough patients/rocks/chip designs/instrument readings, you see that it isn't true after all' (ibid., p. 82). And Feigenbaum comments with Socratic annoyance: 'At this point, knowledge threatens to become ten thousand special cases' (ibid., p. 82).

There are also other hints of trouble. Ever since the inception of artificial intelligence research, researchers have been trying to produce artificial experts by programming computers to follow rules used by masters in various domains. Yet, although computers are faster and more accurate than people in applying rules, master-level performance has remained out of reach. Arthur Samuel's work is typical. In 1947 when electronic computers were just being developed, Samuel, then at IBM, decided to write a checker-playing program. Samuel did not try to make a machine play checkers by brute force calculation of all chains of moves clear to the end. He estimated that if you tried to look to the end of the game with the fastest computer you could possibly build, subject to the speed of light, it would take 10 followed by 21 zeros centuries to make the first move. So he tried to elicit heuristics from checker masters and program a computer to follow these rules. When the rules the experts came up with did not produce master play, Samuel became the first and almost the only AI researcher to make a learning program. He programmed a computer to vary the weights used in the rules, such as the trade-off between centre control and loss of a piece, and to retain the weights that worked best. After playing a lot of games with itself, the program could beat Samuel, which shows that in some sense computers can do more than they are programmed to do, but the program still could not beat the sort of experts whose heuristic rules were the heart of the program.

The checkers program is not only the first, and one of the best, experts ever built, but it is also a perfect example of the way fact turns into fiction in AI. The checkers program once beat a state checkers champion. From then on, AI literature cites the checkers program as a great success. One often reads that it plays at such a high level that only the world champion can beat it. Feigenbaum, for example, reports that 'by 1961 [Samuel's program] played championship checkers, and it learned and improved with each game' (ibid., 179). In fact, in a recent interview, Samuel said that the program did once defeat a champion, but the champion 'turned around and defeated the program in six mail games'. According to Samuel, after 35 years of effort, 'the program is quite capable of beating any amateur player and can give better players a good contest'. It is clearly no champion. He is still bringing in expert players for help but he 'fears he may be reaching the point of diminishing returns'. This does not lead him to question the view that the masters the program cannot beat are using heuristic rules; rather, like Socrates and Feigenbaum, Samuel thinks that the experts are poor at recollecting their compiled heuristics: 'the experts do not know enough about the mental processes involved in playing the game'. (These quotations are drawn from an interview with Arthur Samuel released by the Stanford University News Office, 28 April, 1983.)

The same story is repeated in every area of expertise, even in areas unlike checkers where expertise requires the storage of large numbers of facts, which should give an advantage to the computer. In each area where there are experts with years of experience, the computer can do better than the beginner, and even exhibit useful competence; but it cannot rival the very experts whose supposed facts and heuristics it is processing with incredible speed and unerring accuracy.

In the face of this impasse it seems necessary, in spite of the authority and influence of Plato and 2000 years of philosophy, to take a fresh look at what a skill is and what the expert acquires when acquiring that expertise. One must be prepared to abandon the traditional view that a beginner starts with specific cases and, as he or she becomes more proficient, abstracts and interiorises more and more sophisticated rules. It might turn out that skill acquisition moves in just the opposite direction: from abstract rules to particular cases. Since we all have many areas in which we are experts, we all have the necessary data, so let us look and see how adults learn new skills.

STAGE 1: NOVICE

Normally, the instruction process begins with the instructor decomposing the task environment into context-free features which the beginner can recognise without benefit of experience. The beginner is then given rules for determining actions on the basis of these features. The beginning student wants to do a good job, but lacking any coherent sense of the overall task, he judges his performance mainly by how well he follows his learned rules. After he has acquired more than just a few rules, so much concentration is required during the exercise of his skill that his capacity to talk or listen to advice is severely limited.

For example, consider two variations: a bodily or motor skill and an intellectual skill. The student car driver learns to recognise such interpretation-free features as speed (indicated by the speedometer) and distance (as estimated by a previously acquired skill). Safe following distances are defined in terms of speed; conditions that allow safe entry into traffic are defined in terms of speed and distance of oncoming traffic; timing of shifts of gear is specified in terms of speed, etc. These rules ignore context. They do not refer to traffic density or anticipated stops.

The novice chess player learns a numerical value for each type of piece regardless of its position, and the rules: 'always exchange if the total value of pieces captured exceeds the value of pieces lost'. He also learns that when no advantageous exchanges can be found then centre control should be sought, and he is given a rule defining centre squares and one for calculating extent of control. Most beginners are notoriously slow players, as they attempt to remember all these rules and their priorities.

STAGE 2: ADVANCED BEGINNER

As the novice gains experience in actually coping with real situations, he begins to note, or an instructor points out, perspicuous examples of meaningful additional components of the situation. After seeing a sufficient number of examples, the student learns how to recognise them. Instructional maxims now can refer to these new *situational aspects* recognised on the basis of experience, as well as to the objectively defined *non-situational features* recognisable by the novice. The advanced beginner confronts his environment, seeks out features and aspects, and determines his actions by applying rules. He shares the novice's minimal concern with quality of performance, but instead focuses on quality of rule-following. The advanced beginner's performance, while improved, remains slow, uncoordinated and laborious.

The advanced beginner driver uses (situational) engine sounds as well as (non-situational) speed in his gear-shifting rules, and observes demeanour as well as position and velocity to anticipate behaviour of pedestrians or other drivers. He learns to distinguish the behaviour of the distracted or drunken driver from that of the impatient but alert one. No number of words can serve the function of a few choice examples in learning this distinction. Engine sounds cannot be adequately captured by words, and no list of objective facts about a particular pedestrian enables one to predict his behaviour in a crosswalk as well as can the driver who has observed many pedestrians crossing streets under a variety of conditions.

With experience, the chess beginner learns to recognise over-extended positions and how to avoid them. Similarly, he begins to recognise situational aspects of positions as a weakened king's side or a strong pawn structure despite the lack of precise and universally valid definitional rules.

STAGE 3: COMPETENCE

With increasing experience, the number of features and aspects to be taken into account of becomes overwhelming. To cope with this information explosion, the performer learns, or is taught, to adopt a hierarchical view of decision-making. By first choosing a plan, goal or perspective which organises the situation and by then examining only the small set of features and aspects that he has learned are the most important given that plan, the performer can simplify and improve his performance.

Choosing a plan, goal or perspective is no simple matter for the competent performer. It is not an objective procedure, like the feature recognition of the novice. Nor is the choice avoidable. While the advanced beginner can get along without recognising and using a particular situational aspect until a sufficient number of examples makes identification easy and sure, to perform competently *requires* choosing an organising goal or perspective. Furthermore, the choice of perspective crucially affects behaviour in a way that one particular aspect rarely does.

This combination of necessity and uncertainty introduces an important new type of relationship between the performer and his or her environment. The novice and the advanced beginner applying rules and maxims feel little or no responsibility for the outcome of their acts. If they have made no mistakes, an unfortunate outcome is viewed as the result of inadequately specified elements or rules. The competent performer, on the other hand, after wrestling with the question of a choice of perspective or goal, feels responsible for, and thus emotionally involved in, the result of his choice. An outcome that is clearly successful is deeply satisfying and leaves a vivid memory of the situation encountered as seen from the goal or perspective finally chosen. Disasters, likewise, are not easily forgotten.

Remembered whole situations differ in one important respect from remembered aspects. The mental image of an aspect is flat in the sense that no parts stand out as salient. A whole situation, on the other hand, since the result of a chosen plan or perspective, has a 'three-dimensional' quality. Certain elements stand out as more or less important with respect to the plan, while other irrelevant elements are forgotten. Moreover, the competent performer, gripped by the situation that his decision has produced, experiences and therefore remembers the situation not only in terms of foreground and background elements but also in terms of senses of opportunity, risk, expectation, threat, etc. These gripping, holistic memories cannot guide the behaviour of the competent performer since he fails to make contact with them when he reflects on problematic situations as a detached observer. As we shall soon see, however, these memories become the basis of the competent performer's next advance in skill.

A competent driver beginning a trip decides, perhaps, that he is in a hurry. He then selects a route with attention to distance and time, ignores scenic beauty, and, as he drives, he chooses his manoeuvres with little concern for passenger comfort or for courtesy. He follows more closely than normal, enters traffic more daringly, occasionally violates a law. He feels elated when decisions work out and no police car appears, and shaken by near-accidents and traffic tickets. (Beginners, on the other hand, can perpetrate chaos around them with total unconcern.)

The class A chess player, here classed as competent, may decide after studying a position that his opponent has weakened his king's defences so that an attack against the king is a viable goal. If the attack is chosen, features involving weaknesses in his own position created by his attack are ignored as are losses of pieces inessential to the attack. Removal of pieces defending the enemy king become salient. Successful plans induce euphoria and mistakes are felt in the pit of the stomach.

In both of these cases, we find a common pattern: detached planning, conscious assessment of elements that are salient with respect to the plan, and analytical rule-guided choice of action, followed by an emotionally involved experience of the outcome.

STAGE 4: PROFICIENCY

Considerable experience at the level of competency sets the stage for yet further skill enhancement. Having experienced many situations, chosen plans in each, and having obtained vivid, involved demonstrations of the adequacy or inadequacy of the plan, the performer sees his current situation as similar to a previous one and so spontaneously sees an appropriate plan. Involved in the world of the skill, the performer 'notices' or 'is struck by' a certain plan, goal or perspective. No longer is the spell of involvement broken by detached conscious planning.

There will, of course, be breakdowns of the 'seeing', when, due perhaps to insufficient experience in a certain type of situation or to more than one possible plan presenting itself, the performer will need to take a detached look at his situation. But between these breakdowns, the proficient performer will experience longer and longer intervals of continuous, intuitive understanding.

Since there are generally far fewer 'ways of seeing' than 'ways of acting', having understood without conscious effort what is going on, the proficient performer will still have to think about what to do. During this thinking, elements that present themselves as salient are assessed and combined by rule to produce decisions about how best to manipulate the environment. The spell of involvement in the world of the activity will thus be temporarily broken.

On the basis of prior experience, a proficient driver approaching a curve on a rainy day may sense that he is travelling too fast. He then consciously determines an appropriate lower speed based on such salient elements as visibility, angle of road bank, criticality of time, etc. (These factors would be used by the *competent* driver consciously to *decide that* he is speeding.)

The proficient chess player, who is classed a master, can recognise a large repertoire of types of positions. Recognising almost immediately and without conscious effort the sense of a position, he sets about calculating the move that best achieves his goal. He may, for example, know that he should attack, but he must deliberate about how best to do so.

STAGE 5: EXPERTISE

The proficient performer, immersed in the world of his skilful activity, *sees* what needs to be done, but *decides* how to do it. For the expert, not only situational understandings spring to mind, but also associated appropriate actions. The expert performer, except of course during moments of breakdown, understands, acts and learns from results without any conscious awareness of the process. What transparently *must* be done *is* done. We usually do not make conscious deliberative decisions when we walk, talk, ride a bicycle, drive, or carry on most social activities. An expert's skill has become so much a part of him that he need be no more aware of it than he is of his own body.

We have seen that experience-based similarity recognition produces the deep situational understanding of the proficient performer. No new insight is needed to explain the mental processes of the expert. With enough experience with a variety of situations, all seen from the same perspective or with the same goal in mind, but requiring different tactical decisions, the mind of the proficient performer seems gradually to decompose this class of situations into subclasses, each member of which shares not only the same goal or perspective, but also the same decision, action or tactic. At this point, a situation, when seen as similar to members of this class, is not only thereby understood but simultaneously the associated decision, action or tactic presents itself.

The number of classes of recognisable situations, built up on the basis of experience, must be immense. It has been estimated that a master chess player can distinguish roughly 50,000 types of positions. Car driving probably involves a similar number of typical situations. We doubtless store far more typical situations in our memories than words in our vocabularies. Consequently, these reference situations, unlike the situational elements learned by the advanced beginner, bear no names and, in fact, defy complete verbal description.

The expert chess player, classed as an international grandmaster, in most situations experiences a compelling sense of the issue and the best move. Excellent chess players can play at the rate of 5–10 seconds a move and even faster without any serious degradation of performance. At this speed they must depend almost entirely on intuition and hardly at all on analysis and comparison of alternatives.

The expert driver, generally without any awareness, simply slows when his speed feels too fast until it feels right. He shifts gears when appropriate with no conscious awareness of his acts. Most drivers have experienced the disconcerting breakdown that occurs when suddenly one reflects on the gearshifting process and tries to decide what to do. Suddenly the smooth, almost automatic, sequence of actions that results from the performer's involved immersion in the world of his skill is disrupted, and the performer sees himself, just as does the competent performer, as the manipulator of a complex mechanism. He detachedly calculates his actions even more poorly than does the competent performer since he has forgotten many of the guiding rules that he knew and used when competent, and his performance suddenly becomes halting, uncertain, and even inappropriate.

It seems that a beginner makes inferences using rules and facts just like a heuristically programmed computer, but that with talent and a great deal of involved experience the beginner develops into an expert who intuitively sees what to do without applying rules. Of course, a description of skilled behaviour can never be taken as conclusive evidence as to what is going on in the mind or in the brain. It is always possible that what is going on is some unconscious process using more and more sophisticated rules. But our description of skill acquisition counters the traditional prejudice that expertise necessarily involves inference.

The knowledge engineer might still say that in spite of appearances the mind and brain *must* be calculating—making millions of rapid and accurate inferences like a computer. After all, the brain is not 'wonder tissue' and how else could it work? But there are other models for what might be going on in the hardware. The capacity of experts to recognise tens of thousands of paradigmatic situations, and to see the present situation as similar to one of these, suggests that the brain does not work like a digital computer applying rules to bits of information. Rather it suggests, as some neurophysiologists already believe, that the brain, at times at least, works holographically, superimposing the records of whole situations and measuring their similarity. Karl Pribram has explicitly noted the implication of this sort of process for expertise. When asked in an interview whether holograms would allow a person to make decisions spontaneously in very complex environments, he replied, 'decisions fall out as the holographic correlations are performed. One doesn't have to think through . . . a step at a time. One takes the whole constellation of a situation, correlates it, and out of the correlation emerges the correct response' (cited in Coleman, 1979, p. 80).

Given the above account of skill acquisition we can understand why the knowledge engineers from Socrates to Samuel and Feigenbaum have had such trouble getting the expert to articulate the rules he is supposed to be following. The expert is simply not following any rules! He is doing just what Feigenbaum feared he might be doing: recognising thousands of special cases.

This in turn would explain why expert systems are never as good as experts. If one asks the experts for rules one will, in effect, force the expert to regress to the level of a beginner, and give you the rules he still remembers but no longer uses. If one programs these rules in a computer one can use the speed and accuracy of the computer, and its ability to store and access millions of facts, to outdo a human beginner using the same rules. But no amount of rules and facts can capture the knowledge an expert has when he has stored his experience of the outcomes of tens of thousands of actual situations.

Feigenbaum himself admits in one surprisingly frank passage that expert systems are very different from experts.

> A human expert solves problems, all right, but he also explains the results, he learns, he restructures his own knowledge. . . . Part of learning to be an expert is to understand not merely the letter of the rule but its spirit . . . he knows when to break the rules, he understands what is relevant to his task and what isn't . . . . Expert systems do not yet understand these things. (Feigenbaum and McCorduck, 1983, pp. 84-5)

But because of his philosophical commitment to the rationality of expertise and thus to underlying unconscious heuristic rules, Feigenbaum does not see how devastating this admission is. Once one gives up the assumption that experts must be making inferences, and admits the role of involvement and intuition in the acquisition of skills, one will have no reason to cling to the heuristically programmed digital computer as a model of human intellectual operations. Feigenbaum's claim that 'we have the opportunity at this moment to do a new version of Diderot's *Encyclopaedia*, a gathering up of all knowledge—not just the academic kind, but the experiential, heuristic kind' (ibid., p. 229), as well as his boast that thanks to knowledge information processing systems (KIPS) we shall soon have 'access to machine intelligence—faster, deeper, better than human intelligence' (ibid., p. 236) can both be seen as a late stage of Socratic thinking. In this light, those who claim we must begin a crash programme to compete with the Japanese fifth generation intelligent computers can be seen to be false prophets blinded by these Socratic assumptions and personal ambition. While Euthyphro, the expert on piety, who kept giving Socrates examples instead of rules, turns out to have been a true prophet after all.

REFERENCES

Coleman, D., 'Holographic memory: An interview with Karl Pribram', *Psychology Today*, 1979, *12(9)*, 80.

Feigenbaum, E. and McCorduck, P., *The Fifth Generation: Artificial intelligence and Japan's computer challenge to the world* (Reading, MA: Addison-Wesley/London: Michael Joseph, 1983).

3

On Not-doing and On Trying and Failing

Don Mixon

All of us experience times when, like Hamlet, with 'every motive and cue for passion' we are unable to do the deed. Why can't we? Why the inaction? For inaction and action as complex, as psychologically central as Hamlet's, nothing short of Shakespeare's play will begin to give a satisfactory answer.

But I can make it simpler. Much simpler. Most of the things we are unable to do, or try to do and fail, are less complicated than sorting out the rottenness in Denmark.

Take, for example, sitting down in a chair. Ordinarily I pay little attention to how I get in and out of chairs. Suppose that I form the wish to sit down in a particular manner and find, no matter how hard I try, that I cannot. Why can't I? Given current fashion, should you ask a psychologist any of the above questions, the answer you are most likely to hear is a cognitive one. Not that cognitivists ordinarily address themselves to not-doings. But I assume that those who believe cognitions are acceptable explanations for doings, must believe they can account for not-doings as well. Or they should, if they wish their theories to be taken seriously.

One problem with cognitivism is that is feeds on the illusion that people are organised hierarchically, that something—an information processor, a mind—is at the top and is responsible for what goes on in the ranks below. The illusion is particularly dangerous because, when examples are selected carefully enough, cognitivism can appear somewhat plausible. The plausibility is gained by seeming to come close to common experience. When we, for example, tell our legs to propel us forward and they do, an information processor may seem in command. But this is a special case, is it not? Ordinarily we needn't tell them. Our legs without command simply take us forward. Even the special case is only fairly close to common experience because, though we may be comfortable saying, 'I tell my legs to propel me. . .', we are less likely to say, 'My mind (or my information processor) tells my legs to propel me. . .'

Whatever plausibility cognitive explanations have when the information processor seems in control is lost when the ghost in the machine is not even seemingly in control: when, like Hamlet, we cannot. I shall explore examples of not-doing and of trying and failing.

Given our training and occupation the grip of cognitivism on psychologists is not surprising. We live our lives, at least metaphorically, in our heads. Most of us are scholars and if we no longer as lecturers dispense knowledge, we as students have spent a considerable portion of our lives imbibing knowledge. For a scholar, knowledge, the mind's product, is at the centre of experience. It liberates, it leads to advancement, to action. Coming up with the right words, the right bits of knowledge, at the right time on tests and examinations is what it's all about: ' "Cognitive" belongs to the vocabulary of examination papers' (Ryle, 1949, p. 258).

The importance of knowledge to the lives of academics is clear. What may not be obvious to scholars is that, for most of *social* behaviour, knowledge, while important, takes one only part of the way towards action. To give a broad example (to which I shall return) Liza Doolittle in Bernard Shaw's *Pygmalion* quite rapidly could have absorbed with her quick mind all the knowledge necessary to pass as a Duchess at the Embassy reception. But this knowledge (which could be verified by an exam or an objective test) would not have enabled her to succeed in passing for a Duchess or even emboldened her to try.

Another example involving a common, everyday behaviour comes from the life of the philosopher and psychologist, John Dewey. My choice of Dewey is not accidental. As early as 1922 he wrote an *Introduction to Social Psychology* that gave serious attention to the far from simple connection between trying and doing or not-doing. Dewey at the time of the experience described below was 59 years old, easily the best-known and most influential US philosopher, a man with reason to be confident of his cognitive powers.

> In bringing to bear whatever knowledge I already possessed—or thought I did—and whatever powers of discipline in mental application I had acquired in the pursuit of these studies, I had the most humiliating experience of my life, intellectually speaking. For to find that one is unable to execute directions, including inhibitory ones, in doing such a seemingly simple act as to sit down, when one is using all the mental capacity which one prides himself upon possessing, is not an experience congenial to one's vanity. But it may be conducive to analytic study of causal conditions, obstructive and positive. (1932, p. xvii)

Dewey is describing what happened in the course of a lesson in psycho-physical re-education given by F. M. Alexander. It doesn't matter for the moment why, but what Alexander asked Dewey to do was to inhibit his usual manner of sitting down and to substitute new directions, which if successful would bring him into the chair with his head, neck and back in a balanced relationship (roughly to sit down without tensing his neck or sticking out his buttocks). What could be simpler than sitting down in a chair? Or more difficult than sitting down with the head, neck and back in a particular relationship? The failure Dewey experienced is an everyday occurence in the life of athletes, artists, actors and artisans: everyone whose work involves skill knows that just because you tell yourself to do something in a particular way doesn't mean you can. If all it takes to produce a perfect golf swing, for instance, is to tell yourself how to swing the club, links would be crowded with sub-par golfers. A cognitive command might have been sufficient to get Dewey into the chair, but his brain power proved helpless to enable him to get into the chair in the way he wished. The critical insight for social psychology, worked out by Dewey in *Human Nature and Conduct* (1922), involves extending the notion from athletes, artists, actors and artisans where it is obvious, to social behaviour where it is not. However, once stated, it should become obvious. For whereas Liza Doolittle could quickly learn what a Duchess might say and do at an Embassy reception, she could not pass as a Duchess until she had the skill to say the words and do the movements in a convincingly Duchess-like way. Ways of behaviour cannot be reliably produced until they are mastered much as a skill is mastered.

Why can't anyone who is capable of memorising the lines and pronouncing the words give a convincing stage performance? Why can the performance of an understudy differ so from the performance of the star? They say the same words and do the same movements. Don't they? A close look at the stage actor's task will reveal what is missing from most behavioural accounts. The art of acting involves being able to convincingly produce bodily, vocal, and emotional ways of behaving. The player's task underlines the twofold nature of behaviour: each behaviour has two components—*what* is done and the *way* in which it is done. Everything done must be done in some way. That is, people don't just sit down, they must sit down in some fashion. An actor does not simply say 'O, what a rogue and peasant slave am I!' He says it in the way his Hamlet must say it at that moment, on that night, before that audience.

'People don't just sit down' except when the action is incompletely or abstractedly described. Modern psychology has abstracted, has removed essential features of, both the term 'behaviour' and term 'habit'. Behaviour has come to mean *what* an organism does and habit to mean *what* an organism does repeatedly. The uses are abstractions which both ignore the twofold nature of behaviour and change radically the common language meaning of the terms. None of the five definitions of 'behaviour' in the *Oxford English Dictionary* (1887) refer to what is done. The first definition is characteristic: '1. Manner of conducting oneself in the external relations of life; demeanour, deportment, bearing, manners.' Common use of the term 'habit' (as reported in the *OED*) also emphasises the way things are done.

> Holding, having, 'haviour'; hence the way in which one holds or has oneself, i.e. the mode or condition in which one is, exists, or exhibits oneself, (a) externally; hence demeanour, outward appearance, fashion of body, mode of clothing oneself, dress, habitation; (b) in mind, character, of life; hence, mental constitution, character, disposition, way of acting, comporting oneself, or dealing with things, habitual or customary way (of acting, etc.), personal customs, accustomedness.

Psychologists eviscerated the terms with the highest of motives.

The abstractions no doubt came about in an effort to simplify what goes into a stimulus and a response—particularly in animal work. Motive makes the abstractions no less pernicious. For social behaviour the essential component was excised. Behavioural *whats* have been studied as if the way something is done is of no interest. As if the words of the script and the movements prescribed by stage directions encompassed all of behaviour. As if the way the words are said and movements done are superfluous.

But you don't have to be a psychologist to engage in behavioural abstraction. You can, if you wish, ignore the *way* and 'just' sit down, 'just' swing the golf club, 'just' say the words. Looked at from a social point of view, the *what* component of behaviour can be called a 'discretionary task' (Mixon, 1980). The tasks are commonly at people's discretion because they can do them. That is, anyone can sit down, swing a golf club, pronounce words and do the thousands of other things members of a particular society learn and are expected to do. There are exceptions of course. Some people cannot—because of disability, lack of opportunity, or whatever—do *all* of the things expected. But, generally speaking, societies depend on people being able to do a very large number of behavioural *whats*. And because everyone can do them such discretionary tasks do not need explanation. They are of no psychological interest. A possible exception is interest in exploring differences in the discretionary tasks expected by various societies. But aside from cross-cultural analysis behaviour becomes psychologically interesting only when the *way* component is present. People are not expected to be able to do *whats* in the same way. The *way* we sit down, swing a golf club, say words is habit/skill dependent and varies greatly from person to person.

Cognitive explanations can appear plausible because of the seemingly direct connection between a cognition (that is, a command, intention, or whatever), and the execution *when common discretionary tasks are used as examples*. However, cognitive explanations lose even surface plausibility when we look at behaviour in its full sense. The seemingly direct connection between command or intention and execution simply is not there.

Dewey devoted the entire first section of *Human Nature and Conduct* to ways of behaving (which he called habits) and their workings. The discussion, which is not complete until the book ends, is worthy of any psychologist's attention, even the attention of those who have difficulty with Dewey's way of writing. Dewey contrasted his use of the term 'habit' (which is not unlike the *OED* definition quoted earlier) with the tendency to limit its meaning to repetition.

> Repetition is in no sense the essence of habit. Tendency to repeat acts is an incident of many habits but not of all. A man with the habit of giving way to anger may show his habit by a murderous attack upon some one who has offended. His act is nonetheless due to habit because it occurs only once in his life. The essence of habit is an acquired pre-disposition to *ways* or modes of response, not to particular acts except as, under special conditions, these express a way of behaving. (1922, p. 42)

One of Dewey's chief contributions to the understanding of habit is his insistence on its skill-like nature. Unlike Ryle who had reason to emphasise the *difference* between intelligent capacities and mechanical habits, Dewey wished to point out the element of intelligent capacity or skill in habits. Mere 'blind habit' did not much interest Dewey except as something that might possibly be transformed into a skill (or intelligent capacity).

Habits, as ways or modes of response, unlike abstracted *whats* which can break down easily into stimuli and responses, are not convenient and easy to use as units of analysis. Habits ordinarily do not come in neat, time-bound units. They share a common difficulty with motor skills.

> The difficulty is that while the idea and the reflex are excellent concepts for describing behaviours that naturally break into discrete units, they are not nearly as satisfactory for describing behaviours that are essentially continuous. (Irion, 1969, p. 2)

Difficult or not, habit as a unit of analysis offers decided advantages over the units commonly used by social psychologists. Social psychology throughout most of its history has been a cognitive discipline. The components of its key term 'attitude', for example, are taken directly from the tripartite division of mind: cognitive, emotional and conative. Cognitivism is not avoided by changing the meaning, as some writers do, of conative from 'will' to 'behaviour'. Nor when a person's attitude is measured by a discretionary task—typically by checking an attitude scale. Not just attitude research, but very nearly all of experimental social psychology employs discretionary tasks as dependent variables. Although lack of psychological interest is sufficient reason for not using discretionary tasks as dependent variables, it is not the only reason. Anyone can do them: participants, for example, can check an attitude scale anywhere they please. Thus, rather than being determined by the independent variable or variables, the outcome is in the control of the participant. Experimenters know this so they attempt to trick the participants into giving a 'valid' response by various forms of deceit, but only succeed in producing results impossible to interpret and in creating serious problems for their truthful colleagues (Mixon, 1977). Deception as a 'control' is an ethical and methodological disaster. Luckily for the future of serious research, habit's skill-like nature makes the construction of 'habit scales' on the model of attitude scales unlikely. It would be as absurd as measuring a motor skill by asking people to agree or disagree with statements about their degree of skill.

Gordon Allport hardly could have been more wrong. In an historical essay on social psychology, Allport devotes two paragraphs to Dewey's conception of habit and concludes that Dewey claimed too many attributes for habit and that the notion was too vague. The concept *attitude*, Allport claimed, 'filled the need Dewey felt' (1968, p. 59). But attitude and habit—at least as social psychologists have defined attitude —are radically different concepts. Attitude is cognitive, habits involve the entire psychophysical being.

We can, of course, conceive of cognitive habits. And they appear to pose special difficulties because of the seemingly direct connection between command or intention and acts, when it comes to cognitive acts. Dewey denies a privileged connection.

> . . .we are likely to suppose that. . .control of the *body* is physical and hence is external to mind and will. Transfer the command inside character and

mind, and it is fancied that an idea and the desire to realize it will take immediate effect. After we get to the point of recognizing that habits must intervene between wish and execution in the case of bodily acts, we still cherish the illusion that they can be dispensed with in the case of mental and moral acts. Thus the net result is to make us sharpen the distinction between non-moral and moral activities, and to lead us to confine the latter strictly within a private, immaterial realm. But in fact, formation of ideas as well as their execution depends upon habit. (1922, p. 30)

It may be that the notion of discretionary tasks will help here. When we abstract behaviour, when we 'just' sit down, swing a golf club, pronounce words, there does seem to be a direct connection between command and execution. There is a parallel in cognitive matters, for cognitive behaviour can be abstracted too. When the command is, '2 × 2 = ? or 'Who issued the Behaviourist manifesto in 1913?' the connection between command and execution seems direct. But if the command is 'Write an essay in the style of William Hazlett', or 'Write an essay on the early days of Behaviourism', the direct connection is no longer even seemingly there. Even an exhaustive familiarity with the writings of Hazlett will not guarantee that I can write in his style. And encyclopedic knowledge about Behaviourism is no guarantee that I can write or even think about it in a coherent or lucid way, or in any particular fashion. Ways, styles of thinking, are just as skill-dependent as ways of moving, speaking, etc. If we wish to think in the way a Zen master thinks, for example, we must master the skill. We can't simply decide to do it.

An alternative to cognitivism would be anything that puts cognitive studies in their place. Place is important. As Ryle took care to demonstrate, the Ghost isn't there. Mind should be studied, but should be studied where it lives: 'the chessboard, the platform, the scholar's desk, the judge's bench, the lorry-driver's seat, the studio and the football field are among its places' (Ryle, 1949, p. 51). Ways of thinking are interesting in themselves and are part of behaviour. So much depends upon how they are studied and what's made of them. The claim that behaviour can be *explained* only by appeal to internal cognitive processes cannot be taken seriously. Explanation that leaves out, for example, ways of moving, speaking, feeling and that leaves out all of the external contingencies is curiously impoverished. People simply are not (even by analogy) machines impervious to environment and controlled by cognitive processes. You can think in a particular way only if you can, you can perceive in a certain way only if you can, you can perform an action in a particular way only if you can, you can speak in a certain way only if you can, you can express emotion in a certain way only if you can. . . and no amount of cognitive processing will make a bit of difference to those *cans*. The only way you can do these things in a certain way is to gain the skill. And that, ordinarily, takes time and practice.

Another way of understanding the importance of ways of behaving or habits is in terms of ends and means. A command or intention to do something is to command or intend an end. Habits are the means. Dewey couldn't sit in a certain way because he lacked the skilled means. The same with the golfer and actor. Liza couldn't go straight to the Embassy reception because she lacked the means to succeed. To think that cognitive processes alone can do anything is, in Dewey's term, to engage in magical thinking—to think that the wish alone can produce the end. 'The principle of magic is found whenever it is hoped to get results without intelligent control of means. . .' (1922, p. 27).

An alternative to cognitivism would first of all give up the notion that any part can explain the whole. At least with an organism as complex as a human that lives in an environment as intricate and as encroaching as ours. Cognitive 'explanation' masks the important questions. How can we do what we intend to do? How and why do we fail? How can we develop habits that serve as effective means? How does one type of habit interact with or influence another type? By asking such questions unimagined influences and relationships become subject to study. For example, actors can tell us that the way a character perceives influences expression. And the way a character expresses influences the way and what of perception.

Dewey said that the early lessons with F. M. Alexander produced 'the most humiliating experience of my life, intellectually speaking'. Yet Dewey went on having lessons for the rest of his life—over thirty years. What kept him going? On a vulgar level he persevered because the lessons helped keep him healthy and young (Dykusizen, 1973). And no skill is ever entirely mastered. At another level Dewey stated that ideas he held in an abstract and theoretical way were given concrete significance and substance by study and friendship with Alexander. The effect of the lessons on his philosophy was powerful enough that E. D. McCormack could write a persuasive dissertation (1958) which makes a strong case for the proposition that the key to Dewey's post-1916 writing lies in understanding the work and influence of Alexander.

What did Alexander teach? Well, for one thing, he taught the importance of 'use'—a concept which maps somewhat onto what Dewey called 'habit', and I call 'ways of behaviour'. He wrote of 'faulty sensory appreciation' which means that use (habit) influences, even seriously distorts, perception. That is, for example, my senses may tell me that my neck muscles are free and relaxed when they are in fact shortened and tense. Alexander emphasised the futility of 'end-gaining', which means going directly for an end without mastering the means to gain it. Describing the Alexander experience has baffled the best writers—and Alexander taught some pretty good ones (e.g. Bernard Shaw and Aldous Huxley). It involves a *relationship* between head, neck and back. When the relationship works, Raymond Dart's (1947) simple term 'poise' describes the state. The experience provided for the pupil by the teacher involves being and moving in a lighter, freer and more integrated way than imagined possible. And the lessons are directed towards giving you the capacity to be and move that way yourself. (For a fuller discussion see any of F. Matthias Alexander's four books (1918, 1924, 1932, 1941), or a more recent account of Frank Pierce Jones (1976).)

> The Alexander technique is a method of re-education that is psycho-physical in the sense that it brings about a change in the person as a whole, by introducing a change in his total pattern of reaction. It is not an attempt to reeducate the mind by way of the body or the body by way of the mind. It is a method for changing and redirecting on a conscious level the background of postual tone which underlies and makes possible all orderly motion. A change in this fundamental pattern is a total change, and it affects the character of any activity whether that activity is mental or physical. (Jones, 1953)

I think that Jones' description is a good one. And that

furthermore it provides an apt model for other habit change. A change in any kind of habit will influence the character of any activity. However, in the absence of the kind of study undertaken by Alexander, we cannot assume that a change in habit will be a change for the better. Except, Dewey might argue, in the case of changing a mechanical habit into a flexible one, or what Ryle would call an 'intelligent capacity'. In most cases, how the activity is influenced is an empirical question. How, for example, might a change in the way we speak influence the way we hear.

The ground, as you see, has shifted from one type of explanation (can cognitive processes *explain* behaviour?) to questions of assessing the effects of changes of habit on 'a change in the person as a whole'. And it is, I think, much better ground for social psychology to be on, for it would allow us to look seriously at, for example, Alexander's method of re-educating or reintegrating habits. And to ask questions like: What restrains or limits our capacity to act? (Dewey's 'obstructive' condition). What can enhance our capacities? (Dewey's 'positive' condition). In other words, when we cannot, how can we? Or, to what extent can we take responsibility for our habits and thus our actions? (Mixon, 1980). The shift is from an attempt to use an internal process to explain the doings of a whole to an attempt to understand the workings of the whole; from questions of linear causality, to an interest in negative restraints, and limits on action. That is, one asks 'not why one particular thing happened but instead why everything else did not happen' (Ogilvy, 1979, p.26).

Unfamiliar territory for most psychologists, but not lonely. Many of us are aware that our colleagues in the natural sciences long ago stopped talking the sort of causal language we indulge in. Looking for limits on actions is more interesting, and more useful—especially for those who wish, like Hamlet, to do something they cannot do.

REFERENCES

Alexander, F.M., *Man's Supreme Inheritance* (New York and London: Dutton, 1918).

Alexander, F.M., *Constructive Conscious Control of the Individual* (London: Methuen, 1924).

Alexander, F.M., *The Use of the Self* (New York: Dutton, 1932).

Alexander, F.M., *The Universal Constant in Living* (New York: Dutton, 1941).

Allport, G., 'The historical background to modern social psychology', in G. Lindzey and E. Aronson (eds.), *The Handbook of Social Psychology*, Vol. 1. (Reading, MA.: Addison-Wesley, 1968).

Dart, R.A., 'The attainment of poise', *South African Medical Journal*, 1947, *21*, 74-91.

Dewey, J., *Human Nature and Conduct; An introduction to social psychology* (New York: Holt, 1922).

Dewey, J., Introduction, in Alexander, *The Use of the Self*.

Dykhuizen, G., *The Life and Mind of John Dewey* (Carbondale and Edwardsville: South Illinois University Press, 1973).

Irion, A.L., 'Historical introduction', in E.A. Bilodeau and I.M. Bilodeau (eds.), *Principles of Skill Acquisition* (New York: Academic Press, 1969).

Jones, F.P., 'Psychophysical re-education and the postural reflexes', Lecture given at the Science Weekend, Bard College, NY, May 1953.

Jones, F.P., *Body Awareness in Action: A Study of the Alexander Technique* (New York: Schocken, 1976).

McCormack, E.D., *Frederick Matthias Alexander and John Dewey: A neglected influence*, Unpublished doctoral dissertation (University of Toronto, 1958).

Mixon, D., 'Why pretend to deceive?', *Personality and Social Psychology Bulletin*, 1977, *3*, 647-53.

Mixon, D., 'The place of habit in the control of action', *Journal for the Theory of Social Behaviour*, 1980, *10*, 169-86.

Ogilvy, J., *Many Dimensional Man: Decentralizing self, society, and the sacred* (New York: Harper & Row, 1979).

Ryle, G., *The Concept of Mind* (London: Hutchinson, 1949).

4

Cognitive Psychology, 'Taylorism' and the Manufacture of Unemployment

John Shotter

Since its inauguration as a science 100 years ago, one whole mainstream of psychological research has been concerned to study the supposed 'mechanisms' within us, said to be mediating our activities—where such mechanisms are often represented as in fact doing our seeing, and reasoning, etc. for us. One theorist who actually inveighed *against* such a view is Neisser (1967). While committing himself to the use of what he called 'the program analogy' in the description of psychological processes, he made it clear that he did not think that machines themselves were intelligent: 'It is true that a number of researchers, not content with noting that computer programs are *like* cognitive theories, have tried to write programs which *are* cognitive theories' (ibid., p. 9). But, for Neisser, it is as if people merely *use* something like a computer program to inform their actions. Thus: 'The task of a psychologist trying to understand human cognition is analogous to that of a man trying to discover how a computer has been programmed' (ibid., p. 6). And this is how psychologists in general now see the doing of their science and the nature of the phenomena with which they must deal.

I want to show that, even if one does inveigh, as Neisser does, against the view that people *are* machines, the pursuit of the 'program analogy' in our understanding of ourselves can still lead to a loss of status by people in our society, because it promotes a form of psychology to do with showing how people 'can be replaced by machines'.

THE DIVISION OF LABOUR AND 'SCIENTIFIC MANAGEMENT'

In *The Wealth of Nations*, Adam Smith (1776/1921, vol.II, pp. 301-2) describes one of the more negative results of the division of labour thus:

> The man whose life is spent in performing a few simple operations . . . has no occasion to exert his understanding. . . . He naturally loses, therefore, the habit of such exertion, and generally becomes as stupid and ignorant as it is possible for a human creature to become.

Its positive advantage is, however, the 'great increase in the quantity of work, which, in consequence of the division of labour, the same number of people are capable of performing' (ibid., vol.I, p. 9). Thus, for Adam Smith, its institution was a matter of economics. For F.W. Taylor (1947), the originator of 'Taylorism', however, there were other reasons for the division of labour: (a) the centralisation of control, and (b) the rendering of the work process independent of craft, tradition and the workers' skills. And he succeeded, in fact, in outlining a procedure by which industrialists could appropriate the 'naturally occuring' knowledge in their 'environment', and gain possession of it as a commodity for their own use. Furthermore, he showed how it could be used to separate 'brain work' from 'muscle work', and thus to place the work process under the control of management, with the work of lower management being brought under the control of higher management, and so on.

Taylor, in analysing why it was so difficult to manage and control a workforce, realised that it was because it possessed something that the management lacked: the knowledge and the skill to produce the goods. This left the workers with a degree of bargaining power, for:

> The ingenuity and experience of each generation—of each decade, even, have without doubt handed over better methods to the next. This mass of rule-of-thumb or traditional knowledge may be said to be the principle asset or possession of every tradesman . . . which is not in the possession of the management. (ibid., p. 32)

But this state of affairs can be remedied: by applying the principles of 'scientific management' in which,

> The managers assume . . . the burden of gathering together all the traditional knowledge which in the past has been possessed by the workmen and then of classifying, tabulating and reducing this knowledge to rules, laws and formulae . . . (ibid., p 36)

Because:

> . . . all the planning which under the old system was done by the workman, as a result of his personal experience, must of necessity under the new system be done by the management in accordance with the laws of science . . . (ibid., p. 36)

Thus, through the application of scientific methods (but not to scientific ends), all this 'naturally' occurring knowledge can be quarried, excavated and itself fashioned into a marketable product.

But the process can be applied also to the management as well, as Taylor realised, in the form of 'functional management':

> 'Functional management' consists of so dividing the work of management that each man from the assistant superintendent down shall have as few functions as possible to perform. If practicable the work of each man in the management should be confined to the performance of a single leading function. (ibid., p 99)

And this completes the circle. Management itself becomes subject to a process of manufacture, and can be 'packaged' and marketed as a commodity. We then reach a stage in which, as Taylor says: 'In the past the man has been first; in the future the system must be first' (ibid., p. 7). And to the extent that Taylor's prophecy has come true, instead of the majority of people now living under the domination of the few, all of us live dominated by 'the system', dominated in fact by our own techniques of domination.

This then is 'Taylorism': the procedure by which a communal stock of knowledge can be mined and excavated and refined into a marketable commodity. Where the process of refining can itself, by making use of 'scientifically managed' production processes, be conducted as a manufacturing industry, as a 'knowledge industry'. Taylor's procedures are entirely general:

> The development of the science of doing any kind of work always requires the work of two men, one man who actually does the work which is to be studied and another man who observes closely the first man while he works and studies the time problems and the motion problems connected with this work. (ibid., p. 235)

The first person uses creative imagination, and trial-and-error energies in discovering a way to do the work (and Taylor points out, of course, that not one but a range of workers are observed to find the *best* one), and then the observer works to transform the process created by the first into a product, a commodity which can bought and sold.

PSYCHOLOGICAL RESEARCH

It will be instructive now to see how these aims are also present in current cognitive psychology. Although, of course, it does not present itself in this context as possessing aims of a commercial kind, nor as concerned with the kinds of analysis required by managers to get control of processes of production. It is presented as concerned with discovering a neutral and philosophically respectable analysis of what it actually is for actions to be intelligent and knowledgeable. And as I mentioned earlier, central to the approach currently being pursued is the 'program analogy', and the model of people as 'information processors'. A difficulty in this approach is, however, that it is not obvious how one can actually represent genuinely intelligent activities within such a framework. One solution to it is described by Daniel Dennett (1979, pp. 80-1), a philosopher seen by many psychologists as a supporter of the current 'information processing' view of cognitive abilities. He outlines the 'remarkably fruitful research strategy' of the artificial intelligence (AI) programmer thus:

> His first and highest level of design breaks the computer down into subsystems . . . into a committee or army of intelligent homunculi with

purposes, information and strategies. Each homunculus in turn is analysed into smaller homunculi, but, more important, into less clever homunculi. When the level is reached where the homunculi are no more than adders and subtractors, by the time they need only the intelligence to pick the larger of two numbers when directed to, they have been reduced to functionaries 'who can be replaced by a machine'.

This, he claims, is what intelligent activities *are*.

But in producing this account he executes a sleight of hand which diverts, apparently, even his own attention from the main point, never mind ours: for the point is that what is intelligent here is not the *product*, the program for the activity produced by the programmer, but the *process* of its production by the programmer. For it is that process which requires intelligent decisions as to what the appropriate 'committees' and 'armies' of homunculi should be, what abilities they should have, and how further they should be subdivided. As Margaret Boden (1977, p. 183) points out:

> There are indefinitely many representational schemes one might employ in making sense, of one sort or another, out of a phenomenon . . . [an] interpretative scheme requires an analysis of the phenomenon into the 'parts' that it takes to be significant.

And clearly, programmers must use their intelligence in choosing among possible representations the one which does in some manner represent an activity's 'significant parts'. Plan-following, as Dennett himself says, can be done by a machine. Plan-making or plan-forming, however, is a different kind of activity altogether (see Ryle, 1949). What gets concealed in Dennett's account is the nature of the 'natural' (or not so natural) resources upon which programmers draw in devising their programs. The fact that these resources owe their existence to the ways in which they are produced and reproduced by people in their everyday communal activities goes unmentioned. What captures our attention is that, if they can be subdivided appropriately into hierarchies of sub-tasks, they can be executed by functionaries 'who can be replaced by machines' and removed from communal life.

Now I do not want to argue in any crude sense that, because computers had their origins in commercial life, accounts such as Dennett's represent the result of a conspiratorial union of science and capital; not in the least. It is not people's commercial interests which lead them, necessarily, to theorise as they do; the form their theory takes can arise entirely as an *unintended consequence* (Merton, 1957) of the fact that the theories people produce must reflect the reality in which they live. That they see people as working in terms of hierarchies of domination along mechanical lines should come as no surprise at all, for that is how much of our work has been arranged and managed for some long time now. Hence, whether that is its intention or not, it is clear that AI can contribute to a considerable extent to what might be called a 'people replacement' business.

But what about work in psychology with a less obvious end-result, what might its unintended consequences be? Take, for example, studies by psychologists of 'problem-solving' behaviour: in such studies, people (called subjects) are presented with problems by psychologists (professional experts), and the subjects develop solutions to those problems. Given the requirements of their science, these solutions are theorised by the psychologists as consisting of recognisable elements, lawfully and regularly related to produce predictable results. Thus theorised, the strategies used in solving the problems, *which have in fact been created by the subjects*, are presented as the psychologists' 'findings'. Such studies are perhaps innocuous enough, for contrived problems in the laboratory may not have much relevance to everyday life—the results have little 'market value' to the clients funding the research. In the early 1970s, psychologists clearly began to sense this, and many became 'applied psychologists', turning away from the laboratory to the study of behaviour in everyday life (Broadbent, 1971)—to the extent that, as Howarth (1981, p. 151) put it, with respect to the study of problem-solving, 'this neglect of naturally occuring strategies is now a thing of the past'.

In other words, the process in which many psychologists are now engaged is formally equivalent to 'Taylorism': for they are using a procedure by which the knowledge, which is currently shared out among everyone in the community (transmitted to us in large part from previous generations), can be extracted and expropriated by scientific experts, and re-presented to the community as a scarce commodity, as 'discovered' by them in their studies of Nature. Furthermore, it is re-presented in special terms from the point of view of an outsider, a third-person external observer; the view required by a manipulator or manager, but not by a first- or second-person participant in the activity, for it is terms of forms and not meanings. It is a view which can render ordinary people—those who have been researched upon—even more mystified and helpless than before, for their concern is with coping with their world not as an outsider to it, but as a participant within it.

But it is not just people's knowledge which is under attack in this way, but their very way of life. For sociologists, psychologists, psychiatrists and other such experts are all studying 'the problem' faced by society in socialising its young. And by means of a procedure resembling 'scientific management' in its every detail, they are working to break down the socialisation process into its component parts, and to assign a function to all the 'workers' involved, including themselves of course as the resident 'experts' (Lasch, 1977). 'Cognitive psychology' is now a central contributor to this process.

CONCLUSIONS

I have not attempted here to present an account of what in fact is happening in psychology and in life at large. All I have attempted to do is to uncover the object at which current activity in psychology seems to be directed. And to argue that, whether individual psychologists intend it or not, this object parallels the explicit intention in Taylorism and 'scientific management': the appropriation of a communal resource, people's skills and knowledge; the centralisation of its control; and its embodiment in machines. In other words, cognitive psychology can work to manufacture unemployment. It need not do so, for a technology properly internalised can enhance people's abilities rather than degrade them (Vygotsky, 1978; Ong, 1982). But it *can* do.

The arguments I have presented here are not new. They are presented very much as Braverman (1974) presented them in his *Labor and Monopoly Capital: the Degradation of Work in the*

Twentieth Century, and they may be criticised in the same way: that they underestimate the extent to which workers creatively resist such a form of control by management, and devise strategies to retain some autonomy (see, for example, Wilkinson, 1982; Wood, 1982). To the extent that people's intrinsic intelligence and creativity prevents the total institution of 'Taylorism', to the same extent, the programme of cognitive psychology—to discover the 'programs' in people's actions—must also fail. In fact, people must, of necessity, create new ways of doing things from time to time as new and unforeseeable contingencies arise, and there are no programs to be found for doing that, for if those new ways are to be appropriate to their circumstances, they must to an extent be dependent upon them, i.e. they must be contingent upon some future circumstances which are as yet unknown.

But one must not underestimate the degree to which an untrue doctrine can be *made* true: (a) by the Humpty Dumpties in power refusing to see any view of the world other than their own and decreeing the discussion of any alternatives illegitimate; and (b) by those who are degraded as a result falling into despondency and helplessness, utterly mystified as to the part they can play in their own liberation. Psychologists play a part in this process, whether intended or not; they should be clear as to what their part is, and whether it is as they intend it to be.

REFERENCES

Boden, M. *Artificial Intelligence and Natural Man* (Hassocks Sussex: Harvester Press, 1977).

Braverman, H., *Labor and Monopoly Capital: the degradation of work in the twentieth century* (New York: Monthly Review Press, 1974).

Broadbent, D.E., 'The relation between theory and application in psychology', in P.E. Warr (ed.), *Psychology at Work* (Harmondsworth: Penguin Books, 1971).

Dennett, D.C., *Brainstorms: Philosophical essays on mind and psychology* (Hassocks Sussex: Harvester Press, 1979).

Howarth, C.I., 'The structure of effective psychology: man as a problem-solver', in A.J. Chapman and D.M. Jones (eds.), *Models of Man* (Leicester: British Psychological Society, 1981).

Lasch, C., *Haven in a Heartless World: the Family Besieged* (New York: Basic Books, 1977).

Merton, R.K., *Social Theory and Social Structure* (Chicago: Free Press of Glencoe, 1957).

Neisser, U., *Cognitive Psychology* (New York: Appleton–Century–Crofts, 1967).

Ong, W.J., *Orality and Literacy: the technologizing of the word* (London: Methuen, 1982).

Ryle, G., *The Concept of Mind* (London: Hutchinson, 1949).

Smith, A., *The Wealth of Nations*, vols. I and II (London: Bell and Sons Ltd, 1776/1921).

Taylor, F.W., *Scientific Management* (comprising *Shop Management* (1903), *The Principles of Scientific Management* (1911), and *Testimony before the Special House Committee* (1912)) (New York: Harper & Bros. first edn. 1912/1947).

Vygotsky, L.S., *Mind in Society: the development of higher Psychologigal Processes* (Boston: Harvard University Press, 1978).

Wilkinson, B., 'Battling it out on the factory floor', *New Scientist*, December 1982, 642-3.

Wood, S., *The Degradation of Work? Skill, deskilling and the Labour Process* (London: Hutchinson, 1982).

Section IB:
Intentionality and Classification

Central to cognitivism is a dualism which locates the perception and classification of objects and events outside the world in which they occur and, instead, within a separate, mental realm of ideas, concepts or representations. 'Inputs' from all modalities thus converge upon the mind, where they are interpreted with the aid of prior knowledge about the world, and (eventually) emerge as 'output' or behaviour. The long-standing problem with this approach, identified, for example, by Hume, has been that of who interprets the interpretation or representation, and it has proved hard to avoid the trap of making an implicit appeal to an infinite regress of interpretative homunculi. Modern attempts to solve this problem rest on the cognitivist analogy between minds and computers, which after all manifestly *work*. But can computers ever really show the same *intentionality* towards the world as do biological organisms? Some recent attempts to attribute intentionality to computers are discussed by Palmer (Chapter 5), who finds that they still rest upon the fallacy (inherent in cognitivism or 'the way of ideas') of trying to found intentionality upon entities that are not themselves intentional.

Our abstract systems of classification are so much a part of our thinking that we are apt to treat them as absolutes, and reflections of the timeless structure of the mind itself. But, as Ghiselin (Chapter 6) points out, classification is itself a human acitivity, and one that could be understood in biological terms, as an evolutionary problem. The *activity* gives rise to particular *systems* of classification, and it would clearly be circular to base an explanation of the activity on any one system. But that

53

is just what is attempted by cognitivism, which presents mind as mirroring a world classified according to the western search for ultimate 'essences' presumed to underlie experience of actual objects.

5

Cognitivism and Computer Simulation

Anthony Palmer

There are many aspects to the development within cognitive psychology which work in artificial intelligence exemplifies. My concern is with only one. Claims to be a significant development within philosophy are increasingly being made on its behalf. Daniel Dennett engagingly characterises them in the following way:

> Some AI people have recently become fond of describing their discipline as 'experimental epistemology'. This unfortunate term should make a philosopher's blood boil, but if AI called itself thought-experimental epistemology (or even better: *Gedanken*-experimental epistemology) philosophers ought to be reassured. (Dennett, 1978, p. 117)

A growing number of philosophers can be found who insist that research in artificial intelligence, together with allied work in linguistics, provides a basis for a new philosophy of mind. Essentially, the view is that new techniques and tools have enabled philosophers to return to a style and programme of philosophising which, at least for a while, was thought to have been finally discredited. It is not now unusual to hear philosophers say that they have turned to artificial intelligence because it seemed to present them a means of doing in a systematic way what until then they had been doing unsystematically. It is this thought that lies behind the increasing use of the phrase 'experimental epistemology'. The programme and style of philosophising to which they have returned is itself best viewed as one which in its turn utilised new tools and techniques, those of the formal logician, to revitalise doctrines introduced in the seventeenth century by

55

Descartes. In short they have returned to that conception of logic and language promulgated in the first quarter of the twentieth century by Bertrand Russell of whom, as David Pears (1967) has convincingly argued, 'the truest single thing that can be said is that [his philosophy] stands in the direct line of descent from Hume's [and that he is] the philosopher who gave empiricism an adequate logical framework'. Cognitivism, or the way of ideas, seems to be permanently capable of resuscitation by means of new tools and techniques.

I suppose the first statement of the view is to be found in Descartes' *Rules for the Direction of the Mind:*

> The cognitive power is always one and the same: if it applies itself, along with the imagination, to the common sensibility, it is said to see, feel, etc., if it applies itself to the imagination alone, in so far as that is already provided with various images, it is said to remember; if it does this to form new images, it is said to imagine or conceive; if, finally, it acts by itself, it is said to understand. ... In accordance with these diverse functions the same power is called now pure intellect, now imagination, now memory, now sense; and it is properly called mind when it is either forming new ideas in the phantasy or attending to those already formed.

It must be remembered that for Descartes the imagination and the common sensibility are both bodily. We get a conception of the psychological or mental when we conjoin such physical apparatus with a uniform faculty; a power of knowing or understanding. So began the way of ideas.

When this theory of ideas was first introduced it was clear that one of the benefits it seemed to bring with it was that of providing a means of understanding how language is possible. The having of a cognitive faculty in this way distinguished man from the brutes. Recalling this line of his thought in the *Discourse on Method* Descartes wrote:

> I specially dwelt on showing that if there were machines with the organs and appearance of a monkey, or some other irrational animal, we should have no means of telling that they were not altogether the same as those animals; whereas if there were machines resembling our bodies, and imitating our actions as far as is morally possible, we should still have two means of telling that, all the same, they were not real men. First they could never use words or other constructed signs, as we do to declare our thoughts to others. It is quite conceivable that a machine might be so made as to utter words, and even utter them in connection with physical events

that cause a change in one of its organs; so that e.g. if it is touched in one part it asks you what you want to say to it, and if touched in another, it cries out that it is hurt; but not that it should be so made as to arrange words variously in response to the meaning of what is said in its presence, as even the dullest of men can do.

In short, what such machines would lack is a mode of representation; they are incapable of thinking about things. It is only beings who have such a faculty that can use language to express what they know and indeed only they who can know anything at all, for example, that this object is a piece of wax for example.

> It must be observed that the perception of the wax is not sight, not touch, not imagination; nor was it ever so, though it formerly seemed to me to be; it is a purely mental contemplation; which may be either imperfect or confused, as it originally was, or clear and distinct, as it now is, according to my degree of attention to what it consists in. (*Meditation*, 2)

The advantages of the new cognitivism are difficult to overestimate. Not only did the doctrine free philosophy from the literal unintelligibility of the version of scholastic philosophy that was then being taught (e.g. to Descartes at *La Flèche*), with its 'substantial forms', and 'intentional species'. It also introduced an admirable egalitarianism into conceptions of human beings (since good sense is the most evenly distributed thing in the world) which had powerful ramifications in political and educational spheres in the eighteenth century. However, the doctrine brought with it its own problems which were to prove insuperable, or at least seemed so to prove, until work in artificial intelligence offered hope of escape.

The problems which the way of ideas set for philosophy were epistemological. If knowledge is mediated by ideas, and if words become meaningful by being, as Locke put it, annexed to ideas, then there was a clear need to bridge the gap between ideas and things; to ensure that our ideas are adequate representations of the way things are. For Descartes the gap was bridged by God, whose provable existence and demonstrable goodness guaranteed that, by and large, with exceptions that a right conduct of reason will enable us to avoid, things are as we think them to be. While to Locke, who deplored such a God-based metaphysics, it seemed obvious that some of our ideas—those of the primary qualities of bodies—could not fail to resemble the qualities themselves, and this ensured that a theory of knowledge within the way of ideas could have a firm basis. Soon, however, the distinction between primary and secondary qualities came under attack from Berkeley, and proofs of God's existence were, to say the least, rendered suspect by Hume, who was to inflict an even greater wound which seemed to prove fatal.

The postulation of ideas through which we gain knowledge of things and by means of which we are able to express that knowledge, requires a conception of someone who uses ideas; in short it requires a conception of the self. Yet if all our knowledge is mediated by ideas it seems that the one thing we can have no idea of is a self which uses such ideas. Hume, notoriously, acknowledged that this was a problem he could not solve.

> For my part, when I enter most intimately into what I call *myself*, I always stumble on some particular perception or other, of light or shade, love or hatred, pain or pleasure. I never catch *myself* at any time without a perception, and never observe anything but a perception. When my perceptions are removed for any time, by sound sleep; so long am I insensible of *myself*, and may be said truly not to exist. . . . If anyone upon serious and unprejudic'd reflection, thinks that he has a different notion of *himself*, I must confess that I can reason no longer with him. (*Treatise of Human Nature*, Book I, Part IV, section VI)

Yet if the problem cannot be solved, Descartes' way of ideas is bankrupt. It is this, Hume's problem, which researchers in artificial intelligence claim to have solved, and thus to have at least begun to rehabilitate cognitivism. With that rehabilitation the techniques of computer simulation have come to seem extremely powerful. In what follows I shall use the exposition in Daniel Dennett's paper 'Artificial Intelligence as Philosophy and as Psychology' in his book *Brainstorms* as representative of this line of thinking.

The following is Dennett's modern version of the problem:

> For the British Empiricists, the internal representations were called ideas, sensations, impressions: more recently psychologists have talked of hypotheses, maps, schemes, images, propositions, engrams, neural signals,

even holograms and whole innate theories. . . . [However] nothing is intrinsically a representation of anything; something is a representation only for or to someone; any representation or system of representations thus requires at least one *user* or *interpreter* of the representation who is external to it. Any such interpreter must have a variety of psychological or intentional traits: it must be capable of a variety of *comprehension* and must have beliefs and goals (so it can *use* the representation to *inform* itself and thus assist itself in achieving its goals). Such an interpreter is then a sort of homunculus. . . . Therefore psychology without homunculi is impossible but psychology with homunculi is doomed to circularity or infinite regress, so psychology is impossible. (Dennett, 1978, p. 122)

He then proceeds to give what he considers to be AI's solution to the problem. First of all, he points out that homunculus talk is ubiquitous in AI, but that far from its being harmful there it turns out to be extremely beneficial. The reason why this can be so, he argues, is that they are not invoked to explain abilities wholesale.

Homunculi are *bogeymen* only if they duplicate *entire* the talents they are rung in to explain. If one can get a team or committee of relatively ignorant, narrow-minded, blind homunculi to produce the intelligent behaviour of the whole, this is progress. A flow chart is typically the organisation chart of a committee of homunculi (investigators, librarians, accountants, executives); each box specifies a homunculus by prescribing a function *without* saying how it is to be accomplished (one says in effect: put a little man in there to do the job). If we then look closer at the individual boxes we see that the function of each is accomplished by subdividing it via another flow chart into still smaller, more stupid homunculi. Eventually this nesting of boxes within boxes lands you with homunculi so stupid (all they have to do is to remember whether to say yes or no when asked) that they can be, as one says, "replaced by a machine". One *discharges* fancy homunculi from one's scheme by organising armies of idiots to do the work. (ibid., p. 123)

Offered *this* as a solution to Hume's problem, one wonders how it could ever have been thought to be one. For it is clear that the problem remains even at the level of the stupidest homunculus. The problem was, from the start, one of intentionality. Indeed, Hume's problem is just one way of stating a problem about intentionality. One criterion of an intentional verb is that propositions containing it do not retain their truth value through changes in correct characterisations of their objects. They do not go through the hoops of what

Peter Geach has called Shakespearian inference. While that
which we call a rose by any other name would smell as sweet,
that which we think about or worship or intend would not be
thought about or worshipped or intended if its characterisation
were altered even to something which is true of what is thought
about or worshipped or intended. The Greeks worshipped
Zeus, Oedipus thought about Jocasta and intended to make
love to her, but given that it is true that Zeus is nothing but a
collection of sticks and stones, and Jocasta was the mother of
Oedipus, it will not necessarily be true that the Greeks
worshipped sticks and stones and that Oedipus thought about
his mother and intended to go to bed with her. For this we need
the way in which the Greeks represented Zeus to themselves
and the way in which Oedipus represented Jocasta to himself.
If Hume's problem of internal representations is one of
intentionality from the start, then we shall not solve it by
merely restricting the range of intentionality.

There are, I think, very strong parallels here to the solution
which Descartes himself offered to a problem about mind and
body which his own views generated. Recall his suggestion that
mind only acted upon a very little bit of body, the pineal gland.
The problem (as I suspect he himself recognised) was not one of
size. Similarly, if Hume's problem is that of intentionality, it
will not be solved by making the range of its application
smaller and smaller. Hume's problem really does require that
homunculi are dispensed with altogether, for *remembering* to
say yes or no provides us with just the same problem from a
logical point of view as remembering that two bishops are more
powerful than a knight and a bishop in a restricted end game,
or remembering to say check at the appropriate moment.

There is also a striking parallel here to the way in which
many philosophers of the 1950s and 1960s, suffering from what
has been called the Routledge and Kegan Paul syndrome,
sought to answer the question, 'What must be added to (mere)
bodily movements to turn them into fully-fledged human
behaviour?'. Correctly suspicious of supposing that the answer
was to add a bit of mental stuff, they argued (overinfluenced, I
suspect, by the pressure the analogy with games and in
particular the game of chess was exerting on philosophical
speculation) that what was needed was for bodily movements

to be set in the background of a society with its rules, conventions, institutions, etc. The following passage from A.I. Melden's book *Free Action* is typical.

> [T]he child needs to be trained . . . to recognise *this* bodily movement of its mother in *this* transaction in which it engages, as *this* action, *that* bodily movement in *that* transaction as *that* action. Only in the context of the specific activities which it has been trained to perform . . . is it possible to understand the bodily movements of those participating . . . as the actions they are . . . So one could go on to explore the manner in which the concepts of action and agent are enriched by relating to the wider scenes of social intercourse in which in divers ways various social and moral institutions, conventions, statutes etc., are relevant to the background activities against which bodily movements are understood as the actions they are. (Melden, 1961, p. 190)

However it is clear that setting bodily movements in the background of rules and conventions could not possibly have the effect of turning it into human behaviour. The model does indeed provide us with a way of showing how something which is an action can have a different force or become a quite different action if set in different backgrounds—raising one's arm on the starting grid of a Grand Prix is to do something quite different from raising one's arm before serving in a game of tennis—for raising one's arm is already an action. However, a model which serves well to explain how one action can become another will be a non-starter when used to explain how something which is not an action becomes an action. To use the former as an explanation of the latter is really only an unargued assertion that the latter is no problem. Moreover if we permit ourselves the luxury of thinking of intentionality as being unproblematic, i.e. if we permit ourselves homunculi in our explanations, then, as Elliot Sober (1982) has argued, there is no reason from a logical point of view why the homunculi we import to explain the abilities of human beings should be less intelligent than the human beings whose behaviour they are brought in to explain. It would indeed be an explanation of why I behave in the ways that I do, or of how I am able to do the things that I do, if it were discovered that inside my skull were a miniature genius who for purposes of his own moved my limbs around. This is no doubt not very likely but there would be nothing wrong with it as an explanation. What it would not serve to explain is the problem which Dennett calls Hume's problem.

The upshot of all this is that if we think of AI as thought experimentation within the constraints of a new technology, namely computers, then Hume's problem or any similar problem is not going to be resolved by workers in AI. What we need to do, then, is to ask ourselves what is there about Hume's problem which makes it insoluble by computational means.

Before doing this, however, it is worthwhile considering a prior question. Why, given that the computational psychologist's solution is manifestly no solution, could it possibly have been thought to be so? I think that part of the right answer to this question is that the AI solution would be a proper solution to something which looks like Hume's problem but is not. The computational approach is dependent upon the assumption that philosophical problems about mind and body have been solved in advance. If minds are just brains, i.e. if some sort of thesis of contingent identity of mind and body is correct, then we no longer have Hume's problem. For the thesis of contingent identity is just the thesis that there are no logical problems with regard to the postulation of that identity. It is precisely for that reason that the term 'contingent' is contained in the statement of the thesis. Hume's problem might be stated by saying that we cannot dispense with intentionality. The identity thesis might well be stated by saying that ultimately there are no logical problems which stand in the way of dispensing with intentionality, even though it may empirically be the case that we cannot. Moreover, if the contingent identity thesis is stated in a particular way an added impetus is given to the use of an intentional terminology which is integral to the AI approach. If instead of saying (a) there are brain states that for any person are identical with states of mind, we say (b) for any person there are brain states that are identical with states of mind, this leaves open the possibility that such brain states may differ from person to person, and indeed that they may be different in the same person at different times. If such were the case then the AI approach would be the only sensible approach. Hence given that there are no logical problems in dispensing with intentionality we can reconstruct something that looks like Hume's problem and use a computational approach to solve it for us. We set ourselves the problem of how a large-scale ability whose characterisations would involve intentional descriptions could be a consequence of a series of smaller-scale abilities whose descriptions also involved intentional characterisations and so on, until we have reached the smallest possible abilities. We then add the reminder that we have shown in advance that there is no logical reason why such abilities will not turn out in the end to be identical with certain brain states. Showing how they turn out to be so will be the point at which the so-called computational or top-down approach meets up with the physiological or bottom-up approach. If you are sceptical of the contingent identity thesis then the philosophical problems—in particular Hume's problem—remain untouched. The AI approach has solved no philosophical problems. On the contrary, its adoption presumes that the philosophical problems have been solved.

The identity thesis, albeit in various forms, has rapidly assumed the status of a dogma in recent years. Dennett's version of it seems to me to be peculiarly dangerous. Using the idea that problems of intentionality, problems about the nature of representation, are in principle solved, he argues that we can be quite safe in our psychologising if we utilise the power of our ordinary intentional concepts by moulding them into a system. We can then use such a system not only in the explanation of human behaviour but also to understand the use which we make of our ordinary psychological concepts; a systematised version of belief, desire, intention etc. will help us to understand those concepts themselves.

> Every mental event is some functional, physical event or other, and the types are captured . . . by a regimentation of the very terms we *ordinarily* use—we explain *what beliefs are* by systematizing the notion of a believing system, for instance. (Dennett, 1978, p.xix)

When, however, our ordinary psychological concepts prove recalcitrant to such systematisation, he argues, we should conclude not that there is something radically wrong with our systematic endeavours but that there is something wrong that

we are trying to understand! 'Most if not all of our familiar
mentalistic idioms fail to perform [the] task of perspicuous
reference, because they embody conceptual infelicities and
incoherences of various sorts.'

I now return to the question of why Hume's problem is not
soluble by computational means. My suggestion here hinges
upon the terminology with which I began, i.e. the idea that
work done in AI is correctly characterised as the conducting of
thought experiments. Dennett's view was that while the phrase
'experimental epistemology' smacks of confusion (the confusion of supposing that epistemological problems can be
solved by empirical means), if we can envisage a form of
experimentation *which is not empirical* then the possibility of an
experimental epistemology opens up. It is here that the notion
of thought experiments comes into play. Thought experiments
are experiments all right, but they are precisely not empirical
experiments. They deal not so much with what is the case but
with what might be the case; not so much with actualities as
with possibilities. Possibilities may be unactualised but
actualities are at least possible. *Ab esse ad posse valet
consequentia.* What the computer enables us to do is to be
systematic in our exploration of possibilities. The discipline of
the computer enables us to turn our *a priori* speculations into
thought experiments, computation standing to speculation
about possibilities in the way in which experimentation stands
to speculation about actualities. Computers are the 'prosthetic
regulators' of our *a priori* speculation. Hence to philosophise
without the computer is unreasonably to deny ourselves the
use of such regulators.

With such a characterisation of thought experiments we can
now turn to Hume's problem. We have seen how that problem
turns out to be insoluble by even prosthetically regulated
thought experiments. It follows from this that in so far as
Hume's problem is correctly thought of as a problem about the
possibility of a psychology which utilises the idea of internal
representations then such a possibility is not one which will be
capable of being explored in a prosthetically regulated way.
Similarly, if Hume's problem is correctly thought of as a
conceptual problem it will follow that we shall need to
distinguish between conceptual investigations and thought

experiments even though both might be correctly characterised as explorations of possibilities.

The discipline of the computer will only enable our *a priori* speculations to be turned into regulated thought experiments if the subject matter of our speculation is proper for such experimentation. However, even while Russell and Frege were developing the tools with which the former sought to give empiricism an adequate basis, it was becoming clear that the conception of logic embodied in those very tools was itself the greatest obstacle to such a scheme. The development of what we now know as formal logic began with the depsychologising of the subject. Bradley, who did not contribute to that development, pointed in the same direction when he argued that from the point of view of logic ideas could not be thought of as individuals.

> For logical purposes the psychological distinction of idea and sensation may be said to be irrelevant, while the distinction of idea and fact is vital. The image, or psychological idea, is for logic nothing but a sensible reality. It is on a level with mere sensations of the senses. For both are facts and neither is meaning . . . But an idea, if we use an idea of the meaning, is neither given nor presented, but is taken. It cannot as such exist. It cannot be an event, with a place in the series of time and space. It can be a fact no more inside our heads than outside them. And if you take this mere idea by itself, it is an adjective divorced, a parasite cut loose, a spirit without a body seeking rest in another, an abstraction from the concrete, a mere possibility which by itself is nothing. (Bradley, 1928, Ch. 1, section 8)

Logic, in other words, can have nothing to do with internal representations psychologically conceived, i.e. conceived as psychological entities or indeed as entities of any sort. But perhaps more importantly for our purposes, Frege, the founder of modern logic, became increasingly aware as his views developed that the main source of contamination of what he calls the logical source of knowledge was a tendency to treat concepts as objects. The confusion of psychology and logic is indeed for him just one version of that tendency.

> One feature of language that threatens to undermine the reliability of thinking is a tendency to form proper names to which no objects correspond . . . The definite article [in the expression 'the concept *star*'] creates the impression that this phrase is meant to designate an object, or,

what amounts to the same thing, that 'the concept star' is a proper name, whereas 'concept *star*' is surely a designation of a concept and thus could not be more different from a proper name. The difficulties which this idiosyncrasy of language entangles us in are incalculable. (Frege, 1979, p. 270)

It was this realisation that, from a logical point of view, lay behind Wittgenstein's influential rejection of the picture of language in which 'every word has a meaning. This meaning is correlated with the word. It is the object for which the word stands' (Wittgenstein, 1953, §1). Cartesian and Lockean ideas were just such objects. Bradley and Frege had been the first to realise that ideas so conceived were irrelevant to logic. It was to be another half-century before they were to be proclaimed irrelevant to any subject whatsoever: that, as Ryle so vividly put it, they belonged to the myth of the ghost in the machine. I think it is an accident of history that the development from Bradley to Ryle coincided with the development of various forms of behaviourism. These were much more influenced by the failures of introspectionist psychology and a hankering for the measurable than any considerations of logic. It is sheer confusion to place Ryle's *The Concept of Mind* (even worse, Wittgenstein's *Philosophical Investigations*) within that tradition, and to see it as reinforcing a form of materialism by providing a behaviouristic interpretation of mental concepts. Ryle certainly did reject the way of ideas: 'They belong where "phlogiston" belongs and where "substantial forms" belong, namely the folk-lore of philosophy'. Yet he found its defenders more worthy opponents than the adherents of the materialism which it replaced. 'The Cartesian myth does indeed repair the defects of the Hobbist myth only by duplicating it. But even doctrinal homeopathy involves the recognition of disorders' (Ryle, 1949, p. 330). And yet it is this alternation, either behaviourism or a psychology that utilises ideas (internal representations), which is the largest single impetus behind the current resurrection of cognitivism. Ryle would have urged, indeed he did urge, that this dichotomy, like most logicians' dichotomies, needs to be taken with a pinch of salt.

Hume's problem is a problem about the nature of concepts. He called them ideas. But because he thought of them as peculiar sorts of objects (mental objects) he found himself ensnared in the problem which we have given his name to in this paper. Hume's problem is best thought of as the name we give to the difficulties that ensue when we treat concepts as objects. The characteristic form which such difficulties take is that of an infinite regress.

Hume's talk of impressions and ideas is an attempt to explain the ways in which we think about the world, and we, like him, can ask how it is possible to think of the world in the ways in which we do. We can, for example, ask how it is possible for us to think of it in terms of cause and effect given that necessary connections are never observed. Or we might wonder how it is possible to think of rights and obligations given that these are never observed. We know that Hume's response to these and similar questions was to point to the role of the passions in human affairs. We might produce different solutions. But when in the Appendix to the *Treatise* he raises the question of the self—i.e. when he raises the question we have labelled Hume's problem—he raises a question which he himself recognises is unanswerable in that way. The first two questions do indeed ask us to experiment in thought but the question in the Appendix does not. It cannot do so for it raises quite a different problem about ideas or about the perceptions of the mind, or, to use Dennett's terminology, about internal representations. And this question arises from treating them as objects, a view to which he can see no alternative.

> In general the following reasoning seems satisfactory. All our ideas are borrowed from preceding perceptions. Our ideas of objects therefore are borrowed from that source. Consequently no proposition can be intelligible or consistent with regard to objects which is not so with regard to perceptions. (*Treatise,* Appendix)

The trouble is, as Hume saw, that if ideas are thought of in that way—i.e. if they are thought of as objects, then it is difficult to see how they could play the role that they were invoked to play. How could objects give us the way in which we represent objects (the world) to ourselves? Hence Hume's search for the self which regressed to infinity.

This all important but difficult to articulate distinction between concepts and objects might serve to illuminate the remark at the end of Wittgenstein's *Philosophical Investigations* which has generated so much work in philosophy and which has at the same time served to alienate philosophical research from psychological research. I refer to the remark in which he compares work in psychology to work in mathematics.

> The confusion and barrenness of psychology is not to be explained by calling it a "young science"; its state is not comparable with that of physics, for instance, in its beginnings. (Rather with that of certain branches of mathematics. Set theory.) For in psychology there are experimental methods and *conceptual confusion* (As in the other case conceptual confusion and methods of proof.) (Wittgenstein, 1953, xiv)

On my reading of this remark, it is not so much that psychology presents us with muddled thinking which needs philosophical expertise that will be greatly enhanced by the prosthetic regulation of computer simulation, but rather that in psychology, as in the area of mathematics to which Wittgenstein refers, we are likely to become confused about concepts. In mathematics when thinking about concepts there is an inclination to confuse them with sets or classes, and this is an example of the same sort of error as Hume made when he thought of concepts as mental objects. If Wittgenstein's remark had been read in that way at the time of the publication of the *Philosophical Investigations* then a great deal of what was written about philosophical psychology in the late 1950s and through the 1960s would have remained unwritten—there would have been no Routledge and Kegan Paul syndrome—and in the 1970s and early 1980s we should have been able to see more clearly the limits of AI.

REFERENCES

Bradley, F.H., *Principles of Logic* (Oxford: Oxford University Press, 1928, 2nd edn).

Dennett, D., *Brainstorms* (Montgomery, VT: Bradford Books, 1978).

Frege, G., *Posthumous Writings* (Chicago: Chicago University Press, 1979).

Melden, A.I., *Free Action* (London: Routledge & Kegan Paul, 1961).

Ryle, G., *The Concept of Mind* (London: Hutchinson, 1949).
Sober, E., 'Why must homunculi be so stupid?', *Mind*, 1981, *91*, 410–22.
Wittgenstein, L., *Philosophical Investigations* (Oxford: Blackwell, 1953).

6

Classification as an Evolutionary Problem

Michael T. Ghiselin

CLASSIFICATION AS AN ACTIVITY

Knowledge is organised, virtually by definition. Often its organisational structure is manifested in elaborate systems of classification such as the Linnaean hierarchies of taxonomic zoology and botany. The language of everyday life, if perhaps a bit less sophisticated than that of the erudite, likewise contains a formidable array of groups within groups.

Those who have studied the principles of classification include biologists like myself, philosophers, linguists, anthropologists and cognitive psychologists. Thus the study of classification is a highly interdisciplinary activity. However, the amount of communication between the various areas of investigation has not been particularly effectual, to judge from the many quite different points of view that coexist in the literature. If anything of a general character emerges, it is that everybody tends to oversimplify the subject and take certain rather dubious assumptions for granted.

All too often it is presupposed that the objects of knowledge are immutable entities. The universe is believed to be populated by groups called 'sets' or 'classes', and these correspond to the fundamental elements of knowledge which are said to be 'categories', 'concepts' or 'ideas' that exist 'in the mind'. Accordingly, if we want to understand classification, these are the things we need to study. An evolutionary approach to classification might view matters quite differently, envisaging the universe as populated by concrete entities that change through time: organisms and species, for example, and knowledge itself. When an evolutionary biologist studies the acquisition of some adaptation, such as protective colouration, the appropriate consideration is how a succession of varying generations has been affected by selective processes involving interactions within the environment. When a psychologist studies the acquisition of some learned behavioural feature, an appropriate consideration is how a succession of reinforcements has proceeded. In either case we have what Skinner (1981) calls 'selection by consequences'. Classification too has more than just formal properties. Organisms use it. Thus, although there may be a legitimate place for *Rules and Representations* (Chomsky, 1980), what really matters is *How to do Things with Words* (Austin, 1975).

CLASSES AND INDIVIDUALS

A static view of the world de-emphasises the particular and the concrete. According to Aristotle, for example, all knowledge is of universals or classes, not of single things. More recent students of knowledge have tended, implicitly or explicitly, to echo this claim. Indeed, individuals are treated as so inconsequential that few have bothered to consider what it means when we say that something is an individual. One way to put it is to say that an individual is a single, concrete thing (Ghiselin, 1981). The conventional stereotype of an individual is an individual person, such as you or me, and the term 'individual' is often used as a synonym for 'organism'. But a single, concrete thing can also be a non-living object, such as a chair. It can be a part of something, such as the rung of a ladder. It can also be some larger whole, such as a family, a nation or a galaxy.

That some supra-organismal groups are not classes is clear from the fact that such sentences as 'Burgundy is a France' are nonsensical. Burgundy is a part, not an instance, of France. The distinction is built into our everyday language. But more is involved than linguistic convention. Consider the class *organism*, the members of which are individual organisms. The latter can and do change, but it is impossible for *organism* itself to change. There may have been a time when there were no organisms, and the class may again come to have no members, but *organism* remains *organism* throughout. The thesis that species, as well as organisms, are individuals (Ghiselin, 1981) has practical consequences, as well as theoretical ones. *Homo sapiens* has not always existed. It could change in quite a ꞌvariety of ways, and we rightly fear that it may become extinct.

ABSTRACT AND CONCRETE

Species are not the only groups of interest that turn out to be individuals rather than classes. Many of the basic units in sociology and social psychology are supra-organismal wholes. Families, clubs, clans, tribes, universities and professional societies provide good examples. So do languages and wars. That groups of this sort have psychological importance is apparent from some experimental work by Markman and her collaborators (Markman, 1973; 1979; Markman and Siebert, 1976). Younger children have a hard time reasoning about 'all of the ducks' in a picture, and find it much easier to deal with 'a whole family' of ducks. To put it perhaps too simply, the concrete group is comprehended before an abstraction drawn from it.

Cognitive psychologists seem not to have appreciated the implications of Markman's discovery. For example, Smith and Medin (1981, p. 117) conclude that it does not apply to what really interests them, namely classes. And yet such findings are just the sort of thing one would expect from Piaget's distinction between the concrete operational and the formal operational stages of development (Osherson and Markman, 1974). Even Piaget missed the ontological lesson here. Early in life Piaget became interested in the nominalist–realist controversy. As a biologist he could not accept the notion that species are 'abstractions', which follows if species are classes, and classes are not real. Instead of recognising that species are individuals rather than classes, which would have solved the problem in a straightforward manner, he developed an elaborate and quite unnecessary metaphysical theory. Perhaps more importantly, an excessive emphasis upon classes has led many, including Piaget, to treat concrete operational reasoning as somehow inferior to the formal operational kind. Each has its appropriate sphere of applicability, but age prejudice is not uncommon, even among developmental psychologists. Thus, reversing the usual interpretation, it may be that in some people the wherewithal to deal with concrete objects atrophies with age; such considerations might provide valuable insights into the diversity of cognitive styles within our species. Furthermore, the literature on cognitive psychology is vague and equivocal in its use of the word 'concrete'. First, whatever seems impalpable or not immediately apparent to the senses is treated as 'abstract', though logically any individual whatsoever is 'concrete', including individual events and individual experiences. What is abstract about going to work on 5 January 1986? Second, there is a failure to recognise that concreteness, unlike abstractness, does not admit of degree. The class of geometrical figures is more abstract than the class of triangles, but it is hard to imagine what would be meant by an 'abstract' particular thing. Third, abstraction is often confounded with generality. The more general classes are indeed more abstract than the more particular ones (triangle and scalene triangle), but although the USA might be considered more general than California, both are absolutely concrete. Smith and Medin (1981) insist that a pair of blue trousers is more abstract than a pair of trousers *simpliciter*. But is not every pair of trousers in the real world a concrete, particular object? I suspect that complex propositions are being confused with abstract entities.

Modern philosophy has often had difficulty coping with individuals. A good example is the metaphysics of Bertrand Russell and those influenced by him (see Black, 1944). According to Russell, the only 'individuals' are so-called logical atoms. Only these can have 'logically proper names'. In other words Bertrand Russell is a class. When one embraces such metaphysics, the properties of classes are artificially imposed upon individuals. What is most important about individuals therefore gets screened out, in particular, variability and change.

A crude version of nominalism is also popular among cognitive psychologists. Nominalism, already mentioned in this chapter, is the doctrine that although individuals are real, classes are not. Whether or not classes are real is beside the point when the entity, whose reality is at issue, is actually an individual. But some versions of 'nominalism' attempt to make just about everything in the universe an 'abstraction', so that whether and how a thing exists is supposed to depend upon our thought processes. Keil (1979, p. 144) tells us that 'Categories are in the head, not in the world'. Does this mean that things had no locations before heads evolved? Chomsky (1980, p. 218) makes things quite explicit. 'Even when we speak of "an organism", we are engaged in idealisation and abstraction. One might, after all, study an organism in the world from a very different point of view. Suppose we were to study the flow of nutrients or the oxygen–carbon dioxide cycle. Then the organism would disappear in a flux of chemical processes, losing its integrity as an individual placed in an environment.' How wonderful it would be if I could make mosquitoes and creditors fall apart simply by thinking about them from an ecological point of view! It is curious how many intellectuals believe that words lack objective reference and nothing exists save self and thought.

CATEGORIES

Classes and individuals are two 'kinds of groups' but we need to make further distinctions. For some reason it has become common practice among cognitive psychologists and anthropologists to call any kind of group whatsoever a 'category'. Systematic biologists, however, restrict the use of this term. A 'taxon' means any of the basic units made up of organisms, such as *Homo sapiens*. The term 'category' refers to the level at which a taxon is ranked, such as species and genus. Thus, *Homo* is a taxon, and genus is a category.

Philosophers have used 'category' in yet another sense, to mean the basic headings under which everything is supposed to fall, such as substance, attribute, place and relation. Misapplying the categories leads to what are called 'category mistakes'. If I take a walk and get tired, it makes sense to say that I am tired or that my legs are tired, but not that the walk itself is tired. My legs and I fall under the category of substance, the walk is an event; my tiredness an attribute of me, but not the walk. Often category mistakes can be recognised because they are nonsensical. Even quite young children will say that the statement, 'The distance between Paris and London weighs 10 kilograms' is 'silly'. Thanks largely to the work of Keil (1979), the problems that surround categories are widely appreciated by cognitive psychologists. However, partly because the term 'category' has been so equivocal, a great deal has been overlooked. It is a mistake, but not a category mistake, to say that a human being can change sex. Oysters change sex routinely, and the results of surgery and hormone injections can give a fair approximation. If there is a mistake here, it is a mistake about matters of fact or perhaps the definition of terms. For one individual to become another individual, however, in the sense of the earth becoming the moon, would be unthinkable. It is not just a physical impossibility, but a metaphysical one.

Perhaps it is not desirable to lump all instances of metaphysical error under the rubric of 'category mistake'. At any rate, there are important distinctions here, for example, between what might be called a 'level mistake' and mistakes with respect to applying such categories as substance and place. For example, when it is said that the USA declared war on Germany, it is not meant that each of the 48 states of the Union did so, but the entire nation. Ryle (1949) used such 'level mistakes' to explain what he meant by a 'category mistake'. But what really concerned him was not whether it is an organ or an entire organism that thinks, but whether, for instance, 'mind' denotes a process ('minding') or a substance (such as the nervous system). These are very different issues.

THE STRUCTURE OF KNOWLEDGE

Given such considerations we can find some room for improvement in Keil's (1979) effort to investigate the hierarchical structure of ontological knowledge. Inspired by the work of Sommers (1959; 1963; 1965), he has developed a tree-diagram that purports to show how people classify the

world. I present it, slightly simplified, not as a tree, but as a
hierarchy of the same logical structure (Keil, 1979, p. 160):

  All entities—
    Atemporal structures
    Temporal structures
    Things that occur in space
    Events—
      Intentional events
      Non-intentional events
    Things that can be sensed—
      Things with no mass
      Things with mass
        Non-cohesive things—
          Masses
          Aggregates
        Cohesive things—
          Non-substantial forms
          Substantial forms
            Artefacts
            Living things
            Plants
            Animals
              Non-human
              Human

Examination reveals that the rationale of these subdivisions is
far from homogeneous. At higher levels we do find good
ontological categories. Thus, for both events and things that
can be sensed we can specify where they are located (the
category of place). But we cannot say that a recess (event) is
heavy or that a playground (substance) is an hour long. When,
however, we descend to the level of non-cohesive *versus*
cohesive things, we encounter problems. Consider water. The
test that shows it to fall under things with mass is that 'Water is
heavy' makes sense. That it is non-cohesive is shown by the fact
that it makes no sense to say that 'water is tall'. But what about
ice? A block of ice can be tall. Ice is water in its solid state.
Furthermore we seem to be having trouble with mass nouns
here. Water is one thing, a cup of water another. When we
specify a cup, water becomes a definite amount, and a

particular cup of water could have a definite height, just as an iceberg does. We do not seem to be dealing with basic ontological distinctions here, but rather with an incoherent mixture of defects in our understanding of the material universe on the one hand, and imperfections in the language of everyday life on the other.

Descending to the level of living things, we get still more problems. According to the hierarchy as it is presented, one can say of any living thing that it is alive, but, we are told, only animals can be asleep, only people can be sorry or think. Here we are not dealing with categorial knowledge at all, but with knowledge of taxa, and matters of contingent fact or mere belief. The reason why plants are not supposed to sleep is the same as the reason why non-human animals are not supposed to feel sorry or think—it is a mixture of folk psychology and theology. There exists, in fact, a substantial literature on the sleep movements of plants, and many persons both lay and erudite do attribute thought and emotions to animals not of our own species. Who is right about such matters is irrelevant here. The behavioural entities in question could arise through evolutionary processes, or, some might say by, divine fiat. Such being the case we have nothing even remotely resembling metaphysical necessity.

Keil's tree suggests that there exists but one and only one hierarchical system corresponding to knowledge. This may or may not be Keil's opinion. But it does raise a very important point, for it is common practice to search for a monolithic taxonomy. In biology, evolutionary relationships between all organisms can and should be expressed by means of a single hierarchy. But we also have additional classification systems, so that a mammal may fall under a wide variety of general terms, such as 'homeotherm', 'predator' and 'marine'. If, as would seem to be the case, ordinary language has the same character, there are important implications for cognitive psychology. Consider the fact that what is called 'category membership' (taxon subsumption) is supposed to be transitive. This is indeed the case for simple hierarchies either of individuals and their parts or of sets and subsets. California is part of the USA, and Mendocino County is part of California, and also a part of the USA. Cognitive anthropologists have therefore been somewhat puzzled by what seem to be intransitive relationships among parts. Consider the putative intransitivity of 'mouth'. The mouth is a part of the face. The face is part of the head. The mouth is part of the head. All well and good—the relation is indeed transitive. However, a tooth is part of the mouth, but it is not part of the face. This seems not to be a transitive relation. Note, however, that 'mouth' is equivocal, or, as cognitive anthropologists put it, 'polysemous'. On the one hand, it refers to a slit-like orifice, on the other hand it refers to what anatomists call the buccal cavity and its associated elements. Although McClure (1975) recognises the equivocation, she does not draw the obvious conclusion. An individual can be a part of more than one whole and a member of more than one class, and we have multiple classification systems for different purposes. A tooth is a part of the head, the alimentary canal, the speech-making apparatus and a smile.

The same kind of problem crops up with efforts to study folk-taxonomies. In the formal classification systems of biologists, an organism can fall under only one taxon at any categorical level (e.g. it cannot be classified as both a bird and a mammal, though it can be classified as both a mammal and a rodent). Folk taxonomies tend to have much the same structure. However, the names of folk taxa are often used in more than one sense, and sufficient attention is not always paid to this. Take the word 'animal', for instance. In some cases it means an animal in the technical, zoological sense: one of the Animalia. Often it is used as a popular synonym for Mammalia, or it may mean a 'beast'—a non-human animal. Again it may mean a domesticated animal, such as a 'farm animal'. Sometimes it is used metaphorically, as in the motion picture about a college fraternity entitled *Animal House*. In botany there is a puzzling word called 'berry'. In some cases it refers to an organ, in other cases to the plant that bears it. Technically a tomato is a berry, and most people think of berries as fruits, not vegetables, so this seems odd.

But does this 'polysemy' introduce chaos into the lives of those who classify objects and talk about them? Not as a general rule. Words are uttered in the context of discourse. If I am cooking and ask somebody to fetch me a tomato from the garden, I obviously mean the fruit, not the whole plant. None the less such contextual matters are habitually overlooked in studies of cognitive psychology, even though some workers have done good research on the role of context (Medin and Schaffer, 1978; Roth and Shoben, 1983). There may be more than one reason for such neglect. For one thing we suffer from an atomistic tendency to treat the world as if it were populated by nothing more than classes and their elements. A particular discourse, however, is an individual thing, and itself is part of some larger whole, like an organism in its environment. A second reason has to do with the way research has been carried out. When the subjects are asked to classify a certain kind of object such as a tomato, they are not supplied with information about context. They are simply asked if a tomato is a good example of a fruit. In some cases it would seem that the subjects provide contextual information on their own account. For instance, if asked for examples of tools, they do not give examples in some broad or metaphorical sense such as books being the tools of a scholar's trade.

If any context has been neglected, it has been the knowers' understanding of the things known. The outstanding symptom here is a kind of phenomenalism. It is assumed that objects are grouped together according to their immediate appearances, especially according to the most salient traits. As a result, knowledge is depicted as a hierarchy of things possessing greater or lesser degrees of 'similarity', similarity being understood as a subjective matter, and not as something having inherent existence in things classified. Now of course, people can and do sort things out on the basis of subjective impressions as to how similar things are, and it may play an important role in folk taxonomy. Indeed, younger children classify only on the basis of 'overall similarity', monocriterial classes being formed later in development (Smith, 1979). Adults and computers *can* classify that way, and a bias toward this kind of classification is often built into experiments. Be this as it may, time and again we find what might be called 'aetiological' taxa being overlooked. By this I mean ones defined in terms of some cause. For example, 'family' can be defined phenomenally in terms of 'family resemblance'—who looks like whom. Aetiologically it can be defined in terms of procreation—who is the offspring of whom. With rare exceptions (Young, 1978) it is only begrudgingly admitted that some taxon might be defined in terms of what things do, where they come from, what motivates them, or anything of the sort. Atran (1983) acknowledges the fact that scientific knowledge transcends the merely phenomenal, but he does not extrapolate to everyday life.

CLASSIFICATION AND REPRESENTATION

This phenomenalism accords with a naive, inductionistic, and empiricistic epistemology. We are supposed to acquire knowledge by experiencing a lot of sense impressions, and correlating these into larger and more complicated ideas. Forget about asking questions and doing experiments! Phenomenalism also fits in neatly with the computer as a model of the mind. Material can indeed be stored and retrieved effectively if it is hierarchically organised. But this model is hard to reconcile with multiple hierarchies and extensive cross-referencing. Part of the trouble here is a confusion between the processes of acquiring and using knowledge and its putative mode of representation. Given that the 'categories and concepts' are supposed to constitute knowledge itself, how is 'classification' thought to represent knowledge? Smith and Medin (1981) provide a useful tripartite division into classical, probabilistic and exemplar views. They do not say so, but these represent three different metaphysical positions. The classical view is based upon the sort of traditional logic that was invented by Aristotle. The probabilistic view incorporates some notions derived from the work of Russell, Wittgenstein and other modern logicians. The exemplar view is rather Platonic, featuring an idealized model that gets pictured in the mind. The classical view has the advantage of according with the sort of logic we seem to use in everyday discourse. It applies in a straightforward manner to terms that have what are called conjunctive definitions—a set of defining properties that are shared by all members of the class. For example, a bachelor has to be both unmarried and a man. Everybody agrees that many terms are defined in that way, but how many is debatable. An alternative is disjunctive definition, in which a set of properties is defining, but no two members of the class need share any of them. That we can cope with groups of this sort can be seen from the following example:

    abc bcd def defg efgh

Here we have a continuum of objects linked together by features in common, but with the extremes quite different. Discriminating such groups is sometimes important, as when comparative anatomists trace series of organisms through genealogical trees. Various authors have claimed that the taxa of biology are disjunctively ('polythetically') defined, including some students of cognitive psychology and anthropology (e.g. Needham, 1975). In so far as the taxa of biology are genealogical units sharing a common ancestor, however, this view has had to be abandoned. Biological taxa, at least of this sort, are individuals and have to be defined ostensively, without any defining properties whatsoever. None the less, it would seem that disjunctively-defined groups do play a significant role in classification. Vygotsky (1962) believed that younger children organise groups into concatenary assemblages, and only later are able to form conjunctive classes. Wittgenstein (1958, p. 32) came up with the notion of a 'family resemblance' among the members of such classes as 'games'. The term 'family resemblance' was unfortunate because what makes one part of a family is not resemblance at all, but procreation and social relationships. The notion that folk-taxa are based upon family resemblance has been widely endorsed by cognitive psychologists, though not always uncritically (Smith and Medin, 1981). Anisfeld (1968) in particular urged that although disjunctive sets are easy to come up with in theoretical speculation, they are hard to find in actual practice. Subtler defining properties are often overlooked. Much of the problem results from a confusion between what biologists call 'diagnostic' traits and defining ones (see Ghiselin, 1984). People use certain salient features as convenient, but not necessarily conclusive, evidence that a name applies. By analogy with medicine, the symptoms are not to be confused with the disease, which is defined if possible on the basis of aetiology.

    Often confused with disjunctive definition is the notion that the limits of taxa are vague or indefinite, and that membership is a matter of degree. Actually a disjunctively-defined class can be so defined that everything definitely either does or does not fall under it; for example, the class of women and boys who were born in Hong Kong or Los Angeles. And the problem of delimitation applies to individuals and conjunctive classes as well. Where membership is in fact a matter of degree, some members could be absolutely and unequivocally members while others would have transitional or borderline status. Often the notion of degree of membership is linked to that of 'typicality', with the defining properties best developed in what are thought of as good examples. Where there is only one such focal element it is obvious that disjunctive definition is not involved.

The view that taxon-membership is a matter of degree has been ably supported by Rosch and her collaborators (Rosch, 1975; 1979; Rosch and Mervis, 1975). The evidence brought forth in support of this view is none the less open to question. People feel that some kinds of objects are better examples of, say, 'bird' or 'furniture' than others are. For instance a robin seems to be a better example of a bird than a chicken is. Also it takes less time to verify statements about typical exemplars than about atypical or aberrant ones. However, the whole thesis of degree of membership is cast into doubt by some recent work of Armstrong, Gleitman and Gleitman (1983). They found that not only will people rank different kinds of birds according to how well they exemplify 'bird', they will also rank integers according to how well they exemplify 'odd number' and 'even number'. But 2,228,477 and 1 are both, absolutely and without qualification, odd. I would interpret these results to mean that the subjects were responding as they usually do whenever asked for an example of something. It is common practice to define terms partly by ostensive reference to an example. 'A watch is a small time-piece such as the one on my wrist.' In the context of such definition we want an example that is good in the sense that it is familiar, possesses the defining properties in salient form, does not possess features that might wrongly be taken for defining ones, and so forth. Context is so important that subjects provide it even when not asked to do so.

The notion that group membership is a matter of degree is often related to the theory of 'fuzzy sets' (Lakoff, 1973; Kempton, 1978; McCloskey and Glucksberg, 1978; Jones, 1982; Osherson and Smith, 1982; Zadeh, 1982). In support of this view it is claimed that there exists a continuum with respect to membership. McCloskey and Glucksberg (1978) observe that different people will not place the same object in a particular group, and that the same person will classify it in different ways at different times. But does this tell us that the boundaries of taxa are vague? No, though it certainly is good evidence that they vary. It could mean that the boundaries are delimited rigorously, but at different places by different people, and by the same person at different times. Anthropologists have shown that the speakers of a language do not have identical idiolects (Gardner, 1976), so the apparent fuzziness may result from illicit extrapolation from population averages to single instances—like concluding that somebody really has $2\frac{1}{3}$ children. Lakoff (1973) uses what he calls 'hedges' to substantiate the claim that sets are fuzzy. Such expressions as 'in the strict sense' and 'roughly speaking' are supposed to add fuzziness to taxa. Actually their function in the context of discourse is the exact opposite. They tell us which of many logically possible classes might be designated by an equivocal linguistic symbol. It is only in the context of discourse and reasoning that a term means anything, and this is a matter of particulars. The question is not whether a term might be interpreted in more than one way, but whether an individual act of thinking or communication is affected by such 'fuzziness'.

It would probably help a great deal if the study of classification were disassociated from that of mental representations. The data about how people classify tell us little about how knowledge is represented (whatever that is supposed to mean). Indeed, it is far from clear what students of categorisation are trying to get at when they deal with representation. Suppose, by way of an analogy, we tried to study literature by going to a college library and doing research on the catalogue. No doubt we could learn something about how certain materials are arranged and how we obtain access to them. We might discover that the catalogue is arranged alphabetically by author and subject. And perhaps some titles are more readily located than others. But how close does such information get us to literature itself? Even if we went into the stacks and saw how the books were arranged on the shelves, we would not get much closer. Nor would a formal analysis of the structure of the books themselves. What we really need if we want to understand literature is how people read and write books, and how books relate to culture in general, not how they are arranged and fetched. By the same token, what is worth while in the study of classification has to do with the role that various kinds of groups of objects play in our cognitive processes.

Thus classification comes to be seen as an evolutionary problem when we realise that what matters is how each individual organism copes with the problems of its particular environment. What goes on is concrete, adaptive and contextual, not abstract, formal and intrinsic. It does not seem likely that our ability to deal with the categories in the various senses of that term is an accidental consequence of how Greek philosophers happened to view the world, or that we are otherwise dealing with something arbitrary or merely conceptual. Rather, we seem to have entered into an adaptive relationship with a more ultimate aspect of reality. So if we are going to understand why children do not have to be told that weighing the difference between Paris and London is nonsensical, perhaps we ought to be asking whether their ancestors' reproductive success was affected by an ability to make such judgements. If we are all endowed with the ability to do metaphysics, it is probably because of its utility in the conduct of our everyday lives.

REFERENCES

Anisfeld, M., 'Disjunctive concepts?', *Journal of General Psychology*, 1968, *78*, 223–8.
Armstrong, S. L., L. R. Gleitman and H. Gleitman, 'What some concepts might not be', *Cognition*, 1983, *13*, 263–308.
Atran, S., 'Rendons au sens commun . . .', *Le Genre Humain*, 1983, *7–8*: 81–95.

Austin, J. L., *How To Do Things with Words* (Oxford: Oxford University Press, 1975, 2nd edn).

Black, M., 'Russell's philosophy of language', in Paul Arthur Schlipp (ed.), *The Philosophy of Bertrand Russell* (Evanston: University of Chicago Press, 1944), pp. 227–55.

Chomsky, N., *Rules and Representations* (New York: Columbia University Press, 1980).

Gardner, P. M., 'Birds, words, and a requiem for the omniscient informant,' *American Ethnologist*, 1976, *3*, 446–68.

Ghiselin, M. T., 'Categories, life, and thinking', *The Behavioral and Brain Sciences*, 1981, *4*, 269–313.

Ghiselin, M. T., ' "Definition", "character", and other equivocal terms', *Systematic Zoology*, 1984,*33*, 104–10.

Jones, G. V., 'Stacks not fuzzy sets: An ordinal basis for prototype theory of concepts', *Cognition*, 1982, *12*, 281–90.

Keil, F. C., *Semantic and Conceptual Development: An ontological perspective* (Cambridge: Harvard University Press, 1979).

Kempton, W., 'Category grading and taxonomic relations: A mug is a sort of cup', *American Ethnologist*, 1978, *5*, 44–65.

Lakoff, G., 'Hedges: A study in meaning criteria and the logic of fuzzy concepts', *Journal of Philosophical Logic*, 1973, *2*, 458–508.

McCloskey, M. E. and S. Glucksberg, 'Natural categories: Well-defined or fuzzy sets?', *Memory and Cognition*, 1978, *6*, 462–472.

McClure, E. F., 'Ethno-anatomy: The structure of the domain', *Anthropological Linguistics*, 1975, *17*, 78–88.

Markman, E., 'Facilitation of part–whole comparisons by use of the collective noun "family" ', *Child Development,* 1973, *44*, 837–40.

Markman, E. M., 'Classes and collections: Conceptual organization and numerical abilities', *Cognitive Psychology*, 1979, *11*, 395–411.

Markman, E. M. and J. Siebert, 'Classes and collections: Internal organization and resulting holistic properties', *Cognitive Psychology*, 1976, *8*, 561–77.

Medin, D. L. and M. M. Schaffer. 'Context theory of classification learning', *Psychological Review*, 1978, *85*, 207–38.

Needham, R., 'Polythetic classification: Convergence and Consequences', *Man* (n.s.), 1975, *10*, 349–69.

Osherson, D. N. and E. Markman, 'Language and the ability to evaluate contradictions and tautologies', *Cognition*, 1974, *3*, 213–26.

Osherson, D. N. and E. E. Smith, 'Gradedness and conceptual combination', *Cognition*, 1982, *12*, 299–310.

Piaget, J., *Insights and Illusions of Philosophy* (New York: World Publishing Company, 1971).

Rosch, E., 'Cognitive representations of semantic categories', *Journal of Experimental Psychology: General*, 1975, *104*, 192–233.

Rosch, E., 'Principles of categorization', in E. Rosch and B. B. Lloyd (eds.), *Cognition and Categorization* (Hillsdale: Lawrence Erlbaum Associates, 1979), pp. 27–48.

Rosch, E. and C. B. Mervis, 'Family resemblances: Studies in the internal structure of categories', *Cognitive Psychology*, 1975, *7*, 573–605.

Roth, E. M. and E. J. Shoben, 'The effect of context on the structure of categories', *Cognitive Psychology*, 1983, *15*, 346–78.

Ryle, G., *The Concept of Mind* (London: Hutchinson, 1949).

Skinner, B. F., 'Selection by consequences', *Science*, 1981, *213*, 501–4.

Smith, E. E. and D. L. Medin. *Categories and Concepts* (Cambridge: Harvard University Press, 1981).

Smith, L. B. 'Perceptual development and category generalization', *Child Development*, 1979, *50*, 705–15.

Sommers, F., 'The ordinary language tree, *Mind*, 1959, *68*, 160–85.

Sommers, F., 'Types and ontology', *Philosophical Review*, 1963, *72*, 327–63.

Sommers, F., 'Predicability', in M. Black (ed.), *Philosophy in America* (Ithaca: Cornell University Press, 1965), pp. 262–81.

Vygotsky, L. S., *Thought and Language* (Cambridge: MIT Press, 1962).

Wittgenstein, L., *Philosophical Investigations*. (New York: Macmillan, 1958, 2nd edn).

Young, J. C., 'Illness categories and action strategies in a Tarascan town', *American Ethnologist*, 1978, *5*, 81–97.

Zadeh, L. A., 'A note on prototype theory and fuzzy sets', *Cognition*, 1982, *12*, 291–7.

PART II

Alternatives to Cognitivism

Section IIA

J. J. Gibson's Ecological Approach to Psychology

So far, this book has dwelt upon the limitations and paradoxes of cognitivism. Many of the problems with cognitivism have been acknowledged and discussed within cognitive science itself but with the object of repairing rather than replacing the theoretical foundations. For, the argument goes, the only alternative to cognitivism is a return to mechanistic behaviourism. But there *are* further alternatives. The best-known and most flourishing is that of Gibson's ecological approach to psychology, with its radical conceptual framework firmly based upon Gibson's own expertise as an experimentalist. Gibson himself was uncompromising in his rejection of cognitivism, but there have been attempts, especially since his death in 1979, to assimilate some of his insights into cognitive science. Thus the theory is in danger of distortion beyond recognition, and a detailed statement of Gibson's final position, avoiding the over-simplifications that are current, is therefore timely. Such a statement is provided by the two chapters (7 and 10) by Reed, who draws upon Gibson's unpublished manuscripts and notebooks, and looks ahead to the theory's potential as a *comprehensive account of cognition*, not merely as an alternative theory of perception.

The other two chapters of this section (8 and 9) pursue debates occurring within the framework of ecological psychology. Katz discusses the epistemological problems that arise if Gibson is taken to be a realist in the traditional sense, while Noble argues the need for an adequate account of language in order to realise a complete theory of human psychology.

89

7

Why Do Things Look As They Do? The Implications of J. J. Gibson's *The Ecological Approach to Visual Perception*

Edward S. Reed

INTRODUCTION: GIBSON'S PROJECT

The Ecological Approach to Visual Perception (1979) was James J. Gibson's final book, representing the culmination of more than half a century's experimentation, looking and pondering by the most important student of visual perception of the twentieth century. Because Gibson combined a unique freshness of thought with a deep insight into the fundamental problems of psychology, his work continually evolved, making it difficult for even a diligent reader to be certain of having caught all the implications of any one of his writings. Gibson challenged orthodox psychology on a whole host of issues that no one else had ever considered deeply. He upset the applecart. And he did so repeatedly, often undercutting his previous most radical pronouncements with still more radical arguments and experiments. In this chapter I shall attempt to articulate some of the more fundamental implications of Gibson's last book. I shall thus say very little about how his thought developed (see Reed and Jones, 1982; and Reed, 1986a, for details of this) but a great deal about his last version of a psychology that did not accept traditional assumptions, or what he had come to call an ecological psychology. After briefly contrasting Gibson's last with his previous books, to give at least some of the developing context of his thought, I proceed by discussing each section of *The Ecological Approach*, which provides a convenient overview of the components of ecological psychology.

In *The Perception of the Visual World* (1950), Gibson offered a solution to the centuries-old problem of depth perception.

Although he eventually rejected this solution, it has become common currency among psychologists. Prior to Gibson's work, visual psychology had no plausible account of everyday depth perception, the sort of seeing required to drive a car without crashing. Nowadays Gibson's early ideas of 'texture gradients' and 'motion perspective' can be found in most textbooks on perception as explanations of 'depth' or 'space' perception, along with more classical theories of the 'cues' for depth. It is a measure of Gibson's independent thinking and rigorous standards that he did not remain satisfied with this earlier account, despite the considerable acclaim he received for it. And it is especially significant that the most telling experimental attacks on Gibson's early theory of visual space perception derived from his own laboratory (Reed, 1986a).

In *The Senses Considered as Perceptual Systems* (1966) Gibson offered a solution to the problem of how our several kinds of sensory experiences become transformed and integrated into cognition of the world. He rejected the fundamental assumption of all previous theories of perception, that sensations are expanded into perception by some form of mental activity. He offered instead a theory of perception as based not on sensations, but on information in stimulation. When stimulation is imposed on passive observers, sensations arise; but when active, purposeful creatures are allowed to explore stimulation, they are able to detect information that is specific to environmental sources. Thus, Gibson insisted that the category of exploratory (as opposed to performatory) behaviour be recognised to enable us to understand the behavioural functioning of perceptual systems. However, Gibson's novel distinction between obtained and imposed stimulation (yielding sensations specific to sensory nerves) has been largely ignored, although his work prompted renewed interest in so-called 'sensory integration' (Mendelsohn and Haith, 1976; Mark, 1978), and in the relation of overt attention to perceiving (Neisser, 1976). In his later work Gibson continued to accept his view of the senses not as conduits to the soul or brain, but as information-seeking systems.

The *Ecological Approach to Visual Perception* tackled an even more difficult issue than previously. Gibson asked, 'why do things look as they do?'—echoing Koffka (1935) but giving the question a pragmatic twist: 'How do we see where we are in the environment? How do we see whether or not we are moving and, if we are, where are we going? How do we see what things are good for? How do we see how to do things . . .?' (Gibson, 1979, p. 1). The answer to all of these questions is straightforward, but understanding the answer (much less accepting it!) requires a willingness to dispense with many of the fundamental assumptions of western philosophy and science. We see as we do, Gibson says, because we see what the affordances for behaviour of things are on the basis of information specifying those affordances. Gibson's new solution to this old puzzle will not make much sense until one is willing to doubt that sensations are the basis of perceptions, that there are stimuli for organisms, that there are responses of organisms, that the brain processes or integrates or stores information, that perception without conception is blind . . . to list only a few of the theories Gibson rejects.

Gibson's project is certainly daunting, with metaphysical and epistemological consequences as well as scientific ones. This is what is so exciting about his work: right or wrong, he tackled big problems and asked new and insightful questions. Although his answers to these questions are controversial, even someone who holds views diametrically opposed to Gibson's will appreciate his questioning of fundamental assumptions.

ONTOLOGY

Gibson's ontology is new and unfamiliar. It is not a science of Being or Form, but a science of persistence and change. Gibson rejects both the dichotomy of Being versus Becoming and that of Substance versus Form. He rejects both the battle between Parmenides and Herakleitos, and the battle between Aristotle and Plato. These dichotomous battlefields are the basis of western scientific and philosophical thinking. The separation of a thing's 'being' from its 'becoming' manifests itself in many ideas about how growth and motion are separate processes from that which grows or moves. Psychological activity, such as perceiving and acting, we almost automatically assume to be separate from the physical and biological aspects of an organism. Gibson rejects this separation of psychology from the natural, but he does this without falling into the trap of reductionism. None of the myriads of ontologies based on the traditional dichotomies will work for psychology, so a new approach is needed.

For Gibson, although there are no Beings, there are things which persist, and some things which are almost permanent with respect to human lives (e.g. the Earth). The idea of unchanging 'atoms' of matter or mind has often been invoked as the stuff of which the mental or physical world is composed. By virtue of being unchanging Beings, these atoms supposedly underlie the variations and changes of awareness (see e.g. Julesz and Schumer, 1982). An alternative proposal, popular since Kant, is that unchanging forms or schemata organise the otherwise chaotically changing mental world. Gibson simply abandons these old dichotomies of Being and Becoming. For him persistence is reciprocal with change (Gibson, 1979, p. 76; see also Reed and Jones, 1982, Ch. 4.7). There are no mere persistences, for change is partially constituted by non-change, and vice versa. If there are no pure permanences or pure fluxes, then there is no need for an atomism of either thing or process, nor is there a need for forms, whether immanent or transcendent, mental or physical.

More radical still is Gibson's rejection of the concepts of space and time. (In this regard it should be noted that in psychology space and time are still thought of as the permanent receptacles of less permanent objects.) 'Space and time will not often be referred to in this book, but a great deal will be said about permanence and change. . . . It will be assumed that the layout of the environment is both permanent in some respects and changing in some other respects' (pp. 12–13).

This aspect of Gibson's ontology has profound implications for his account of perception. Gibson (1950) once tried to explain space perception, but he now denies that space is something that organisms perceive, so there can be no 'space perception' (or depth perception or, as will become clear, form perception). Organisms perceive not space and time, nor things in space and events in time; rather, they perceive persistent aspects of their environment and also changing aspects of their environment.

This reorientation of ontology is not mere verbal magic. 'Space perception' implies that organisms perceive 'space', i.e. that which geometry describes. People who believe in space perception do experiments on 1-D, 2-D and 3-D perception, on how 2-D perception is 'transformed' into 3-D (the problem of 'depth' perception) and on whether visual space is Euclidean or not. For Gibson these are all fruitless endeavours based on a bad assumption. This is an echo of William James' old hobby-horse, the 'psychologist's fallacy' (James, 1890, 1: p. 196; II: p. 281 ff.). James was irked that, so far as most perceptionists were concerned, 'mere acquaintance with space [is treated] as tantamount to every sort of knowledge about it, the conditions of the latter are demanded of the former state of mind, and all sorts of mythological processes are brought in to help.' Yet Gibson went beyond James, arguing that there is no evidence that organisms are acquainted with space.

The 'space' of physical science and of geometry is one way (actually several ways) of describing the world. If perceivers exhibit some knowledge about the world, they may appear to exhibit some knowledge about 'space', but it is surely an empirical question whether the knowledge is really 'of space' or of something else. Experiments which manipulate a 'spatial variable' of a display and obtain a variation in performance would demonstrate perceptual knowledge of space if and only if the performance variations were some clear function of the spatial variations. It has been more than obvious to perceptionists since the time of Mach's *Space and Geometry* that no such functions have ever been found. Orthodox perception research still follows Mach's interpretation of these findings. Organisms are said to 'organise' the spatial characteristics of sensory input into a 'subjective' or 'psychological' space. (Hence, there are separate visual, auditory and tactile spaces which require to be integrated; cf. Mark, 1978.)

However, Gibson read these results quite differently. If spatial variables do not seem to covary lawfully with perceptual variables then so much the worse for 'space'. Instead of arguing that there 'must be' organisational processes 'coding' the spatial input, Gibson suggested that the description of what is perceived as 'spatial' is a conjecture which has been falsified by innumerable experiments. For this reason he proposed that psychologists attempt a new conjecture, a new way to describe what organisms perceive. To make scientific hypotheses about what is perceived requires careful consideration of the evolution and ecology of perceiving organisms. Gibson's ontology is based on this decision to look more closely at what might exist that organisms would have evolved to see it.

Animals live in an environment of persistences and changes: things are always involved in events. One sort of persistence–change pairing are animals themselves, active creatures. Gibson claimed that 'psychology begins with the division between the inanimate and the animate'; psychology is not the science of mind, or the study of behaviour, or the analysis of information-using systems. Psychology's subject matter is the sort of persistent things which are animated; that is, animals, as agents. These agents are persistent within an ecological scale of reality: 'The size-levels of the world emphasized by modern physics, the atomic and the cosmic, are inappropriate for the psychologist' (p. 9). At the ecological level of reality there are things which can be looked at or touched or tasted. Individual atoms are of no importance to most creatures, nor are galaxies. Similarly, the ecological time-scale is not that of physics: the duration of organism-relevant properties in the environment should be measured by sunrise and set, tidal cycles and seasons. Ecological psychology is concerned not with 'the flow of abstract empty time' but with changes in the environment, especially changes relevant to animate existence. As far as Gibson was concerned, space and time exist, but that ontology is of little or no use to psychologists.

Pragmatic realist that he was, Gibson's ontology does not stop with the abstract level of mere persistence and change. He develops an ontology of the *substance* and *surfaces* of the animate environment, and of the *media* through which animals move to locate things—an ecological physics, as it were. A medium is rarefied and affords locomotion. Media are also transparent, allowing light to reverberate through them, so that homogeneous media afford looking through as well as moving through. (Similarly, a medium allows reverberation of vibrations from a mechanical event and diffusion from chemical events, thus affording listening and smelling.)

The most important point about media for perceptual theory is that they can become 'filled' (at least locally) with light, sound, or odour. Thus 'any point in the medium is a possible point of observation for any observer who can look, listen, or sniff'. This makes each point in a medium *unique* (for it will have a unique relationship to the *sources* of light, sound, and odour), unlike points in space. Gibson urges that although this account is *consistent* (Gibson, 1979, p. 17) with physics as now known, it is nevertheless at a 'higher order', being environmental science. There are more things in Gibson's environment than dreamed of by physical science, even in the physics of solid states or of non-reversible thermodynamics, or even in 'systems theory'. A re-evaluation of the importance of the sciences of the existing world of geology, surface science, rheology, materials science, and so on, is long overdue, and perhaps Gibson's work will motivate such reappraisals.

Substances are the combinations of chemical elements which are not rarefied, but comprise things. 'They are compounded and aggregated in extremely complicated ways and thus do not tend towards homogeneity' Gibson (1979, p. 22), as do media. Usually, substances are relatively resistant to deformation, relatively impenetrable and relatively stable in shape. At our level of the environment they are usually opaque to light, but Gibson neglects to mention that this is not the case at the level of micro-organisms, most of which can be damaged by excessive light energy. Substances are *nested* into various levels and components, many of which afford behaviour for animals, such as eating or nest-making.

Surfaces are crucial for visual perception. This is because 'the medium is separated from the substances of the environment by *surfaces*' (p. 22), and each locale embodies a *layout* of surfaces which can change. At our size level, these surfaces 'soak up or throw back the illumination falling upon them', in other words, surfaces are *potentially visible*. Gibson's ontology is tailored to fit his epistemology and psychology, but there is some independence among these things. Surfaces exist without being seen, nor is their purpose to be seen—it is just that they are, in large part, what is seen, when something is seen. Gibson lists nine laws of surfaces (1979, pp. 23–4) which detail the properties relevant to seeing things (e.g. resistance to deformation, texture, reflectance). Gibson also lists seven qualities of substantial surfaces (1979, p. 31) which are intended to replace the qualities of visible appearances handed down to us from Descartes, Locke and Berkeley: colour on the one hand and form, size, position, solidity, duration and motion, on the other hand (cf. Reed and Jones, 1982, Ch. 1.8).

This rejection of the distinction between 'primary qualities and secondary qualities' runs counter to three and a half centuries of physics and psychology, and it should be studied most carefully (Reed, 1982b). If Gibson is correct, then when we say 'That banana looks good to eat' we are not speaking figuratively, but literally; nor are we somehow 'associating' a visual with a taste quality, we are simply seeing the fact of ripeness and edibility. If such a mode of description became scientifically acceptable, it would mark a significant change in modern thought.

Modern science is based on the assumption, denied by Gibson, that the world is a congeries of matter in motion to which meaning is added by our minds (Whitehead, 1926; Burtt, 1932). Hume long ago noted that the fundamental doctrine of modern (post-Galilean) science was that we are not aware of things (not even of our own bodies) but merely of 'certain impressions, which enter by the senses' (Hume, 1739/1964, p. 191). It is only by associations among these impressions or by the interpretive powers of our minds that meanings evolve. The distinction between the natural and social sciences now so strongly felt is based on this assumption that subjects invest the world with meaning—that there are (natural) sciences of what *exists* and (social) sciences of what is *meaningful*. 'The theory of affordances . . . begins with a new definition of what value and meaning *are*. The perceiving of an affordance is not a process of perceiving a value-free physical object to which meaning is somehow added . . . it is a process of perceiving a value-rich ecological object. Any substance, any surface, any layout has some affordance for benefit or injury to someone. Physics may be value-free, but ecology is not' (Gibson, 1979, p. 140). To reject this assumed distinction between a value-free world and value-imposing minds is to call into question the basis of modern western scientific cosmology, not by vague references to the supernatural or the social basis of scientific ideas, but through a specific attack on fundamental assumptions about the place of mind in the world.

Gibson is aware of the importance of his argument, and devotes an entire chapter to 'The Meaningful Environment'. There is one important problem with his project, however, that becomes obvious at this juncture of the argument. In all previous ontologies there has been a distinction between existence and existence-for-a-subject, yet this distinction breaks down, or so it seems, in Gibson's ontology. The surface of water on a pond, for example, is *smooth* to me, but *rough* to a water mite, yet 'smooth' and 'rough' are two of Gibson's seven qualities of existents. In fact, what counts as a surface for an animal of human size will not necessarily count as a surface for a micro-organism, but surfaces are things which exist. Gibson's rejection of Being versus Becoming engenders a rejection of 'objective existence' as invariance *tout court*. In Gibson's ontology, what exists is a 'persistence across certain changes'. Hence, existents are historically and circumstantially constrained without being any the less real. Whether such an ontology can be developed fully and explicitly without self-contradiction remains to be seen.

The most profound implication of Gibson's ontology is with respect to meaning. Although Gibson's existents are not existents-for-some-subject, they are meaningful and useful. Nor must these utilitarian and semantic properties be conferred upon the things; rather, meanings must be discovered (Gibson, 1979, p. 33). Meanings for Gibson are primarily potential uses for animals. These potential uses of things are what things *afford for behaviour* (p. 36). It turns out that affordances are what is perceived by animals, and that animals are very selective about their perceiving. For example, a land turtle perceives that a cliff is dangerous, and affords stoppage of locomotion, whereas an aquatic turtle does not (see Walk and Gibson, 1961).

Elsewhere (Reed, 1985) I argue that Darwin's basic insight was that the biological environment (as distinct from the physical world) is made up of *resources*. Biological processes, on this view, are modes of competition for resources. Specific kinds of processes are determined by the specific resources for which there is competition. For Darwinians, I would therefore argue, animate behaviour and perception should be defined as modes of resource usage. Gibson's ecological psychology is the first systematic expression of this aspect of the Darwinian revolution in psychology.

Gibson's affordances are more than existents-for-a-subject. Affordances exist whether or not they are utilised, much as oil in the ground is a resource whether or not it is being used. Affordances thus constitute a bridge between ontology and epistemology because they refer to the mutuality of animal and environment. Because an affordance is a resource, or a 'use-value', it does not exist unchanged throughout space and time, but only exists under certain conditions of animal–environment interrelation. Yet, because an affordance is a use-value, it does exist independently of being utilised. After all, even untapped oil reserves are a valuable resource. Hence, although an affordance can be partially constituted by an environment, it is not 'objective' in a straightforward way; nor is it 'subjective', although it is partially constituted by an agent. For these reasons Gibson (p. 129) states that 'an affordance is neither an objective property nor a subjective property; or it is both if you like. An affordance cuts across the dichotomy of subjective–objective and helps us to understand its inadequacy. It is equally a fact of the environment and a fact of behavior. It is both physical and psychical, yet neither.'

The affordance concept is extremely difficult to grasp, yet appears worth the effort. I reconstruct Gibson's reasoning as follows: If what exists are 'persistence–change' pairs, then an object in the environment, taken by itself, is not an existent. What does exist is that object considered in relation to all the changes which leave it persistent in some way. An apple may be eaten or thrown, it may rot or ferment. It affords eating only once, but it may be thrown several times; if it rots it is so changed as to afford very little, but if it ferments it affords a new form of eating, which is intoxicating. Apples exist as substantial surfaces comprising objects, but it is the affordance of such objects which are seen. (In philosophical jargon, affordances are intentional objects.) My account is unsatisfactory, however, for it does not answer a number of important questions, such as whether affordances are relations or potentialities. Robert Shaw (Shaw and McIntyre, 1974;

Turvey *et al.*, 1981, Shaw, Turvey and Mace, 1982) has tried to resolve some issues in the theory of affordances by using Leibniz's laws of individuation, plenitude and sufficient reason, but even this seems to me unsatisfactory. Much work needs to be done on affordance.

It has recently been argued that the concept of affordance is of little value as it does not 'constrain' behaviour (Cutting, 1982; Ben-Zeev, 1984). For example, an apple neither constrains one to throw it, jump on it, ferment it, or any other specific action. This criticism misses two important points. First, affordances constrain not behaviour but ontology. For an animal to eat something it must be edible and ingestible. Birds simply do not bother to try to eat trees, and rarely dine repeatedly on poisonous fruits, even though they will eat leaves, insects, fruit, and other foods that grow on trees. Second, the affordance concept is not useful as an *explanation*, but is useful in *describing* behavioural situations. The existence of an edible item does not entail that that item is seen or eaten. But the *non*-existence of an edible item guarantees that a bout of eating is not in the offing.

Another criticism of the theory of affordances is that it exaggerates the separation of the observer and environment (see Noble, 1981, for perhaps the best statement of this argument). Did the ground really afford terrestrial locomotion prior to the existence of terrestrial creatures? Noble and others would answer 'no', claiming that affordances are a *relation* between organism and environment, and that their value is as much a function of the organism as of the environment. This objection reduces affordances to Lewinian valences, which misses one of the great advantages of the affordance concept: 'The affordance of something does *not change* as the need of the observer changes . . . An affordance is not bestowed upon an object by a need of an observer and his act of perceiving it. The object offers what it does because it is what it is' (Gibson, 1979, pp. 138–9). Because affordances are aspects of the environment of *all* observers, and not just of a single observer (Gibson, 1979, p. 43), an affordance can exist even though no specific user of that affordance exists. A cache of food affords eating even if the animal that squirrelled it away dies and no other one come along. To reduce affordances to a relation between a particular organism and its habitat is to explain away the intentionality of perceiving and acting, for intentionality is not a relation (see Reed, 1983). Furthermore, if affordances are mere relations, then one loses the evolutionary connection of ecological psychology. Populations of animals can adapt only to what exists in the environment. If affordances are *created* by organisms (instead of *realised* and *altered* by them) no adaptation could occur. 'The organism depends on its environment for its life, but the environment does not depend on the organism for its existence' (p. 129).

EPISTEMOLOGY AND PSYCHOLOGY

Gibson's implicit distinction between epistemology and psychology is classical in many ways. What I am calling epistemology Gibson calls the study of stimulus information—in the case of vision, ecological optics. This is the study of what makes vision *possible*. The psychosomatic process of information pick-up make awareness actually occur, but the factors allowing for seeing can be studied independently of particular observers. Epistemology for Gibson is the study of what makes knowing possible, while psychology must also study the processes that make knowing happen. However, for Gibson, the observer-independent factors allowing for vision are neither physical nor psychological, they are ecological (see below, on occlusion). The new science of ecological optics is thus a key to Gibson's project.

Gibson's epistemology is a theory of *direct cognitive contact with existents*. This is not a theory wherein the mind or sensorium is touched by things, but a theory wherein animals hunt for meanings. The fundamental problem for a theory of direct perception is the apparent fact of perceiving at a distance. A human smile means friendliness even across a room. Classical Greek and medieval direct realists proposed a theory of 'forms' or 'species' which each object transmitted to human minds. Newton's *Opticks* (1704) echoes these views, but by then nominalistic science had devastated such theories. In Descartes' *Dioptrice* (1637) even the role of the retinal image in seeing is played down. Forms were replaced by physical percussions in the optic tract and brain. The philosophical, physiological and psychological dogma of the next three centuries was that our perceptual contact with the environment is limited to the feelings aroused in the mind/brain by rays of light (sound, odour, etc.). Of Gibson's (1960; 1963; 1966; 1979) reasons for rejecting this dogma, the best is that, if it is taken as a conjecture (roughly, 'secondary qualities must be explained as interactions among primary qualities in the world and in the brain'), then it is one that has been refuted time and again.

Repeated attempts have been made to identify sensory (secondary) qualities with the activity of specific receptors, afferent fibres or central neurons, but none of these has met with much success. The currently fashionable notion of 'feature detectors' modifies this ancient conjecture, but to no avail. Are the 'features' to be detected in the environment, or in the proximal stimulation? The facts seem to be as follows: certain patterns of proximal stimulation (e.g. the double transition of light intensities that defines an 'edge') set off a sometimes sharply defined sometimes diffuse gradient of central nervous activity in passive, purposeless (often drugged) animals. This gradient is modulated by prior stimulation—especially by prior stimulation involving 'similar features' or 'dimensions'. Some writers argue that the central regions so excited are comprised of 'feature detectors' and others use these data to support the idea of sensory 'channels' that are 'tuned' to various dimensions of stimulation (Uttal, 1973; Mark, 1976). Either way, the basic idea of uniquely mapping primary qualities into secondary by way of uniquely specific brain events has been abandoned implicitly, though not explicitly. Gibson's willingness to reject this traditional account deriving sensory qualities from primary physical/ physiological interactions will seem reasonable to those who are aware of the countless puzzles to which it has led. Because Gibson's rejection of sensationalism has aroused much controversy, readers of his last book may be disappointed to see no defence against critics of Gibson's anti-Müllerian views. Apparently, Gibson decided that the best defence is a good offence.

In the present case, the offence is a systematic theory describing with what a visual system is in contact. According to this theory, visual systems are in contact with ecological information contained in light. Information for Gibson is not 'information theory' information. There is no 'channel', there are no 'bits', there is no 'coding' (1979, pp. 62–3). Instead, information is optical structure and deformation generated in a lawful way from environmental layout and events. This optical structure is not similar in any way to the environment, but it is 'specific' to it. By this Gibson seems to mean that optical structure is uniquely and nomically dependent on environmental structure. Gibson's fundamental hypothesis was that structure in the optic array is specific to its environmental sources, so that an observer whose perceptual system detects some optical structure is therefore aware of what that specifies—the environment, not the array. In the classical theory of Johannes Müller, sensations are said to be specific to their receptor inputs so that instead of being aware of each neural event, observers are aware of specific sensory qualities associated with those events. But Gibson says, 'I have rejected this theory of specificity and substituted another that is quite radically different' (1979, p. 115). Whereas Müller's theory has motivated generations of research on the nervous correlates of sensation, as mentioned above, Gibson hoped to motivate considerable research on the environmental information available in the patterns of energy in the media of the environment. Much of his own work was devoted to an analysis of the information available in ambient light.

Light from the sun fills the air (the terrestrial medium) densely so that it is in a 'steady state' of reverberation. Therefore, at each physical point in the environment, there is a densely nested set of 'solid visual angles' which are comprised of inhomogeneities in the intensity of the light. These inhomogeneities are nomically dependent on the optical properties of the layout of the surfaces and substances in a particular locale.

The structure of an optic array, so conceived, is without gaps. It does not consist of points or spots that are discrete. It is completely filled. Every component is found to consist of smaller components. . . . This means that the array is more like a hierarchy than like a matrix and that it should not be analyzed into a set of spots of light, each with a locus and each with a determinate intensity and frequency. In an ambient hierarchical structure,

loci are not defined by pairs of coordinates, for the relation of location is
not given by degrees of azimuth and elevation (for example) but by the
relation of inclusion. (1979, p. 68)

This analysis of the structure of ambient light requires an
entire new discipline, which Gibson has named 'ecological
optics'. The sorts of measurement-operations engendered by
ecological optics are very different from the measurements of
other branches of optical science, which have analysed rays of
light and their intersections with each other and with planes
('spots' or 'points' of light). Previous analyses of light are
inadequate because they do not describe the structure in light
which enables organisms to see. Traditional visual science has
relied on physical optics, geometrical optics, and physiological
(retinal receptor and image) optics, but these are not good
enough, Gibson argued, for a theory of how we see the
environment. Physical optics can tell us about how rays of light
are detected: geometrical optics about refraction, reflection
and the laws of incidence; and physiological optics can tell us
about the sensations aroused by light rays stimulating
receptors. None of these disciplines, nor all of them in
combination, can explain how a person sees the environment,
its surfaces, substances, objects, events and meanings. None of
these disciplines is of much use in explaining such important
visual tasks as visually guided walking. Walking requires
locating the *ground surface*, seeing that it *affords footing*,
avoiding *obstacles* and steering around them. Whatever the
flaws of Gibson's work, he has offered the first satisfactory
account of such visual activities as walking.

It is impossible to give a satisfactory account of ecological
optics in a short space, for it is an entire discipline, and an
unfamiliar one at that. In what follows I shall only attempt to
present a vague outline of ecological optics and its philosophical consequences.

The primary philosophical consequence of ecological optics
is to engender a perceptual theory which eschews the
distinction between sensory data and intellectual operations
that has been central to modern philosophy and psychology
since Descartes. Ecological information is not sense data:
information is limitless, meaningful, publicly available and

enduring, whereas sense data are finite, meaningless, private and short-lived. If ecological information is uniquely and nomically dependent on its source, then an organism which can detect the information perceives at least one aspect of the source as well, without any further ado. There is no distinction between seeing and 'seeing as' in Gibson's epistemology (Reed and Jones, 1978).

Even more radically, Gibson denied that there are percepts conceived of as mental products of a sensory process. Information can be detected and used, but it does not 'flow' from one place to another. The brain does not form representations of information or of the environment; rather the brain and eyes and body together form a perceptual system capable of *looking around*. The 'product' of this perceptual 'process' is not a percept, but a new state of the perceptual system (Gibson, 1979, Ch. 14; see also Neisser, 1976).

For example, when any terrestrial animal locomotes, there is a particular optical structure (Gibson, 1979, pp. 122–6) called 'streaming perspective' which has within it structures and relations specifying the direction and velocity of locomotion. This information exists in the optic array, not in the organism. An organism which can attend to this information can guide its locomotion (Gibson, 1979, pp. 232–4) by modulating the optical structure. The information here does not 'flow' from the world to the brain, but is rather a lawful *consequence* of the movements in that layout. Because ecological information is nomically dependent on both the animal's behaviour and the environment's structure, it specifies some of the persistences and changes of the entire animal–environment system. Moreover, because ecological information is a lawful consequence of the animal–environment system it need not flow from environment to the animal—it is already where it need be.

The modern idea of 'information flow' is a lineal descendant of the traditional view that the mind operates on the 'deliverances of the senses' to engender perception. Gibson rejects this whole approach (1979, p. 238) and tries to start afresh, basing his epistemology and psychology on his ontology. What is perceived are affordances for behaviour. How they are perceived is by information which specifies them (note that information for an affordance must specify qualities of both the animal and the environment.)

A second important epistemological consequence of ecological optics is a new test for the reality of a thing. Since
Berkeley and earlier, the idea has been that, if one is unsure
whether or not something is real, then one should try to touch
it. As there are tactile hallucinations, and as many things
should not be touched (e.g. fire), this test for reality encourages
various forms of phenomenalism and idealism. Ecological
optics replaces this test for reality with *the law of reversible
occlusion* (Gibson, 1979, pp. 76–8, 191–9, 243–4; Gibson,
1970).

This law of nature is based on two facts of ecological optics
(Gibson, 1979, p. 193): (1) 'Given an illuminated medium, a
surface is unhidden at a fixed point of observation if it has a
visual solid angle in the ambient optic array at that point. If it
does not (but has it at another point of observation), it is
hidden'. (2) 'For any fixed point of observation, the persisting
layout of the environment is divided into hidden and unhidden
surfaces. Conversely, for every persisting surface, the possible
points of observation are divided into those at which it is
hidden and those at which it is not.'

From these two facts it follows that 'any movement of a
point of observation that hides previously unhidden surfaces
has an opposite movement that reveals them.' This is the law of
reversible occlusion, which states that the hidden and
unhidden real things in a locale can be interchanged by moving
around. Going out of sight is not the same as going out of
existence. The perception of persistence does not rely on
persistence of perception, but on tests using reversible
occlusion.

The occlusion of one surface by another is a ubiquitous fact
of the environment. The *interchangeability* of the visible and
invisible surfaces is a ubiquitous fact of *ambulatory vision*,
vision during locomotion. Surfaces are not just seen as surfaces
or as 'near and far' but as *covering* or *being covered*. It is this
ecological fact of going out of sight that has confounded
philosophers for centuries. Hume and other sceptics have
taunted us with the astonishing fact that no one can explain
why things persist even when they are momentarily unper-
ceived. Gibson's theory offers the first hope of solving this

problem, by distinguishing going out of sight from going out of existence (1979, p. 194; cf. Reed, 1986b). To make this distinction requires showing that the perception of persistence is not based on the persistence of perception, and this is exactly what Gibson and Kaplan's crucial experiment (based on Michotte's pathbreaking work) shows (Gibson *et al.*, 1969). The unique pattern of deletion of texture in the optic array specifies a *covering* of one surface by a second; that is, the persistence of the covered surface is specified not by its persistent sensory (or even optical!) representation, but by a uniquely specific deformation of the optic array. The difference between going out of sight and going out of existence can be *seen*, and the optical information specifying these events can be isolated and displayed experimentally. The twin puzzles of the existence of the outside world and of solipsism can begin to be resolved empirically.

Occlusion is one of the most important facts of perception, and Gibson devoted much of his later thinking to it. Epistemologists might profit from studying the data for and concept underlying Gibson's theory of occlusion. It has long been a scandal of epistemology that existence and perceived existence have not been conceptually separable. Few philosophers are adherents of solipsism, but fewer still can argue against that position persuasively. Reversible occlusion cannot solve the problem of objectivity versus subjectivity, but it can solve the problem of public versus private knowledge.

The privacy of the self is specified by the unique arrangement of concealed and revealed surfaces in a layout. At the same time, the public environment is specified by the invariant interchangeability of concealed and revealed surfaces during locomotion. The environment is simultaneously the environment of one observer and that of all observers (Gibson, 1979, p. 43) moving through it. Occlusion is thus neither a physical nor a psychological fact, but an *ecological* one. Occlusion exists only when the layout of the environment is taken with reference to a line or path of sight.

Using his theory of affordances and ecological information Gibson went on to demonstrate how meaningful action requires perceptual guidance. Affordances do not constrain behaviour, but information for affordances exists and information also exists for *realising* affordances, as Gibson described in his study of locomotion and manipulation (1979, Ch. 13), two of the most basic of human activities. Gibson's theory of action rested on his account of the 'rules' of perceptually guided behaviour, in which he rejected both the S-R concept of mechanistic behaviourism and the motor program concept of cognitivism:

> Locomotion and manipulation are neither triggered nor commanded but *controlled*. They are constrained, guided or steered, and only in this sense are they ruled or governed. And they are controlled not by the brain but by information, that is, by seeing oneself in the world. Control lies in the animal–environment system. Control is by the animal in its world. . . . The rules that govern behavior are not like laws enforced by authority or decisions made by a commander; behavior is regular without being regulated. The question is, how can this be? (p. 225)

I suspect that this is the best formulation yet of how to study behaviour scientifically. We need to understand and develop the implications—experimental as well as theoretical—of formulating the question of control and purpose in this way (see Reed, 1982a, for a tentative attempt to do this).

PHILOSOPHICAL ANTHROPOLOGY

Since Kant, philosophical anthropology has been conceived of as a study of the philosophical basis of relationships among human beings: human communication, intercourse, play, symbolising, and so on. In the section on 'Depiction' in his last book, Gibson (1979) adumbrated a new view of symbols, although he was concerned primarily with pictorial displays, which he did not equate with descriptions or symbols. To some degree, Gibson's account of depiction addresses itself to the traditional distinction between 'natural' and 'conventional' representation; however, Gibson makes this old dichotomy a dimension, and he offers a very novel account of 'natural representation'.

Despite this, Gibson's theory of pictorial displays is less well worked out than his other ideas. Static pictures are a problem for a perceptionist who emphasises the information obtained by a moving observer in an extended environment. Even though we are normally observing while moving around in a layout, a photograph can appear to represent a scene vividly. Gibson tried to explain how, but remained convinced that more work is required.

Gibson's account of 'natural depiction' is that *some* of the information in an optic array can be *captured* by a photographer or artist, and *displayed* upon a surface for other viewers. However, not all of the original information can be captured (for mathematical reasons). Hence, 'there is no such thing as literal re-presentation of an earlier optic array' (1979, p. 279), although *motion* pictures can present a great deal of the information utilised by mobile observers (1979, Ch. 16).

'A picture is not an imitation of past seeing' (1979, p. 280), but it is more like seeing than is utilising a verbal (spoken or written) description. There is here a dimension (or is it a transition?) from *tacit* to *explicit* knowing, direct to indirect perceiving. Seeing involves tacit knowledge (1979, pp. 260–1). A child may know tacitly the law of reversible occlusion and enjoy playing with it in the game of 'peek-a-boo', but she has no explicit knowledge of that law. A picture displays information and the information within it may be seen, without explicit knowing being involved. But the artist who draws a picture may know explicitly how to capture information, and may even write it down in a treatise on painting.

What makes seeing some pictures more like seeing than like reading, and what makes seeing some pictorial displays more like reading than like seeing? The answer lies on a picture's surface: Some surfaces are treated so as to provide optic information (e.g. a photograph) for a *second* scene, whereas some are treated so as to provide optic information for a marked surface (e.g. a Jackson Pollock painting). When a 'picture is both a scene and a surface, and the scene is paradoxically behind the surface' (1979, p. 281), then that is an information-carrying, 'realistic' display.

To make a representation is *not*, contrary to widespread assertion, to make an object 'stand for' another. It is, instead, to provide selected information for other people so they may be become aware of the depicted or presented object. The graphic act, like the speech act, is a basic human skill allowing for mutual awareness of the environment. The mystery of representation in psychology will only begin to be solved when we become clear about what enables something to *function* as a representation—when we understand what actions serve to make explicit and public the implicit and private awareness of the environment we all have. Gibson takes very seriously this human predilection for attempting to make implicit knowledge explicit. He wants to have a theory of the graphic act (pp. 275–6), not just a theory of drawing, and this surely is a step in the right direction.

There are many hints in Gibson's later work about the nature of explicit knowledge, human praxis and communication. Some of these hints will be worth expansion. The concept of explicit knowing, and especially of graphic traces, as a *recording* in more persistent form of tacit knowledge, is an intriguing idea (1979, pp. 273–4). It is one of the very few conjectures about the *function* of explicit knowing, and as such it is related to Popper's concept of 'world 3' (Popper and Eccles, 1977), although there are several important differences. For one thing, Gibson tried to explain why people engage in making such things as books or pictures, whereas Popper just accepts that they do, without conjecturing why they do. Popper's 'world 3' items are re-representations of mental data which are already like explicit knowledge—in fact, Eccles' account of the mind 'reading' the brain's activities misleadingly treats mental data as if they were explicit knowledge. Gibson's graphic acts are attempts to make fleeting tacit knowledge more persistent. For Gibson 'representation' is not a mental process underlying all perceiving, acting and knowing; it is simply one kind of activity, and the graphic act is a paradigm case. A systematic account of Gibson's theory of cognition and representation can be found in my 'James Gibson's ecological approach to cognition', Chapter 10 of this volume.

Gibson's philosophical anthropology was enhanced by his own realism. He refused to 'reduce' things out of existence. His strategy was always one of respect for facts at their own level. Cognising is not reduced to perceiving, as in positivism, nor is perceiving reduced to cognising, as is currently faddish. There are no simple 'nothing but' formulas in Gibson's work: People are not likened to machines or animals, movements are not likened to responses or reflexes, picturing is not likened to verbalising, nor is verbalising likened to picturing, and awareness is not reduced to behaviour or brain states. Gibson abhorred explaining by explaining away, and refrained from that all too common practice. He was also eager to criticise his old views, and sensitive to deficiencies in his current approach. In fact, the word 'approach' occurs in the title of his last book because he apparently felt that he did not yet have a theory even though this book is his most complete work on vision.

CONCLUSION

Gibson says things look as they do because they afford what they do, that we have evolved so as to perceive affordances and there is optical information available specifying those affordances. This answer contrasts markedly with the traditional answer that things look as they do because that is how the mind interprets the brain movements, or because the fields of force in the brain so organise the proximal stimuli, or because the brain computes the visual properties of things from retinal images.

It is very much an open question whether Gibson's new answer, or any theory along similar lines, can succeed. To be consistent, Gibson must reject most of the concepts and dichotomies of our intellectual heritage (Agassi, 1977). Such a wholesale rejection will not succeed without satisfactory rebuilding. Gibson supplied considerable empirical support for his views, but philosophers as well as scientists should question the conceptual foundations and implications of his work to see how well his rejections and replacements really work.

In this chapter I have touched on many of the issues addressed by Gibson's final ideas, but I have not done justice to the depth and breadth of Gibson's project. In producing his final book, Gibson worked through American realism, pragmatism, behaviourism, phenomenology, Gestalt theory, systems theory, act psychology, evolutionary theory and ecology, sifted the wheat from the chaff and produced not a muddled eclecticism, but a surprisingly clear new approach. It is a new approach to all of psychology, and it has many implications for the human sciences in general.

The psychology of perception is an old science. It has not changed fundamentally since Descartes' day, although the puzzles and mysteries have deepened and darkened across the years. Gibson's ideas are surely wrong in many ways, but I venture to suggest that they are far more correct than any previous ideas, and that they are incorrect in ways which will prove to be fruitful and innovative. Above all, Gibson's ideas are new in a good way: they are not merely novel, but profoundly challenging.

Even if they prove to be wrong, Gibson's ideas will not lead to the old dead-ends and puzzles but will open up to us unexplored vistas of thought, and important new conceptual terrains. Anyone interested in perception and psychology, whether or not they agree with Gibson's arguments, will provide us with further enlightenment by heeding the advice of Gibson's final words: 'These terms and concepts are subject to revision as the ecological approach to perception becomes clear. May they never shackle thought as the old terms and concepts have!'

ACKNOWLEDGEMENTS

The writing and revision of this paper was supported by grants to the Center for Research in Human Learning, University of Minnesota, from the National Science Foundation (NSF/BNS-77-22075), The National Institute for Child Health and Human Development (T36-HD007151, to the author from the National Science Foundation (SES-8204863) and a Fellowship from the National Endowment for the Humanities (FA84-24240).

REFERENCES

Agassi, M., *Towards a Rational Philosophical Anthropology* (The Hague: Martinus Nijhoff, 1977).

Ben-Zeev, A., 'The Kantian revolution in perception', *Journal for the Theory of Social Behaviour*, 1984, *14*, 69–84.

Burtt, E., *The Metaphysical Foundations of Modern Physical Science* (New York: Basic Books, 1932).

Cutting, J., 'Two ecological perspectives: Gibson vs. Shaw and Turvey', *American Journal of Psychology*, 1982, *95*, 199–222.

Gibson, J.J., *The Perception of the Visual World* (Boston: Houghton-Mifflin, 1950).

Gibson, J. J., 'The concept of stimulus in psychology', *American Psychologist*, 1960, *15*, 1–15.

Gibson, J. J., 'On the relations between hallucination and perception', *Leonardo*, 1970, *3*, 425–7.

Gibson, J. J., Kaplan, G., Reynolds, H. and Wheeler, K., 'The change from visible to invisible: A study of optical transitions', *Perception and Psychophysics*,1969, *5*, 113–16.

Gibson, J. J. *The Ecological Approach to Visual Perception* (Boston: Houghton-Mifflin, 1979).

Hume, David, *A Treatise on Human Nature* (1739), ed. L. Selby-Bigge (London: Oxford University Press, 1964).

James, W., *The Principles of Psychology* (New York: H. Holl, 1890).

Julesz, B. and Schumer, R., 'Early visual perception', *Annual Review of Psychology*, 1982.

Koffka, K., *The Principles of Gestalt Psychology* (New York: Harcourt, 1935).

Mark, L., *Sensory Processes: The new psychophysics* (New York: Academic, 1976).

Mark, L., *The Unity of the Senses* (New York: Academic, 1978).

Mendelsohn, M. and Haith, M., 'The relation between vision and audition in the human newborn', *Monographs of the Society for Research in Child Development*, 1976, *41*, no. 4.

Neisser, U., *Cognition and Reality* (San Francisco: Freeman, 1976).

Noble, W., 'Gibsonian theory and the pragmatist perspective', *Journal for the Theory of Social Behaviour*, 1981, *11*, 65–85.

Popper, K. and Eccles, J., *The Self and its Brain* (New York: Springer, 1977).

Reed, E. S., 'An outline of a theory of action systems', *Journal of Motor Behavior*, 1982a, *14*, 98–134(A).

Reed, E. S., 'Descartes' corporeal ideas hypothesis and the origin of scientific psychology', *Review of Metaphysics,* 1982, *35*, 731–52(B).

Reed, E. S., 'Two approaches to the intentionality of perception', *Synthese*, 1983, *54*, 85–94.

Reed, E. S., 'The ecological approach to the evolution of behavior', in T. Johnston and A. Pietrewicz (eds.), *Issues in the Ecological Study of Learning* (Hillsdale, N.J.: Erlbaum, 1985).

Reed, E. S., 'James Gibson's revolution in perceptual psychology: A case study in the transformation of scientific ideas', *Studies in The History and Philosophy of Science*, *17*, 65–98, 1986a.

Reed, E. S., 'Why ideas are not in the mind: An introduction to ecological epistemology', in A. Shimony & D. Nails (eds.), *Naturalist Epistemology* (Boston: D. Reidel, 1986b).

Reed, E. S. and Jones, R. K., 'Gibson's theory of perception: A case of hasty epistemologizing?', *Philosophy of Science*, 1978, *45*, 519–30.

Reed, E. S. and Jones, R. K. (eds.), *Reasons for Realism: Selected essays of James J. Gibson* (Hillsdale, N. J.: Erlbaum, 1982).

Shaw, R. and McIntyre, M., 'Algoristic foundations to cognitive psychology', in W. Weimer and D. Palermo (eds.), *Cognition and the Symbolic processes* (Hillsdale, N. J.: Erlbaum, 1974).

Shaw, R., Turvey, M. T. and Mace, W., 'Ecological psychology: The consequences of a commitment to realism', in W. Weimer and D. Palermo (eds.), *Cognition and the Symbolic Processes*, Vol. 2. (Hillsdale, N. J.: Erlbaum, 1982).

Turvey, M., Shaw, R., Reed, E. and Mace, W., 'Ecological laws of perceiving and acting: A reply to Fodor and Pylyshyn (1981)', *Cognition*, 1981, *9*, 237–304.

Uttal, W., *The Psychobiology of Sensory Coding* (New York: McGraw-Hill, 1973).

Walk, R. and Gibson, E. J., 'A comparative and analytical study of visual depth perception', *Psychological Monographs*, 1961, *75(15)*, Whole No. 519.

Whitehead, A. N., *Science and the Modern World* (New York: Basic Books, 1926).

8

Is Gibson a Relativist?[1]

Stuart Katz

Socrates: Rather, when I become a percipient, I must become percipient *of something*, for I cannot have a perception and have it of nothing, and equally the object, when it becomes sweet or sour and so on, must become so *to someone*—it cannot become sweet and yet sweet to nobody.
Theaetetus: Quite so.
Socrates: Nothing remains, then, I suppose, but that it and I should be or become—whichever expression we are to use—*for each other*. Necessity binds together our existence, but binds neither of us to anything else, nor each of us to himself; so we can only be bound to one another. Accordingly, whether we speak of something 'being' or of its 'becoming,' we must speak of it as being or becoming *for someone* or *of something*, or *toward something*, but we must not speak, or allow others to speak, of a thing as either being or becoming anything just in and by itself. That is the conclusion to which our argument points.

(Plato, *Theaetetus*)

In 1967, J. J. Gibson wrote: 'It seems to me that these hypotheses [his theory of perception] make reasonable the commonsense position that has been called by philosophers direct or naive realism' (p. 168). This quote merely appears to confirm what virtually every commentator on Gibson, critic or supporter, already assumes, namely that Gibson *is* a direct realist. The attribution 'direct realism' to Gibson's work, therefore, seems not only uncontroversial but unquestionable. I think, however, that this attribution can be questioned. Gibson, in my opinion, does have a direct theory of perception, but it is a relativistic not a realist theory of perception. It is my purpose in this chapter to show why I believe this to be the case. If Gibson is a direct realist, then his theory cannot explain perceptual error. Many have made this point (Epstein, 1980: Gyr, 1980; Rock, 1980; Fodor and Pylyshyn, 1981; Gregory,

115

1981; and others).I share some of their reasons (though none of their theory). However, I argue that a close scrutiny of Gibson's last work, *The Ecological Approach to Visual Perception* (1979) reveals that he is not a realist after all, but a relativist.

REALISM AND ERROR

Realism—or more specifically epistemological realism—rests on two assumptions. First, the external world is *independent* of the perceiver in the sense that it exists autonomously, and is not of the perceiver's manufacture. This is, shall we say, the onto-logical assumption. Second, despite independence, what the perceiver perceives is more or less *about* the world, *true* of the world. This is the epistemological assumption. Now most per-ceptual theorists are realists, but only a handful are direct realists, and all the rest are of another sort, called indirect realists. Whence the difference? One answer to this question lies in the treatment of a set of psychological facts grouped under the heading of 'perceptual error'.

The story in which perceptual error plays so prominent a role is a very old one, and it goes as follows. There is a causal chain in the act of perception which begins with a remote cause called the 'distal stimulus'. The distal stimulus is a part of the external world—an event, an object—which is, from the realist point of view, independent of any perceiver. The distal stimulus gives rise to a proximate cause, the 'proximal stimulus', which is the input to the sensory apparatus. The proximal stimulus is also part of the external world, and it is presumed to carry information about the distal stimulus, though the information is always deficient. There is, as Epstein (1980) has put it, 'an irreducible uncertainty' in the input. Now according to the indirect realist, the distal stimulus is the ultimate object of perception, and yet cannot be perceived directly, since the perceiver must rely on the proximal stimulus alone. Therefore the perceiver employs the proximal stimulus, meagre as it is, and past representations (memories) of remote stimuli, to construct a percept, an up-to-date representation of the distal stimulus. It turns out, according to the theory, that the percept most often corresponds to the distal stimulus. But 'most often' is not the same thing as 'always'. If there is 'an irreducible uncertainty' in the proximal stimulus—if, that is to say, the input is ambiguous with respect to its remote causes—then on occasion perceivers will go wrong; they will experience something other than what the distal stimulus actually is. This is perceptual error, and according to the indirect realist it reveals two things: It first shows that perception is a product of input *and* the perceiver's inference. Second, it shows that on occasion what is constructed differs from what is.

Now the other epistemological realist, the direct realist, denies this story and offers another. It goes like this: There is, roughly, the same tripartite division in the causal chain: distal stimulus, proximal stimulus, perceiver. And the distal stimulus is again the remote cause of perception, a part of the external world. But here the similarity ends. For the direct realist, the proximal stimulus is sufficient for perception. Hence mediating entities are superfluous (as well as logically objectionable).

To the indirect realist, however, direct realism's treatment of error is at least puzzling, and possibly paradoxical. If perception is direct then perception, by definition, *cannot* be in error. Yet there are certainly experiences which are *apparently* in error. What ontological status are we to give to them? If an experience *is* in error, then it cannot be of what is actual, though it is, after all, an experience. But an experience of *what*, if not of what is? Inner objects are no part of the direct realist account, and so the experience cannot be of these objects. And yet, I repeat, the experience cannot be of real objects, for then there would be no error. It follows that *if* Gibson is a direct realist, then his account of error, too, cannot be correct (see Gibson, 1966b, Ch. 14; 1979, Chs. 14 and 15). My solution to this dilemma is to deny that Gibson is a realist.

GIBSON AS RELATIVIST

Why do I think Gibson is not a realist? Nearly everyone else seems to think he is (for exceptions, see Noble, 1981; Costall,

1983). Consider the following statements from his *The Ecological Approach To Visual Perception* (1979):

> The fact is worth remembering because it is often neglected that the words *animal* and *environment* make an inseparable pair. Each term implies the other. No animal could exist without an environment surrounding it. Equally, although not so obvious, an environment implies an animal (or at least an organism) to be surrounded (p. 8).

> [Water] is the medium for aquatic animals, not a substance, but it is a substance for terrestrial animals, not the medium. It is insubstantial when taken with reference to the aquatic environment but substantial when taken with reference to the terrestrial environment. This difficulty, however, does not invalidate the distinction but only makes it depend on the kind of animal being considered. The animal and its environment, remember, are reciprocal terms (p. 21).

> The *affordances* of the environment are what it *offers* the animal, what it *provides* or *furnishes*, whether for good or ill. . . . I mean by [affordance] something that refers to both the environment and the animal in a way that no existing term does. It implies the complementarity of the animal and the environment (p. 127).

What we find in these lines is, in the modern ecological idiom, what Plato's Socrates, speaking for the Sophist Protagoras, says to Theaetetus. The terms are different, but the relativistic conception is the same. The knowledge relation, as always, is a relation between a subject and an object, but unlike realism, relativism does not take the two sides of the relation as independent of the other. Rather, subject and object are mutually defining—the organism in terms of environment, the environment in terms of organism.

Relativism, therefore, cannot be realism, because the environment cannot be specified independently of the organism. But it also cannot be subjectivism because the environment is not a mental creation. Epistemology, in the relativistic way of thinking, does not begin with either the subject or the object, from which the other is derived. As Gibson says: 'an affordance is neither an objective property nor a subjective property; or it is both if you like. An affordance cuts across the dichotomy of subjective-objective . . It is both physical and psychical, yet neither' (1979, p. 129). But if Gibson is a relativist and not a realist, is his theory of perception still a *direct* theory of perception? He has certainly said so, explicitly and repeatedly, down through his final work. Is, then, a direct theory of perception consistent with a relativistic epistemology? The answer to this question, by the logic of relativism, is also yes. The *in*direct theory of perception requires a complicated relation among several terms: a subject, a representation, a proximal stimulus and a distal stimulus. The distal stimulus is the absolute standard, independent of any perceiver, against which the result of any perceptual act must be measured. But it is precisely this idea of a standard that is problematic for any indirect theory of perception. A standard is meant to be a basis for comparison. But if it cannot serve that purpose, what *is* its purpose? So have sceptics, ancient and modern, always reasoned—until they have reasoned away the external world.

But a relativistic epistemology requires none of this baggage. Here one finds a simple complementary relation between subject and world. The nature of the relation requires but two terms. There is no representation, and no meagre proximal stimulus. And by virtue of complementarity, the relation is direct, for there are no other entities interposed between subject and world. The relation, moreover, must be mutually constraining, because, as with any 'internal relation', any 'system', each side of the relation frames the other, brackets its possibilities, constrains what can and cannot be, for both subject and object.

Now, it appears, we have a tidy conceptual package. Epistemological relativism is preferable to realism and to subjectivism because it rejects both the absolute and the skeptical. But what advantages, specifically, does relativism confer on Gibson's theory? Where does it have definite application here? Well, there is that persistent and vexing problem of perceptual error. Can a Gibsonian relativism deal with it? Let us see.

Although the traditional literature of perception might lead us to think otherwise, perceptual error is an issue with a broader scope than the textbook commonplaces we know as illusion and kindred phenomena. One might, for example, ask the more far-reaching question: Why does one animal species perceive differently from another? The most naively realist answer to this is that species do *not* perceive differently. All species, this argument goes, live in a common world (though they may occupy different parts of it); and in any particular place at any particular time, the substitution of one species for any other will give rise to identical perceptions. On a different view, however, (e.g. von Uexkuell, 1957) this answer is rejected. Under similar conditions, different organisms, like bats and frogs and human beings, *do* perceive differently, and the task of the naturalist is to explain why this is the case. The naturalist's answer is not that some species perceive veridically while others do not, or that some species come closer to apprehending things-in-themselves than do others. Species perceive differently because, as von Uexkuell would have put it, *each lives in a different world.* For example, water, Gibson tells us, is a substance for terrestrial species, not a medium, whereas for aquatic species it is a medium, not a substance. Do terrestrial animals perceive water correctly and aquatic species incorrectly, or vice versa? Gibson as relativist tells us no. Each lives in a different world and, complementarily, each perceives differently. Water is a substance in one world and a medium in the other; it is not absolutely substance, nor is it absolutely medium. 'The animal and its environment, remember, are reciprocal terms.' One could never say what water is, without saying for whom it is, and conversely.

There is, however, a realist response to this relativistic alternative which goes beyond the naive view. Different species, it would be conceded, do perceive differently, and perhaps, in some metaphorical sense, live in different 'worlds', but that is no barrier to realism. Every species is, as it were, tuned differentially by evolution because in different habitats the constraints of the external world have different consequences, including perceptual consequences. One may, for example, think of the perceptual world of each species as a simplification or 'homomorphism' of an ultimate reality (Ashby, 1956; Wilcox, 1983). 'Ultimate reality' here refers to the complete articulation of the external world into indivisible constituents and fundamental laws of relation—the venerable Parmeidean–Democritean world view. 'Perceptual world' means a less-articulated (or more simplified) version of the ultimate reality, a failure to make all the distinctions there are. Some species have a relatively well-articulated perceptual world (e.g. the human), others a poorly articulated world (e.g. the clam), still others, an articulated world that lies somewhere between exalted *Homo* and lowly clam (e.g. the housefly or the frog). All perceptual worlds, however, are derived from the ultimate reality. Thus even if perceptual worlds differ among themselves, that does not mean that they do not *accord* with the external world. And if, moreover, perception happens to disaccord with reality, the unlucky species who inherits this aberration may just suffer the consequences, namely extinction. This, I think, is the reply the realist must make to the relativist. But the relativist will then be moved to ask the ultimate relativistic questions: What is this standard, this absolute reality, of which every perceptual world is supposed to be a simplified derivative? How could one conceive an ultimate structure that applies in all conceivable circumstances, from every imaginable point of view? These are, of course, rhetorical questions. The relativist believes that the absolute is myth, itself contextually appropriate or inappropriate, for there are no context-free foundations. Perception is a matter of circumstances, those circumstances determined jointly by subject *and* by object.

The same relativistic conception applies to comparisons made within as well as across species. One might, however, miss the similarity because the individual members of a species share a common habitat. From the realist perspective, a common habitat means common evolutionary pressures, hence common perceptual equipment. It is therefore not at first easy to make sense, from a realist perspective, of multiple ways of perceiving within such a community, and less obvious still, within a single individual at different times. None the less, it is a fact that at least one particular species, *Homo sapiens*, has individual members who have different points of view, and also a fact that any one member of this species has different points of view at different periods of its life. These facts are currently explained, of course, by what we call 'developmental' theory. According to it, different individuals, and a single individual at different times, apprehend the world differently, the latter through a restructuring of experience brought about by epistemic disequilibrium. This is the essence of Piaget's 'genetic epistemology'.

But the theory of development *qua* genetic epistemology is, or at least appears to be, realist. Development here has a distinctly ratiocinative cast, by which I mean that a point of view is explained as an intellectual achievement where *reason* operates on *facts*. This is not unlike the position set forth by Shaw and his colleagues (Shaw, Turvey and Mace, 1982; Shaw and Bransford, 1977), and it is very like, if not simply a variant of, indirect realism. The mechanisms of change moreover are, as with indirect realism, representational. The disequilibrium of development is the clash of inner scheme with outer world. For these reasons, traditional developmental theory, though it recognises point of view, is not relativistic.

How might Gibsonian conceptions remedy this? An answer requires extrapolation, for Gibson himself never discussed the general problem of development in a systematic way. We have only hints. The most singular of these is his analysis of what he called 'sequential structure' (Gibson, 1966a; 1979). Events, Gibson argued, can be perceived directly, although events may be ordered through time. The past, the present (and by extension, the future) are part of an unfolding structure, of which every element, whether occurring in the past, present or future, influences every other. The notes of a melody are part of a sequential structure in which the character of each note is integrated and reintegrated as the melody unfolds. For the problem of error, this means that as the perceiver 'develops', its relation to what it perceives changes, so that what was at one point in time apprehended in one way, is later apprehended in another, because what follows changes the character of wha⁺ went before, and conversely. Put differently, the complementary relation of the developing individual to the world itself changes as events unfold. Both perceiver and world evolve together: 'we must speak of [something] as . . . becoming *for someone* or *of something* or *toward something*, but we must not speak, or allow others to speak, of a thing as . . . becoming anything in and by itself.' And from the developmental point of view, this must be as true of the perceiver as of the world.

I do not think it necessary to go any further here into these unusual (to say the least) implications of Gibson's concept of sequential structure, except to mention its even wider application to the problem of memory, where he scotches the concept of the stored mental representation (see Wilcox and Katz, 1981), and to the problem of occlusion (perceiving without sensing), where Gibson breaks completely with the idea of sensation-based perception (for further discussion see Chapter 7). There is enough in the present discussion, I think, to show how development might be construed in relativistic terms. At any stage of development, what is perceived is, shall we say, 'correct' for that place in the unfolding structure; a point of view is never errant, but appropriate to the circumstances. When an earlier point of view is no longer held, 'error' can only mean what is different from, and therefore inappropriate to, the current point of view. In short, perception, for the relativist, can never be true or false absolutely. Of course, it remains to work out the precise conditions, historical or contextual, that cause changes in perception when it is 'illusory', 'ambiguous' or 'deficient'. The theory of sequential structure, with its radical reinterpretation of time, memory and development must figure prominently in such an explanation, though it is not my place here to advance such a project. But I do think it can be done, and I do think it is necessary if we are to solve the problem of perceptual error, which hangs persistently and forbiddingly over all of epistemology.

IS GIBSON CONSISTENT?

I have tried to make a case in this paper for Gibson as a relativist, but the task cannot be an easy one. It must be made in the face of a realist tradition virtually untouched by a century of pragmatism, functionalism, phenomenology or ordinary language analysis, and then complicated by Gibson himself, for he wrote over a long period of time and, as with all pathfinders, substantially reworked his ideas (see Costall, 1982). Many of his critics, we have seen, have taken him as a realist, a supposition which, if true, makes it difficult for his theory to satisfactorily explain perceptual error. None the less, there are *apparent* inconsistencies in Gibson's work which play easily into realist hands. The Gibson quote in the very first line of this paper is one example. Are there others? Remember that

the epistemological realist assumes, first, that the external
world exists independently of the perceiver but, second, that
the perceiver can yet come to know the world. Consider first
the following quote, once again from Gibson's last book.
Think of it in two parts, the second beginning with 'But note
also that the environment . . . ':

> The natural environment offers many ways of life, and different animals
> have different ways of life. The niche implies a kind of animal, and the
> animal implies a kind of niche. Note the complementarity of the two. But
> note also that the environment as a whole with its unlimited possibilities
> existed prior to animals. The physical, chemical, meteorological, and
> geological conditions of the surface of the earth and the pre-existence of
> plant life are what make animal life possible. They had to be invariant for
> animals to evolve. (1979, p. 128)

The second part of the quote seems to convey, quite explicitly,
the independence—in fact, the temporal priority—of the
physical world. Then how can it be squared with the words
preceding it? Gibson makes similar assertions in at least two
other places in the book as well (pp. 8, 129). Is he therefore
contradicting himself? Is he a realist *malgré lui*? Let us at least
assume that these statements are a rejection of subjectivism.
There was, as Gibson asserts, a physical world prior to animal
life, and if that is so, then the physical world could hardly
depend on animal life in the same sense that existence can
hardly depend on perceiving. But if Gibson's intent is to reject
subjectivism, does this mean he embraces realism? Well, if the
pantheon of the theories of knowledge contains only two
members, subjectivism and realism, then the answer, by
elimination, would be yes. But the pantheon is larger than that.
Another member is relativism. Perhaps Gibson's rejection of
subjectivism is an affirmation of relativism and not realism.
What reasons might we give for this? I have two. The first is
that Gibson explicitly rejects the dichotomous distinction we
call the subjective-objective. We have already seen this in a
passage quoted from p. 129 of his last book. Gibson also says
this:

> There has been endless debate among philosophers and psychologists as to
> whether values are physical or phenomenal, in the world of matter or only

in the world of mind. For affordances as distinguished from values, the debate does not apply. Affordances are neither in the one world or the other inasmuch as the theory of two worlds is rejected (1979, p. 138).

A rejection of subjectivism is, therefore, not an endorsement of realism, because the fundamental distinction by which the two are derived is rejected. Gibson is neither a subjectivist nor a realist. He is apparently something else.

The second reason is that Gibson propounds relativism, explicitly and frequently, as we have seen in the many passages I have taken from his last writings. Worlds are neither in the minds of perceivers nor independent of them. But how then is it possible for a physical world to exist *prior* to the perceiver, as Gibson seems to assert in the above passages, if there is a complementary relation between them—if, that is, each requires the other?

The relativistic answer is this: the world must always be taken with reference to an observer, but the 'perceiver' is not the only kind of observer there is. The 'external world' encompasses, in addition to the phenomenal world of the perceiver, the set of habitats in which all life has evolved, the world as a geologic entity apart from all life, and the world as a cosmological entity (the 'universe'). How can these worlds be taken with reference to a living observer when they come both before and after any single observer, and in the geologic and cosmic cases, all observers? It is certainly true that the 'perceiver' is absent from these contexts, but there are others to take his or her place, namely the *evolutionist*, the *geologist* and the *cosmologist*. The history of the origin and change of life forms, the history of the earth, and the history of the universe are taken with respect to points of view different from the ecological, and without these different points of view, there would be no such worlds, and vice versa. And so too for all spatial and temporal scales of observation since, contrary to realist assumptions, there are no incorrigible atoms, either of matter (the fundamental particle) or of time (the specious present). The observer always finds himself in the middle of things, never at the top or bottom, beginning or end, for there are no such termini. There is only some problem for the observer to resolve, some task to complete, some action to engage in, and the solution can only be found in a context. There are no absolute foundations. Of course, in the last analysis our 'perceiver' and our 'evolutionist' and our 'geologist' and our 'cosmologist' comprise a single philosophical species called a 'being-in-the-world', but the scope of their being is narrow or broad, depending on the worlds these members of the 'species' respectively complement. The realist mistake is to think that there is a single world before there is any point of view. But there cannot, I have argued that Gibson has argued, be one without the other.

So is Gibson consistent? If the interpretation given to his theory here is right, then he is. But the interpretation completes a painting that the artist himself had not yet finished, and there are too many other possible strokes of the brush for any of us to divine what the finished work would have been like. I can only opine that, thematically, Gibson was moving in a definite direction. It seems plausible to assert that had he been able to go further, he would have finally given the appropriate name to his epistemology, the name which appears in the title of this chapter.

REFERENCES

Ashby, W. R., *An Introduction to Cybernetics* (London: Chapman and Hall, 1956).

Costall, A., 'On how so much information controls so much behavior: James Gibson's theory of direct perception', in *Infancy and Epistemology*, G. Butterworth (ed.) (New York: St Martin's Press, 1982).

Costall, A., 'On the mutuality of organisms and environment', (unpublished, 1983).

Epstein, W., 'Direct perception or mediated perception: a comparison of rival viewpoints, *The Behavioral and Brain Sciences*, 1980, *3*, 373–415.

Fodor, J. A., *The Language of Thought* (New York: Thomas Y. Crowell, 1975).

Fodor, J. A. and Pylyshyn, Z. W., 'How direct is visual perception?: Some reflections on Gibson's "ecological approach" ', *Cognition*, 1981, *IX*, 161.

Gibson, J. J., 'The problem of temporal order in stimulation and perception, *Journal of Psychology*, 1966a, *62*, 141–9.

Gibson, J. J., *The Senses Considered As Perceptual Systems* (Boston: Houghton Mifflin, 1966b).

Gibson, J. J., 'New reasons for realism', *Synthese*, 1967, *17*, 162–72.

Gibson, J. J., *The Ecological Approach To Visual Perception* (Boston: Houghton Mifflin, 1979).

Givner, D. A., 'Direct perception, misperception, and perceptual systems: J. J. Gibson and the problem of illusion', *Nature and System*, 1982, *4*, 131–42.

Gregory, R. L., *Mind In Science* (Cambridge: Cambridge University Press, 1981).

Gyr, J. W., 'Visual perception is underdetermined by stimulation', *The Behavioral and Brain Sciences*, 1980, *3*, 386.

Noble, W. G., 'Gibsonian theory and the pragmatist perspective', *Journal for the Theory of Social Behavior*, 1981, *11*, 65–85.

Rock, I., 'Difficulties with a direct theory of perception', *The Behavioral and Brain Sciences*, 1980, *3*, 398.

Shaw, R. and Bransford, J., 'Introduction: psychological approaches to the problem of knowledge', in *Perceiving, Acting, and Knowing*, R. Shaw and J. Bransford (eds.) (Hillsdale, New Jersey: Lawrence Erlbaum, 1977).

Shaw, R., Turvey, M. T. and Mace, W., 'Ecological psychology: the consequence of a commitment to realism', in *Cognition and the Symbolic Processes*, Vol. 2, W. Weimer and D. Palermo (eds.) (Hillsdale, New Jersey: Lawrence Erlbaum, 1982).

von Uexkuell, J., 'A stroll through the worlds of animals and men', in *Instinctive Behavior*, C. H. Schiller (ed.) (New York: International Universities Press, 1957).

Wilcox, S., 'A realist account of perceptual relativity' (unpublished mss, 1983).

Wilcox, S. and Katz, S., 'A direct realist alternative to the traditional conception of memory', *Behaviorism*, 1981, *9*, 227–39.

NOTE

1. I should like to thank Scott Kleiner, James Peterman, Stephen Wilcox, and the editors for very helpful criticisms of an earlier draft of this paper.

9

Perception and Language: Towards A Complete Ecological Psychology

William Noble

In an earlier essay (Noble, 1981) I pointed to certain problems with Gibson's ecological theory of perception (sometimes called a 'direct' theory—see Michaels and Carello, 1981, for a recent overview of the paradigm). It was argued that the place where this theory gets itself into trouble is at the interface between perception and language. For all the power of the theory to account for 'natural world' perception, it comes unstuck in the face of human perception mediated as it is by language. At a 'low' level (language as information at second-hand) the theory takes account of the language-perception connection, but it does not begin to address itself to the way language actually 'goes on' in the real world. Thus, the theory can make little headway towards accounting for the general run of human experience, even though it is trying to aim for such generality. (Reed, in this volume, argues a case for Gibson's treatment of language and perception as more thoroughgoing than what has just been implied. Gibson recognises that language functions in fixing and expanding awareness, in socializing through training and teaching. And Gibson brings language, as expression, into the material and out of the idealised realms. Missing still, however, is appreciation of the normative and rhetorical functions of language in the control of conduct.)

In the course of thinking further about the above problem I began to form a view that the articulation of the perception-language issue seemed to present a concept of the psychological reality of the person complete in itself. That is to say the person as psychologically taken (the person might also be taken economically, sociologically, physiologically), is explicable in terms of just two functions: perceiving and language-using. All the rest of what we understand by the idea of the person in psychology follows as derivative from those two, and their interactions. What I aim to do in this chapter is spell out that thesis in more detail. The actual structure of the essay is as follows: I begin with a very brief treatment of Gibson's ecological theory of perceiving, and go from there to recent cognitivist criticisms of this type of theory. I show the inadequacy of these criticisms and in so doing clarify the (functional) nature of a theory like Gibson's. Next I consider language in the everyday world and try to develop an adequate account of the interaction between perception and language. Finally I discuss language as account-making and the role of audience in that process.[1]

GIBSON'S THEORY OF PERCEPTION AND ITS CRITICS

Gibson's theory is ecological in this sense, that it focuses on the characteristics and features of the environment to be perceived, and its project is the adequate specification of those features at a level matching the sensory sensitivity of 'typical' organisms, particularly humans. It was Gibson's major achievement to propose an optics that matches the scale and performatory scope of human and like organisms. Analysis is at the level of structure consonant with the human frame, its locomotive and prehensory repertoires. By this means the information there in the structure of ambient light to specify features of the environment for such organisms could be described.

The theory has been opposed by adherents to mainstream psychological accounts of perception, who insist that perception is the first stage of 'mental processing', wherein data from the world, via the senses, are analysed and drawn upon by a variety of computational and constructive devices, to provide a plausible representation of the world for the benefit of the 'higher mental processes' (of recognising, understanding, memorising, thinking, and so forth). Gregory (1974), for example, delivered what many have taken to be a broadside upon the ecological model. It turns out, on closer inspection, however, to be a paradigm-based critique in which certain 'facts' are taken as incorrigible propositions rather than as the currency of his cognitivist theory. The irony in Gregory's paper is that he draws on the work of Kuhn (1970), and indeed uses the term 'paradigm' in his article's title, yet he fails to realise that his efforts at demolishing Gibson are paradigm based, hence he *fails* to take note of Kuhn's vital point, that:

> When paradigms enter . . . into a debate about paradigm choice, their role is necessarily circular. Each group uses its own paradigm to argue in that paradigm's defence. (Kuhn, 1970, p. 94)

The technique Gregory (1974) uses is to confront a range of models of perception with a series of 'facts' and demonstrate thereby the apparent inability of the ecological model to account for these facts. The facts in question are largely to do with picture-plane effects (so-called 'illusions'; 'reversible' figures; 'subjective' contours). It is becoming increasingly clear that the picture plane of western post-Renaissance culture has a special ecology of its own (Gibson, 1971; 1979; Wachtel, 1977/78; Wartofsky, 1980, 1981). It is simply not satisfactory, therefore, to accuse a model whose main target is the world of real surfaces, of being somehow less than adequate in relation to the picture-plane. It is in this way that Gregory's 'facts' are paradigm-based. Curiously, Gregory (1970) is entirely awake to the fact that pictures are 'peculiar'; he just doesn't seem to grasp (in his 1974 work) the significance of this. The ecological model can actually be applied more successfully to these picture-plane effects than Gregory (1974) allows. In particular, the three-dimensional reversible 'Necker cube' (and its cousin, the 'Mach figure') that Gregory (1970) and Ullman (1980) point to as showing the role of 'mental' mechanisms in perception, are entirely explicable on the basis of their structural features and on the 'visual posture' needed to achieve such reversal (Noble, 1986). These factors effectively remove the objects in question from the domain of the real to that of the depicted world. This is a distinction cognitivist psychologists either do not notice or, as with Gregory, do not grasp the significance of. As regards the reversible cube, for instance, it goes unnoticed that L. A. Necker's report (1832) specifically refers to 'a figure' of a crystal or geometrical solid, not to an actual crystal or solid, objects, that, in virtue of their structure, are irreversible (Noble, 1986).

Akin to Gregory's strange treatment, we find a similar kind of self-serving argumentation among other cognitivist critics of the ecological model. A recent debate occurred in and around Ullman's 1980 paper. Throughout Ullman's critique is a complaint that Gibson fails to argue from the structure of the nervous system toward a function for that structure. Of course, Ullman and other proponents of artificial 'intelligence' are naturally interested in that form of analysis. But Gibson, emerging as he does in part from a pragmatist and a Gestaltist–phenomenological tradition, is interested in producing a *functional* account of perceptual systems and what is available to them. There is nothing in what is described by these critics *structurally* that detracts from an ecological (functional) account.

Ullman, and some of his supporting commentators, also devote a good deal of attention to elaborating the sorts of problems that a cognitivist account generates for itself in trying to explain the business of perceiving. There follow more criticisms to the effect that nowhere does Gibson apply himself to these problems. Such argument overlooks the fact that Gibson did not use a computational metaphor for perception in the first place, hence he has no need to lose sleep over problems peculiar to that model.

An illustration of the absence of meaningful contact between the ecological model and its cognitivist critics is discernible in the remarks of one of the commentators (Bridgeman, 1980) on Ullman's paper, who, in support of Ullman, and taking himself to be undermining Gibson, states:

> I suggest that the emphasis (in Gibson's theory) be changed from 'direct' perception to 'primary' perception . . . In this reformulation primary perception is defined by those processes that take place quickly and without special attention or cognitive effort . . . [I]n vision these processes might include binocular vision, transformations of solid objects, constancies, and so on, while in hearing they might include the several mechanisms of binaural localization, and the like. Perceptual tasks which require special effort, such as counting the number of objects in a large

array, would require alternate nonprimary models of perceptual
processing, but the processes need not be qualitatively different. The task
of ecological optics, and analogous concepts for other senses, is then to
discover what properties of the world are primary for the perceptual
system, what information in the world the system is built to extract.
(Bridgeman, 1980, p. 381)

Leaving aside the questionable theoretical nature of the
'processes' exemplified, Bridgeman does not seem to realise
what is being 'given away' in this listing of the kind of things to
be included under the heading of direct perception, as against
those things to be retained for explanation under a different
rubric. Bridgeman is saying in effect that the whole gamut of
ordinary sensory contact with the world is subsumable under a
'direct perception' label, while tasks like 'counting objects' are
regarded as in a different basket. I am sure Gibson would have
been quite content to see this distinction honoured, the point
being that 'counting objects' is a linguistic skill, not a
perceptual one, though no doubt for its success it depends on a
confluence of perceptual and linguistic attention to the
environment.

PERCEPTION AND LANGUAGE

The foregoing is all to establish credentials, if you like, for an
ecological model of perceiving. Protagonists of the model are
trying to extend its generality, principally to the arena of so-
called 'social perception' (Knowles and Smith, 1982;
MacArthur and Baron, 1983). Such a move usefully calls
attention to the features of persons and their relations that can
be directly perceived by others, and hence form a key aspect of
how one may act in social life. There is much scope, indeed, for
bridge-building here between Gibson's and Goffman's fans. I
remain of the view, however, that efforts such as those referred
to will lack the power of the model in its original application (to
'natural world' perception) because the issue of language and
its interaction with perception remains undealt with or
inappropriately dealt with in connection with the model.

I think the general neglect of language in his treatment of
perception derives from the Gestalt background of Gibson's

theory. One of the strengths of Gestalt theory was in pointing to the fact of *a*linguistic awareness which is characteristic of all sentient life, which allows successful navigation in the environment—the sort of achievement displayed by ducks and dogs. As a result, on the basis of the observation that creatures with little by way of 'central brain power' can readily get about their environments, the ecological approach starts the analysis with 'how we are able to see what there is to be seen', rather than with 'how we mentally construct "percepts" on the basis of "raw sense data" '. Among Gibson's many achievements has been the successful mounting of a case against perception as based on sensation, and instead arguing that perception is the extraction (in his words, the 'pick-up') of information.

Now, the traditional stumbling-block for people who 'worry' about perception has ever been the sheer fact of our awareness of the world—our consciousness of the quality of our experience. How can I see the desk, the page, the pen, my hand? Where in my consciousness are these images displayed? Why do they have the quality they do? Gibson gives part of the answer to these time-honoured questions by responding as follows: 'Appearances' are as they are because the world is as it is. Such 'appearances' are not displayed in any 'consciousness'; the visual system is merely resonating to the features in the ambient optic array to which it is attuned. The capacity to see the different features and facets of the world is an (evolutionary and developmental) 'achievement' of a visual system sensitive to ecological optical characteristics of ambient light.

If we are to write a theory of experience more completely we must add to Gibson: The awareness of all this perceptual experience is the further (social-interactive) 'achievement' of organisms with the capacity to make accounts to each other and to themselves of the features of the world, including (and this is vital) accounts of that feature of the world which is designated 'themselves'. I don't want to get side-tracked here but it must be noted that the 'self' is a construct having had to do multifarious duty in the history of recent western thought (see Lyons, 1978). It is to the self, to the interior of the self, that cognitivist theory has attributed such things as 'mental structures' and 'information processing systems'.

In Gibson's theory the business of (visual) perception is the extraction of information available in the structure of ambient light. This means that the process under consideration is one in which objects and events are differentiated in the course of organismic interaction with the environment. Such differentiation is enabled by the fact that the sort of perceptual systems which are sensitive to typical energy forms in the world (vibration, radiation) are attuned to invariant features that specify such objects and events. In the visible world (or 'the world available for vision'), the 'self' is specified directly by a constant set of features that can roughly be characterised as a continuous elastic surface that divides and subdivides into limbs and digits, typically occluded by 'garments'. The perception of this complex and highly mobile surface in relation to other features of the environment is crucial in conveying 'the self' in that environment. It should be noted that the 'self' available to the auditory system, or to the basic orienting, haptic and taste–smell systems, in the absence of visual information (as for blind people), is specified differently to a 'self' available for visual notice and inspection, but it is uniquely and consistently specified none the less.

Even at the non-linguistic level (and I am going beyond our own species here), the relationship between organism and environment may be much more than with immediately adjacent surfaces and substances. Certain navigational achievements of many animals seem to be enabled by their sensitivity to gross terrestrial, astral and geomagnetic features of their surroundings as well as to more proximal features.

At the linguistic level, the human 'self' is conveyed within the environment in several ways at once (I leave out the matter of language in non-humans for purposes of present discussion as an issue too complicated to be included in the present chapter).

First, language critically marks to us the objects of our perception. It is this above all else, I believe, that has created all the puzzles. If we did not have language our perceptions would not be intruded on by this reflective capability of remarking on what we perceive. A feature of perceptional experience is thus the 'world as perceived', the noticing of the fact that we perceive the world. 'The monitoring of our self-monitoring' is how Harré and Secord (1972, p. 89) describe it. It is this capacity to point out the objects of the world to ourselves, to name, to elaborate them, to 'think about' them (what they are made of; if manufactured, how it was done, and so forth), it is this same capacity that allows us to notice ourselves, as a constant, hence as the 'obvious' candidate to be put forward as 'the seat of perception'. This can be called the *significatory* field of language, acknowledge by Gibsonians.

Secondly, because language is a social product, to know the 'meaning' of a term in one's language is to have mapped into the set of social (cultural) rules surrounding and penetrating the object designated by the term. When I perceive an object which has a name that I both 'know' and 'understand the meaning of', I am mapping into a set of implicit rules to do with that object. In the earlier essay (Noble, 1981), I referred to the example of the post-box, an object whose use is limited (by social rule) to the containment of a specific class of objects. If I know and understand the word 'post-box' what that means is that I can follow the implicit rule that limits the use to which I put the object referred to. (Equally, if I 'know the meaning' of the term 'self', I know it to be in the class of things to which "personal feelings" can be ascribed.) This is the normative field of language, not generally recognised by Gibsonians.

Thirdly, language is itself perceived and is the 'account system' of humans. Thus, I convey myself successfully in the environment not only to the extent I grasp the language as 'understood' by the people to whom I am speaking (i.e. follow social rules), but also to the extent that I 'know the world' as conveyed by language (i.e. knowledgeability *vs.* ignorance of, for instance, accounts of the world). Thus, my 'knowledge of the language' enables me 'correctly' to perceive those objects of the environment that are linguistically (socially) sustained (the post-box). And further, my knowledge of the language enables me to tap into that vast array of accounts about 'how the world works' (stories, articles, first-hand accounts, theories, and so forth). This is the rhetorical field of language, also untheorised by ecological investigators.

Thus language seems to mark our perceptions, to sustain social rules and, being itself perceived, it is marked as an 'account' system. Verbrugge (1985) notes that language is perceivable as such—as against being what we perceive 'through', the point I am emphasising here. He notes too, it has regularity, and hence seeks to categorize it in the realm of 'events'. This is no doubt faithful to Gibson's project but it does not do justice to how language goes on in the everyday world. To see the point at which language emerges from and interacts with perception, and forces us to extend Gibson's theory, I consider some distinctions made by Toulmin (1982) in a recent essay on consciousness. Toulmin identifies three awareness states: sensibility (in effect, wakefulness or sleep), attentiveness and articulateness. On the basis of the foregoing remarks it follows that language is implicated in humans at the level of attentiveness (after language has been 'guidedly reinvented', to borrow Lock's (1980) admirable term). When we attend to something, when we *notice* it, what we are doing is elaborating it linguistically, that is, identifying it, naming it, even if tacitly.

Toulmin (1982) makes a useful distinction in talking about his notion of attentiveness, namely, that the terms 'consciousness' and 'unconsciousness' may be defined, with respect to this level of awareness, as states of monitoring or of non-monitoring of the environment. Thus, the person driving on the highway may be on 'automatic pilot', their consciousness distracted by other matters. I would say they are perceiving, but not linguistically mediating that perception. They are achieving *a*linguistic information extraction that allows them to successfully convey themselves in the environment. It is feasible to invoke Wundt's construct of *apperception*, as illuminated by Danziger (1980, p. 104), to apply to my construct of *linguistically-mediated* perceiving. It must be noted, too, that *conscious attentiveness* (Toulmin's term) is the equivalent of tacit, linguistically-mediated perceiving (i.e. the linguistic activity is itself *un*monitored, it is the environment that is monitored).

Toulmin (p. 59) goes on to ask a question most pertinent to this feature of my thesis, 'Can infants and animals be "conscious" in the second sense?' (the sense of attending to, or monitoring the environment: the sense I have called linguistic). And he responds as follows:

> The answer to that question is not obvious. When a wakeful dog starts up with its ears cocked, and 'points' in the direction of a distant footfall, we

may be tempted to conclude that it is conscious of its master's imminent arrival. But this second usage cannot be extended from humans to animals as unambiguously as the first, 'sensibility' usage. The same is true for infants. A mother's eye of faith may very early perceive in her infant a 'consciousness' of her identity, presence, and facial expressions, but the reliability of her perception is open to discussion, even though nobody was in any doubt whether the child was asleep or awake, i.e. "conscious" in the first sense. (Toulmin, 1982, p. 59)

Toulmin's hesitancy about consciousness, at his level of 'attentiveness', as a feature of non- or pre-*linguistic* beings is, I take it, implicitly supportive of my argument about the (tacit) linguistic character of conscious attention. Of Toulmin's third category, 'articulateness', of course, there would be no dispute that we are clearly talking about linguistically-mediated action. But it is at the level of attention that language must be brought in to extend Gibson's account of perception. And to bring in language is to bring in the linguistic community and the role of 'audience'.

LANGUAGE AS ACCOUNT-MAKING AND THE ROLE OF 'AUDIENCE'

If, as Berger and Luckmann (1967) argue, language functions in the maintenance of reality, then language has to do with sustaining humans as members of social formations (see Noble, 1983). To maintain such membership means tapping into networks and relationships that acknowledge and respond to one's accounts and overtures; it means to establish *audiences* for one's performances. An audience provides itself to an utterer only in so far as one's utterance goes on having meaning for (has the consent of) that audience. Utterances that negate such meaning damage the 'structure of the life-world'—the everyday world taken for granted (Schutz and Luckmann, 1974) and can lead, in extreme cases, to complete withdrawal of speaking rights (sending to Coventry, referral to a psychiatrist). Loss of audience is a common feature of 'growing up'—the confusions of adolescence are due to uncertainty about who one's 'natural' audience is (children? adults?). Sullivan (1953) recognises throughout his work the paramount issue of audience and the power of audience (through selective withdrawal) to affect (indeed, *control*) the utterances of the other (the parent chastising the child for improper speaking). This and similar experiences at the hands of mentors and peers, leads to the cautiousness (in extreme cases the bashful withdrawn-ness) of so much human life. The fear of (valued) audience loss is considerable because it is the loss of human being.

In contrast, the increasing power and clarity of our utterance (spoken and written) as we mature is due to an increasing knowledge of, and hence confidence in, our audiences. And, what's more, even if the 'present' audience is unappreciative, with increasing experience we know there are others which have been and hence would be. In his theatrical model of the person, Mixon (1983) elaborates a theory of the actor and points to the critical role of the 'official' audience in the theatre. But he also discusses the even more critical role of listening (auditing) among the *actors* as productive of spontaneous and authentic playing. The actors must be audiences for each other in order to successfully convey their combined performances to the auditorium.

The evidence for 'audience' as crucial in the ongoing business of experience comes from multiple and varied sources. A key point to notice is that we have come full circle and are once again looking at an aspect of perception. Audiences need to be accurately identified and discriminated if one's utterances are to have meaning. That in turn means one needs to achieve clear perception—effectively to extract the information there which specifies the audience before one. The function of such information-extraction is to afford the ongoing success or otherwise of one's human (social) being, for we survive and prosper by perceiving and by accurately accounting for what we notice through whatever means is at our disposal. Language entails a new world of perception, the social, and a theory must account for this, not simply extend perception from that of ducks and dogs. It must show how language both reveals and rests upon the social reality within which human 'selves' exist, and human life is lived.

REFERENCES

Berger, P.L. and Luckmann, T., *The Social Construction of Reality* (Harmondsworth: Penguin Books, 1967).

Bridgeman, B., 'Direct perception and a call for primary perception', *The Behavioural and Brain Sciences,* 1980, *3*, 382-3.

Danziger, K., 'Wundt's theory of behaviour and volition', in R.W. Rieber (ed.), *Wilhelm Wundt and the Making of a Scientific Psychology* (New York: Plenum Press, 1980), pp. 89-115.

Gibson, J.J., 'The information available in pictures', *Leonardo*, 1971, *4*, 27-35.

Gibson, J.J., *The Ecological Approach to Visual Perception* (Boston: Houghton Mifflin, 1979).

Goffman, E., *Behavior in Public Places* (New York: The Free Press of Glencoe, 1963).

Gregory, R.L., *The Intelligent Eye* (London: Weidenfeld Nicolson, 1970).

Gregory, R.L., 'Choosing a paradigm for perception', in E.C. Carterette and M.P. Friedman (eds.), *Handbook of Perception*, Vol. 1 (New York: Academic Press, 1974), pp. 255-83.

Harré, R., and Secord, P.F., *The Explanation of Social Behaviour* (Oxford: Basil Blackwell, 1972).

Knowles, P.L. and Smith, D.L., 'The ecological perspective applied to social perception: Revision of a working paper', *Journal for the Theory of Social Behaviour*, 1980, *12*, 53-78.

Kuhn, T.S., *The Structure of Scientific Revolutions* (Chicago, University of Chicago Press, 1970).

Lock, A. *The Guided Reinvention of Language* (London: Academic Press, 1980).

Lyons, J.O., *The Invention of the Self: The hinge of consciousness in the eighteenth century* (Carbondale: Southern Illinois University Press, 1978).

MacArthur, L.Z. and Baron, R.M., 'Toward an ecological theory of social perception', *Psychological Review*, 1983, *90*, 215-38.

Michaels, C.F. and Carello, C. *Direct Perception* (Englewood Cliffs N.J.: Prentice Hall, 1980).

Mixon, D., 'A theory of actors', *Journal for the Theory of Social Behaviour*, 1983, *13*, 97-110.

Necker, L.A., 'Observations on some remarkable optical phæno-menon seen in Switzerland; and on an optical phænomenon which occurs on viewing a figure of a crystal or geometrical solid', *The London and Edinburgh Philosophical Magazine and Journal of Science* (3rd series), 1832, *1*(5), 329-37.

Noble, W., 'Gibsonian theory and the pragmatist perspective', *Journal for the Theory of Social Behaviour*, 1981, *11*, 65–85.

Noble, W., 'Hearing, hearing impairment, and the audible world: A theoretical essay', *Audiology*, 1983, *22*, 225–338.

Noble, W., 'Conditions for reversal and nonreversal of perspective of three-dimensional cubic forms', Ms. in preparation, University of New England: Department of Psychology, 1986.

Reed, E.S., 'James Gibson's ecological approach to cognition', Chapter 10 this volume.

Schutz, A. and Luckmann, T., *The Structures of the Life-World* (London: Heinemann, 1974).

Sullivan, H.S., *The Interpersonal Theory of Psychiatry* (London: Tavistock, 1953).

Toulmin, S., 'The genealogy of "consciousness" ', in P.F. Secord (ed.), *Explaining Human Behaviour* (Beverly Hills: Sage Publications, 1982), pp. 53–70.

Ullman, S., 'Against direct perception', *The Behavioural and Brain Sciences*, 1980, *3*, 373–81; 'Open peer commentary', 381–408; Author's response, 408–15.

Verbrugge, R.R., 'Language and event perception: steps toward a synthesis', in W.H. Warren, Jr and R.E. Shaw (eds.), *Persistence and Change* (Hillsdale, N.J.: Lawrence Erlbaum Associates, 1985).

Wachtel, E., 'The influence of the window on western art and vision', *The Structurist*, 1977–78, *17/18*, 4–10.

Wartofsky, M., 'Cameras can't see: Representation, photography, and human vision', *Afterimage*, 1980, *7*, 8–9.

Wartofsky, M., 'Visual scenarios: The role of representation in visual perception', in M.A. Hagen (ed.), *The Perception of Pictures*, Vol. 11 (New York: Academic Press, 1981), pp. 131–52.

ACKNOWLEDGEMENTS

I am indebted to Brian Byrne and Bronwyn Davies for their critical comments on an early draft of this chapter; and to Arthur Still and Alan Costall for their involvement throughout the gestation of the essay.

NOTE

1. I use a simplified model of language in this essay, namely, intended vocal utterance, but by the term 'language' I wish the reader to understand me as including any kind of bodily expression that has meaning adhering to it by virtue of its being marked by members of the sign-exchanging community—bodily gestures and body posture included. I go further and include forms of bodily expression that are usually *un*intended yet meaning-laden (cries, sweating, flatus, tics, changes of bodily colour) and which therefore have some sort of linguistic status. I see Goffman's (1963) distinction between information 'given' and information 'given off' as characterising the former and latter types of expression. I exclude, obviously, all forms of bodily activity that are imperceptible and hence outside of the psychological reality of the person.

10

James Gibson's Ecological Approach to Cognition

Edward S. Reed

INTRODUCTION

James J. Gibson was a highly controversial figure in modern psychology, who excited great passion among proponents and detractors of his theory alike. About the only matter on which Gibson's adherents and opponents have agreed is that his is an anti-cognitive theory of perception (compare e.g. Michaels and Carello, 1981, with Ullman, 1980). As it turns out, this sentiment—however widely promulgated—is simply and utterly false. Gibson thought of his as a cognitive psychology and of perception as a cognitive function. It is a fact that Gibson (rightly) dismissed modern 'cognitivism' (e.g. information-processing models, artificial intelligence, cognitive science), with its archaic yet incoherent theory of mental representations operating on stimulus inputs. But Gibson's dismissal of these facile, modish theories was not his position on cognition as such. Ever since the 1950s, when he self-consciously abandoned the response theory of cognition and behaviourism (Reed, 1986), Gibson considered his account of perception as a theory of how animals come to *know* their environments—a theory of cognition. Gibson's last two books (1966, referred to hereinafter as SCAPS; 1979, referred to hereinafter as EAVP) are replete with explicit discussions of the psychological issues concerning cognition, language, memory and imagination, discussions which have been ignored or worse throughout the entire secondary literature on Gibson's work.

In this chapter I attempt to reconstruct Gibson's cognitive

psychology. My account is based primarily on SCAPS, EAVP and other published sources. Where necessary for context and clarification I have used unpublished material of two sorts. First, I have used passages from Gibson's 'purple perils', spirit-duplicated (hence the 'purple') memoranda Gibson used in his weekly seminar and which he distributed to interested colleagues (see the introduction to Gibson (1982), referred to hereinafter as RR). Second, I have used manuscript material housed in the Gibson archives at Cornell University. Purple perils are cited as 'PP' followed by a date. Archival material is cited by a date (a question-mark following the date means that the attribution is uncertain, but few dates used here are incorrect by more than two years) and a file number.[1]

When writing EAVP, Gibson (1975, 5–52) made the following note to himself:

Fields of Cognitive Psychology
I. The perception of the environment and its affordances for behaviour
    Learning and the education of attention
    Control of locomotion and manipulation
    Orientation to the far environment
II. Perception and knowledge at second hand
    Pictures, models, toys, (Images)
    Experiments with graphic *displays*
III. Knowledge available in language
    Speech, writing, concepts, words
    Association, traces, memory, learning
    Experiments with *verbal* items.

This review will cover all of these areas (though not in this order) except the control of locomotion and orientation to the far environment (cognitive mapping, so-called) which deserve separate discussions. I have also brought some of Gibson's ideas about knowledge at second-hand and about the role of language in knowing under the single rubric of 'representation systems', a term of my own invention, although the idea for it derives from SCAPS. Criticism of Gibson's ideas is here kept to a minimum. My goal in this chapter is to expound a set of profound and novel ideas that deserve serious discussion, not the kind of ignorant dismissal they have received.

THE COGNITIVE REVOLUTION

Modern cognitive psychology has its roots in behaviourist learning theory. Already in the 1930s and 1940s, Edward C. Tolman was developing his 'cognitive' interpretations of rat maze-learning experiments. In the 1950s, as the ideas of cybernetics and computation theory became widely known, there were the beginnings of a full-scale revolt against the stultifying assumptions of classical learning theory. Cognitive psychology's equivalent of storming the Bastille was Noam Chomsky's (1959) attack on B.F. Skinner's *Verbal Behavior* (1957). Chomsky showed that Skinner's view of language was missing an important aspect of language, namely its *cognitive* function. A language is more than a system of labels or associations, it is more than a complex lexicon of phrases called up at appropriate times by experience and circumstances. A language is also a system of *predication*, which requires a grammar as well as a phrasebook. Language is an evolved specialisation for sharing knowledge about the world.

Chomsky's attack on learning theory, and the contemporaneous developments in computation theory, led to a growing realisation that the psychology of stimulus, response and association had severe limitations. Human behaviour could not be cut off from human knowledge, which was more than a mere linking of stimuli and responses. Apparently human beings 'processed' stimulus inputs, creating grammar-like, rule-based structures for *interpreting* other stimuli, or for *planning* future actions (Miller, Galanter and Pribram, 1960). These structures, linked by grammar-like hierarchies of rules and not by experienced associations, came to be called *mental representations*, and cognition came to be viewed as the formation and use of representations according to rule (Chomsky, 1980; Johnson-Laird, 1983).

The so-called cognitive revolution in psychology has thus *not* challenged the truly basic assumptions of S-R psychology, so much as it has added a new set of assumptions. Cognitive psychologists who study perception do not deny that it is based on stimuli (as Gibson does), but they do deny that association of stimuli (or even Gestalt organisation of inputs) is *sufficient* to explain all of perception (Neisser, 1967; Pinker, 1985).

Something else is needed: the rule-based processing of inputs into representations. Cognitivists who study action do not deny that it is based on responses, but they question whether the association of responses through innate linkages and learning is all there is to action. Isn't action also based on the rule-governed implementation of routines based upon stored knowledge, such as locomoting around the environment with the aid of a cognitive map (Gallistel, 1980; Requin, Semjen and Bonnet, 1984)? The cognitivists' idea is that a stimulus-response psychology can be made complete only by adding to it a psychology of mental representations or mental models that turn stimulus inputs into knowledge, and organise responses meaningfully (Johnson-Laird, 1983; Pylyshyn, 1984, Fodor, 1985).

Gibson's cognitive psychology also emerged from a critique of S-R psychology, but a very different critique. And, where cognitivists attempted to modify and supplement S-R principles, Gibson tried to overthrow them and replace them with an entirely different approach to psychology. The cognitivist critique of learning theory started with the problem of language and the kind of knowledge gained through language, whereas Gibson's critique of behaviourism started with perception and the kind of knowledge it facilitates. Gibson thought his perception-based critique was deeper than the other, and that is why he called for the replacement of S-R psychology, not its supplemention.

GIBSON'S CRITIQUE OF BEHAVIOURISM

The behaviourist or response theory of perception—which Gibson, following his teacher Holt (1915), espoused for years—involves the kind of associative principles which Chomsky and others have criticised so effectively. The basic idea is that one does not perceive an object until one has made a discriminative, specific response to it. This may sound odd, but it is actually just a more sophisticated version of the classic and widespread 'touch teaches vision' theory. The child is said to learn to see that a tennis ball is soft by having experience in touching it and subsequently associating those tactile experiences with the visual experiences of round, white (or orange), and so on. Meaningful perception is thus learned perception, and learned perception requires associating sensory stimuli with previous experiences, an association based on behaviour (see Gibson and Gibson, 1955/RR for a critique). Just as words are supposed to gain meanings through experienced association, so are sensory inputs.

There are many problems with such response theories of perception. First of all, as Gibson (1933; 1937) long ago showed, visual experiences of the same stimulus can change without *any* responses being made. Second, perceptual learning can be shown to occur without any reinforcement linking stimuli to responses (E. Gibson, 1953). This raises the question (at least for behaviourists) of, third, what kind of reinforcement does occur in perceptual activity (Woodworth, 1947; Gibson, 1958)? In behaviour, animals and people supposedly repeat and learn those responses which succeed; in perception, observers tend to learn *what is the case*, regardless of the outcome. The *exploratory* behaviour involved in perception would seem to be of an entirely different order than the *performatory* responses studied by behaviourists (SCAPS, Ch. 2). Fourth, there is the vexed problem of what should count as a stimulus. Behaviourists tended to be glib about this, referring to objects and other animals as stimuli just as readily as they referred to physical energies as stimuli (Gibson, 1960/RR). Gibson's (1961/RR) discovery that complex energy patterns counted as *information* for perception, combined with his critique of the stimulus concept, and his novel idea of exploratory action, led to his complete rejection of S-R psychology (Reed, 1986).

For Gibson, perception now became not a response to stimuli, or the awareness of the mental representations caused by stimuli; rather perception was defined as an observer's awareness of the environment, based on information and the active, exploratory pick-up of information. Information is the basis for contact with the environment because it is specific to its sources in the environment. It is *external* to the animal, and various exploratory actions of perceptual systems are required for perception to occur. Observers look, listen, sniff, taste and feel by orienting and moving their heads, hands and other sensory organs. *Neither* the sensory inputs nor the motor responses of these organs count as the information, they are simply what enables an observer to detect external information. One can track a moving object by moving one's eyes with a stationary head, or by moving one's head and keeping one's eyes steady, or by combining these two procedures. In each case there are very different stimuli and responses, but the awareness of the moving object can be the same if the information picked up is the same (see Gibson *et al.*, 1958 for experimental evidence.)

On this information-based theory of perception the meaningfulness of perception does not derive from any form of association, only from the information actually detected by an observer. Whereas cognitivists explain perceptual knowledge of the world as a construction out of stimulus inputs, Gibson explains it as the ability of the nervous system to home in on useful information: 'Instead of postulating that the brain constructs information from the input of a sensory nerve, we can suppose that the centers of the nervous system, including the brain, resonate to information' (SCAPS, p. 267). This resonance is a circular process that can achieve a state of equilibrium when the information being sought is detected. Perceptual learning is the process of becoming able to differentiate more and more kinds of information, and to increase the range and economy of the detection process (SCAPS, Ch. 13; E. Gibson, 1969). Perceptual learning is thus a change in both behaviour and awareness, and, according to the Gibsons, it is the fundamental cognitive process.

The modern proponents of cognitive psychology started with certain traditional principles: that stimuli and responses are the building-blocks of behaviour, that stimuli lead to sensations or sensory experiences, and that these stimulus inputs are the basis of our contact with the environment. These assumptions led them to treat cognition as the processing or interpretation of inputs into stored knowledge (representations) which can be accessed or re-called for use in language, memory and thinking. Gibson's rejection of these same assumptions resulted in a radically different definition of both perception and cognition. The novel and unusual definitions he proposed have led to the common contention that Gibson did not have a theory of the psychological processes underlying perception and cognition (see e.g. Heil, 1979; Ullman, 1980, and see the replies by Reed, 1980; Reed and Jones, 1981). The problem here is that what cognitive psychologists call psychological processes are processes Gibson treated as irrelevant or incidental to cognition, and cognitive psychologists have not yet even considered the processes of cognition discussed by Gibson:

> Associating, organizing, remembering, recognizing, expecting, and naming—all these are familiar psychological processes, and all of them have been appealed to in the effort to explain the growth of knowledge. But all of these processes were first conceived as operations of the mind upon the deliverances of sense, and they still carry some of this implication. They have now been examined, one by one, and I have suggested that, as commonly understood, they are incidental, not essential to the developing process of information pickup. They need to be reinterpreted. The deeper, underlying kinds of perceptual development seem to involve exploration and attention. (SCAPS, p. 283)

To understand Gibson's argument here requires first distinguishing and defining two kinds of cognition—direct and indirect; and, second, analysing the psychological processes involved in each of these kinds of knowing.

DIRECT COGNITION AND THE VARIETIES OF INDIRECT COGNITION

As Gibson's ecological theory of perception developed, he began to realise just how radical a change in thinking about perception he was proposing. Heretofore, virtually all theories of perception had assumed that the objects of which we are immediately aware are sensory objects, sensations. These subjective objects give us knowledge about the external world, but only after a complex process of inference, association and interpretation is applied to them. In other words, most perceptual psychologists held (and still hold) that what we directly perceive are mental ideas or representations, and it is only indirectly, through the mediation of these representations, that we perceive the external world. Gibson's theory that the perception of environmental objects, places and events is based on ecologically available information challenged this widespread consensus. Thus Gibson began to call his theory a form of direct realism, in that he held it possible to perceive the surrounding environment directly, on the basis of information, and not indirectly, on the basis of sensations and mental representations (Gibson, 1967/RR; Gibson, 1972).

In arguing that it is possible to perceive the world directly, Gibson never argued that mediated, or indirect awareness was impossible—although he was forced to an entirely new definition of indirect perception. Gibson repeatedly made a strong distinction between perception based on information and perception based on language, pictures or other symbols. In SCAPS (p. 91) he wrote, 'In this book, a distinction will be made between perceptual cognition, or knowledge of the environment, and symbolic cognition, or knowledge *about* the environment. The former is a direct response to things based on stimulus information, the latter is an indirect response to things based on stimulus sources produced by another human individual.' In EAVP (p. 147) he is perhaps more blunt:

> Direct perception is what one gets from seeing Niagara Falls, say, as distinguished from seeing a picture of it. The latter kind of perception is *mediated*. So when I assert that perception of the environment is direct, I mean that it is not *mediated* by *retinal* pictures, *neural* pictures, or *mental* pictures. *Direct perception* is the activity of getting information from the ambient array of light.

This process of detecting information is a complex one, unfamiliar to most psychologists or neurophysiologists, who have studied only how sensory inputs are processed or transduced, not how external information is detected by active observers. Gibson devoted the major portion of his second book, SCAPS, to an analysis of the process of pick-up, so only a few of his leading ideas can be summarised here. Most importantly, information pick-up is a process carried out by a functional system distributed throughout an animal's nervous system. Adjustments of peripheral organs, such as turning the eyes and head, play as significant a role in direct perception as the activity of the higher brain centres. Awareness of the environment is based on the adjustment of the animal's entire perceptual system to the information surrounding it. This adjustment includes a range of processes, all of which may be described as the simultaneous extraction of persisting and changing properties of stimulation, invariants despite disturbances of the array of information (EAVP, p. 249). Observers can perceive themselves, their environments, and the changing relationship between themselves and their surroundings. This requires component processes such as delimiting the range of variables in stimulation, establishing covariations of information across different perceptual systems, distinguishing information specifying the self from information specifying the environment, and extracting information about the affordances of the objects, places, events and other people in one's habitat. All of these processes are described in SCAPS (especially Chapter 13). As Gibson emphasises, these processes are 'postulated to be very susceptible to development and learning. The opportunities for educating attention, for exploring and adjusting, for extracting and abstracting are unlimited' (EAVP, p. 250).

The fundamental hypothesis of Gibson's ecological approach to perception is that, where specific information about environmental objects, places, events and people is available and picked up, then observers will perceive these things. This is what Gibson means by direct perception, or 'knowledge *of*' the environment. It is tacit knowledge. It is not formulated in pictures or words, for it is the knowledge that makes the formulation of pictures and words possible. However, even though it is tacit, this knowledge of the environment obtained through direct perception is not personal, subjective or private. Information is *available* in the environment, and it can be picked up by many observers. Even a point of view is not private: 'your perception and mine can be identical even though your sensation and mine can never be identical at the same time. The same invariants over time are available to both of us.' When you move around the rectangular table the changing angles of its corners as projected into the optic array covary so as to keep the cross-ratio invariant, and the same is true for the optic array at my eyes, although I am not in your position at any given time. 'I cannot occupy your point of observation now, but I can in the future and I could in the past' (RR, pp. 411–12). Because we live in a *shared* environment, a social environment inhabited by others of our kind, direct perception is not necessarily private. Privacy of perception and action is possible, by means of occluding edges and their use in preventing information from becoming available to others, but that is another story (see EAVP, p. 136).

Any group of socially living animals thus perceives their habitat in common and can, to some degree, perceive the affordances of their environment for their fellows as well as for themselves. Under certain evolutionary conditions they may also develop the ability to act so as to make their fellows aware of relevant environmental facts. Through gestures and displays information can be selected and presented to others. Humans specialise in the making of optical displays, through facial, manual and postural gestures, and through modifying surfaces with incisions and/or pigments. Humans also specialise in a unique kind of vocal display, speech. According to Gibson (EAVP, p. 42),

> a display . . . is a surface that has been shaped or processed so as to exhibit information for more than just a surface itself. For example, a surface of clay is only clay, but it may be molded in the shape of a cow or painted with the profile of a cow or incised with the cuneiform characters that stand for a cow, and then it is more than just a surface of clay.

Similarly, a sound stream can be modified to provide linguistic information for a cow, and then it is more than just a vocalisation, it is a reference to a cow. These 'images, pictures, and written-on surfaces afford a special kind of knowledge that I call *mediated* or *indirect*, knowledge at second hand' (ibid.). This indirect knowledge is intrinsically shared, because it involves the *displaying of information to others*. Even when one is talking to oneself, or scribbling notes, information is being made potentially available to other observers. (The special case of so-called 'internalised' speech and imagery will be discussed separately below.)

All displays are made up of *samples* of information in various forms. The following is a tentative list of the modes of mediated visual perception (Gibson, 1976?, 5–75):

1. A sample of the optic array is magnified or minified by an optical device, or its energy level is amplified by a device.
2. Some of the frozen structure in a sample of an optic array is reproduced photographically, or recreated chirographically (drawing, painting, etc.).
3. Samples of optical information are *converted* or *coded* into verbal descriptions.
4. Samples of optical information are *indexed* by an instrument, as with a meter stick.

In all these cases the information on which direct perception can be based is *selectively* adapted and modified in a display. A microscope or a photograph sample a *sector* of the global array even if they do not necessarily distort that sample. The value of these selected samples of information lies not in the displays themselves, but in what they refer to or *represent*. These mediators are representations, they do not have affordances as objects do, but rather have 'referential meaning' (5–75). They 'consolidate the gains of perception'—a favorite phrase of Gibson's—'by converting tacit knowledge into explicit knowledge' (Gibson, 1976, 5–61).

The knowledge of the shared environment gained through direct perception can itself be selected, highlighted, made explicit and shared. A picture can make you aware of something I have seen that you have never seen, and a word can label unknown things for you, as well as refer to known ones. Often words and representations tend to delimit and stereotype our knowledge of the world. This is because the environment, and the ecological information available in it, is infinitely rich, whereas lexicons are finite and must therefore select and categorise (SCAPS, p. 281). When perception depends on such labels alone it, too, will tend to be stereotyped. For example, the Nazi stereotype of the 'Jew' had profound and horrifying social consequences on the actions and consciousness of Germans (Gibson, 1939). Luckily, perception can depend on information as well as mediating representations, so it is not inevitably stereotyped.

Indirect awareness has a variety of modes which all have in common the function of making observers aware by means of selecting and sampling information. That sampling may be accomplished through tools, like a telescope or a telephone; or by displays, such as a photograph or a page of text; or through complex coding of ecological information, as in all forms of language (EAVP, Chapter 13). In all cases the awareness can be called indirect because it is different from but based on the direct perception of the display, tool or vocalisation. One directly perceives a picture as a marked surface (even though one rarely attends to that aspect of it) and indirectly perceives that it is, say, a portrait of one's mother. The great variety of processes involved in indirect perception therefore have in common this one process of a 'dual awareness'—a simultaneous awareness of the mediator and what it represents. There are thus many levels of visual cognition,

> At all four levels, (1) seeing the man, (2) seeing his picture, (3) reading his name, and (4) reading about him, the information has to be carried in structured light. There has to be an array with borders, textures, patterns or forms, and this is why the problem of defining the structure of an [optic] array is so fundamental. (SCAPS, p. 244)

INDIRECT AWARENESS CONSOLIDATES THE GAINS OF DIRECT PERCEPTION

The various processes of indirect cognition—the uses of depictions, descriptions, symbols and tools for extending awareness—are quite diverse and have barely begun to be studied. They cannot be analysed here in any depth. Instead, I shall focus on Gibson's fundamental hypothesis, that indirect modes of cognition consolidate the capacities of direct perception, that mediators allow one to make explicit previously tacit knowledge. It is this hypothesis about the relations between indirect awareness (especially through language) and direct perception that sets Gibson aside from the modern consensus in cognitive psychology. It is virtually a dogma of modern psychology that all meaningful perception is indirect, and is in some ways analogous to language and the use of symbols and representations (Luria, 1973; Fodor, 1975; Marr, 1982). Simply put, the idea is that perception of the world is based on sense inputs. We have direct access to the sense inputs, but these are not meaningful in themselves, they become meaningful only after a complex form of quasi-grammatical or computational processing. Thus, it is argued, meaningful intercourse with the world requires that an observer already has some stored knowledge (either innate, acquired, or both) that can be used to interpret inputs. On this theory there is *no* direct experience that is truly meaningful. The relation between direct and indirect processes in cognition is analogous to the old idea of the relation between matter or substance and form: the sense inputs are the matter out of which meanings are carved by 'higher' psychological processes (Fodor, 1985).

The ecological approach to direct perception rejects the basic assumptions from which this cognitivist consensus has sprung. *If* ecological information is available, and *if* animals have evolved nervous systems capable of picking it up, then—or so Gibson's hypothesis goes—meaningful direct perception of the environment will occur when such information is detected. The role of explicit knowledge, and the processes that make knowledge explicit, is not to *create* knowledge out of merely potentially meaningful input, nor even to *select* meanings to assign to inputs. The role of indirect forms of cognition is to *make others aware*, is to share knowledge. (This can be extended to a reflexive mode, as in reminding oneself, making oneself aware.)

Gibson's theory of information-based perception thus forces a rethinking of the nature of all forms of cognition. *For a cognitivist like Chomsky (1959; 1980) a spoken word is simply a stimulus, just as it is for a behaviourist like Skinner (1957).* Neither theory has the concept of stimulus *information*, and both are therefore forced to treat utterances as merely verbal stimuli. Chomsky rightly pointed out that any reduction of a language to a system of associative labellings is untenable, for the very production of speech is 'creative'. One produces that which one has *not* heard (as well as what one has heard) more or less according to the rules of the language. The child's language may mirror that of its parents, but it is also much more than a mirror, as the child learns to ask questions, say what it wants and what it thinks and, in general, produce utterances never before spoken. Whereas for Skinner the contingencies of reinforcement are sufficient to explain learning, for Chomsky they are inadequate, and it is from this inadequacy that Chomsky argues for an 'innate universal grammar'—an inborn inability to make sense out of not completely meaningful stimuli. Each human child must be born with such knowledge, Chomsky asserts, to explain how, given mere verbal stimuli, he or she comes to know how to speak their language properly.

When children learn to produce language creatively, as when they invent grammatically regular constructions that happen not to exist in a language ('I goed to my friend's house'), this is sometimes called 'active learning' to distinguish it from mere passive learning or mirroring (DeVilliers and DeVilliers, 1978). What is striking about the theory of direct perception is that it accounts for such active learning as a kind of *perceptual* learning based on *information*, not a cognitive learning, based on inputs and experience. There is now abundant evidence that infants actively learn about their world through visual perception: experience with objects, events and actions (such as reaching, grasping or sucking) leads to a kind of active learning of the properties of things (E.J. Gibson, 1984). For example, experience with the differences between certain rigid and non-rigid optical motions provides even a five-month old with the knowledge that enables it to distinguish previously unseen kinds of motions (E.J. Gibson, *et al.*, 1978). If perception is based on information, and not on stimulus inputs, then, James and Eleanor Gibson have argued, the debate between the cognitivists and the behaviourists over language learning is simply misguided. The problem is *not* how to explain the active learning of language based on the paucity of the verbal stimuli. Rather, the problem concerns *information*, and specifically the use of the *dual* information in speech: how can children learn to hear not only the utterance, but also what it denotes? According to Gibson (SCAPS, p. 281),

> For the child who is learning to use language and at the same time learning to perceive the world, words are *not* simply auditory stimuli or vocal responses. They embody stimulus information, especially invariant information about the regularities of the environment. They consolidate the growing ability of the child to detect and abstract the invariants. They cut across the perceptual systems or 'sense modalities'. The words are like the invariants in that they are capable of being auditory or visual . . . . They even cut across the stimulus–response dichotomy, for they can be

vocal–motor or manual–motor. Hence, the learning of language by the child is not simply the associative naming or labelling of impressions from the world. It is also, and more importantly, an expression of the distinctions, abstractions, and recognitions that the child is coming to achieve in perceiving.

The newborn infant exposed to speech gets information about the sounds being made, but little or no information about their meanings, and must learn about her world directly. As the infant develops, two kinds of language learning then take place, the 'learning of the language code as a vocabulary' and 'learning to consolidate . . . knowledge by predication' (SCAPS, p. 282). The first involves the learning of complex associations, of words as labels for objects, places, events and actions that the child perceives. This is not behaviouristic learning by associating stimuli with responses, it is instead the learning *of* associations between ecological information and verbal information. Gibson (1975?, 5–52) contrasts his own list of meanings thus learned with those of Brown (1973) and Schlesinger (1974) (Table 10.1). Each of Gibson's categories is based on optical information analysed in EAVP, with the exception of negation (for which, see below). Although these meanings are *derived* from ecological information, they are still *attached* meanings, as opposed to affordance meanings (Gibson, 1980). That is, they are not intrinsic to the words. 'Words, written or spoken, are like arbitrary signs . . . in having *reference to something else*. The meaning is attached and can therefore be detached. Affordances of things, however, have not been attached and cannot be *detached* (not added, associated, remembered)' (Gibson, 1975?, 5–52). Evidence for this comes from the phenomenon of 'lapse' or 'recession' of meaning of words that are repeatedly uttered or stared at—a phenomenon Gibson studied and returned to repeatedly throughout his career. (See PPs for December 1968, January, 1971 [5–5]; Gibson, 1931–35, 1–39–1.41; for the original studies of this phenomenon, see Severance and Washburn (1907), Bassett and Warne (1919), Don and Weld (1924); see also Gibson, 1950, p. 204, where it is argued that all meanings are attached, a position he soon abandoned.)

The second kind of language-learning involves the consolidation of direct perception and attached meanings through

Table 10.1: 'Structural Meanings' in Early Utterances

Brown's Classification

I. Operations of reference
    Nominations: e.g. 'that book'
    Notice: 'Hi children'
    Recurrence: 'More meat, 'nother raisin'
    Nonexistence: 'Allgone juice', 'no more dog'

II. Relations
    Attributive: Ad. + N (big train)
    Possessive: N + N (Mommy lunch)
    Locative: N + N (sweater chair)
    Locative: V + N (go store)
    Agent-action: N + V (Adam write)
    Agent-object: N + N (Mommy sock)
    Action-object: V + N (Ate meat)

Schlesinger's Classification of Relations

Agent-action: N + V
Action-object: V + N
Agent-object: N + N
Modifiers
Negation
Datives ('throw Daddy')
Ostension (Here, there, see)
Locatives

Gibson: Pick-up of structure or relations (meaning)

Appearance
Disappearance
  occlusion vs. 'going out of existence' (allgone, no more)
Reappearance
  recurrence or return
Attribution
  of a property, e.g. size, colour
Possession
Location
Causality
Temporal relations
  before, after, yesterday, etc.
Negation?

predication. A mere list of labels can only serve the needs of categorising and pointing (ostension). The fact that these labels can be *systematised* into stating facts, questions, commands, etc. removes the limits of mere association. This discovery of the predication of environmental facts was one of the greatest of human discoveries, celebrated by Chomsky and many others as implying a uniquely human cognitive skill. It is predication that allows the knowledge of the environment gained via perception to be made explicit and shared:

> Perceiving helps talking, and talking fixes the gains of perceiving. It is true that the adult who talks to a child can educate his attention to certain differences instead of others. It is true that when a child talks to himself he may enhance the tuning of his perception to certain differences rather than others. The range of possible discriminations is unlimited. Selection is inevitable. But this does not imply that the verbal fixing of information distorts the perception of the world. The curious observer can always observe more properties of the world than he can describe. (SCAPS, p. 282).

Whereas cognitivists see language-learning as the child's construction of a meaningful world out of stored 'rules' for the interpretation of not yet meaningful inputs, Gibson saw language as a process of stabilising, making explicit and sharing the meaningful information we all use in our direct perception of the world. Direct perception is thus our basic mode of cognitive contact with the environment, and indirect modes of awareness extend and amplify this cognitive contact, but do not alter it. Thus, as opposed to the theory of a mental construction of a meaningful environment, Gibson proposed a process of discovery: meanings and values are available to observers in their environment. There is always more meaning implicit in perception than has been made explicit by words, pictures, maps, or other symbols. The key difficulty with any theory of meaning as based on discovery is to show that sufficient meaningful information is available to be discovered. Gibson began to do just this with his theory of ecological information for vision, but he also recognised specific problems in attempting to extend his account from perception into language. One fundamental problem is to explain the source of information for negation, as Gibson (1974, 5–42) pointed out:

Information in the form of predication can be a *truth* or a *falsehood*. A person can misinform in the sense of *lie* (not to be confused with fiction). Information in the form of *stimulation* (a flowing *array* of energy) *cannot lie*—cannot be false in this sense (see below). The light and sound from the environment do not say untruths about the environment, only men do that. Information in the form of a *picture* can be *contradictory* or *equivocal* (e.g. goblet-face . . .) but cannot be *false* in the above sense. Pictures do not *predicate* or state an *equation* ([as in] logic or mathematics) and cannot lie (e.g., all swans are black; $2 + 2 = 5$).

Negation requires a system of information in which statements are made about the way the world is, in which properties are ascribed to things. In direct perception, the use of information is not to make statements—the world does not communicate to us—but to facilitate awareness and action. In direct perception the difference between real and imaginary or illusory can be tested for, by means of tacit processes. Of these, Gibson singled out 'the most decisive test for reality is whether you can discover new features and details by the act of scrutiny. Can you obtain new stimulation and extract new information from it. Is the information inexhaustible? Is there more to be seen? The imaginary scrutiny of an imaginary entity cannot pass this test' (EAVP, p. 257). Now, whereas a *display* itself is real (one can scrutinise the surface of a picture and discover ever-finer details) the *information captured* in a display is finite (as one approaches a photographic portrait ever closer, or blows it up with a magnifier, eventually all one can see is the graininess of the surface; when one approaches a person ever closer, one can discover more and more details about their skin, etc.). The tests for reality of representations thus extend beyond the individual scrutiny of the displays and include social norms for the use of the displays, norms for the *sharing* of information. An individual alone can test for the difference between real and imaginary in direct perception, but in indirect perception, where the information has been sampled and selected,

the difference between the factual and the fictional depends on the social system of communication and brings in complicated questions. Verbal descriptions can be true or false as predications. Visual depictions can be correct or incorrect in a wholly different way. A picture cannot be true in the way that a proposition is true, but it may or may not be true to life. (EAVP, pp. 261–2)

Because indirect modes of cognition serve to help share knowledge, many of these modes of awareness have evolved into socially specific systems of representation. The most obvious example is language, each particular language being specific to a certain historico-cultural community (SCAPS, p. 91). But social conventions exist for a wide variety of representation systems: picturing, time-measurement, numbering and mensuration, mapping, etc. When awareness becomes socialised, the learning process also becomes socialised, marking a significant difference between direct and indirect perception. 'I say,' Gibson wrote in a short essay tucked into his copy of Arnheim's (1969) *Visual Thinking*, 'that perceiving does not involve the "assimilating" of new impressions to prior knowledge as traditional theory maintains (Kant). It only involves an increasing sensitivity to available information. But learning in the sense of being told or being taught, learning by communication, depends on *learning the language*. You have to know the language before you can know the world mediated by language. But if you look and listen and feel for yourself you don't *need* any words, concepts, schemas, or preperceptions.' To understand fully indirect apprehension, one needs to go beyond the process of learning inherent in individuals' perceptual systems and investigate the process of socialised learning, or learning about the world via a community's representations systems.

FROM PERCEPTUAL SYSTEMS TO REPRESENTATION SYSTEMS

The primary act of animal cognition is direct perception of the objects, events and places around one. But among these objects there are other animals who are also perceiving the environment. When one observer perceives another, what is perceived is not merely an object in some place, but an observer who is situated at a point of view and aware of the surrounding habitat and what it contains (Gibson and Pick, 1963). The perceived environment is an animate and social environment.

The child begins, no doubt, by perceiving the affordances of things for her, for her own personal behavior. She walks and sits and grasps relative to her own legs and body and hands. But she must learn to perceive the affordances of things for other observers as well as for herself. An affordance is often valid for all the animals of a species, as when it is part of a niche. I have described the invariants that enable a child to perceive the same solid shape at different points of observation and that likewise enable two or more children to perceive the same shape at different points of observation. These are the invariants that enable two children to perceive the common affordance of the solid shape despite the different perspectives. . . . Only when each child perceives the values of things for others as well as for herself does she begin to be socialized. (EAVP, p. 141)

Two or more animals sharing their environment can share their awarenesses as well. Animals can gesture so as to communicate, either about their own state or about environmental states of affairs. A predator may move so as to appear non-threatening, and a harmless creature may attempt to look fierce. One member of a group may vocalise or gesture so as to warn another of danger, a parent may make comforting noises or gestures to its child, mates make alluring gestures and poses to one another. In all such cases, where the function of the act is truly communication, one animal is making a display (optical, acoustical, chemical, mechanical or otherwise) so as to provide information to another. This provided information is the basis of all mediated knowledge. Your agitated vocalisation may inform me directly of your nervous state, but it also may warn me *indirectly* of imminent danger. My direct perception of your emotional state is based on an individual process of information pick-up. My indirect awareness of the danger is based on a group process of selecting and displaying information to be picked up, a social process of representing the environment. Gesturers must make movements that are not merely perceptible by observers in their group, but the gestures must somehow effectively *indicate* environmental facts. There is considerable evidence that there is strong selection pressure for such movements to become differentiated into clearly categorisable patterns (Darwin, 1872; Daanje, 1950; Mayr, 1972) and some evidence that such communicative categories are learned, at least among primates.

At some point in human evolution—quite possibly as recently as 40,000 years ago, according to Lieberman

(1984)—humans began to create vocalisations that indicated environmental facts independently of the state of the speaker or listener. Human vocalisation thus evolved into *verbalisation*, sounds that contained 'symbols which carry the meanings of things in the common environment of *all* individuals. These enable men to think of the same things, to have concepts in common, and to verify their concepts jointly. The cry "wolf" has an entirely different function from either the cry of alarm at seeing a wolf or the howling of the wolf itself' (SCAPS, pp. 90–1). The optical or acoustic information specifying a wolf, or even specifying a dangerous animal is embodied in ecological laws of specificity (Turvey *et al.*, 1981). But the exact optical or acoustic properties of the word for wolf 'depend on a *linguistic community*, which is a unique invention of the human species' (SCAPS, p. 91). The laws of ecological information have emerged from general evolutionary processes operating throughout the ecosystem—there is selection pressure on most animals to adapt to this information (Reed, 1985). But the traditions of a community's symbolisations have emerged from particular evolutionary or historical lines, and the ability to use those symbols is correspondingly limited.

In contrast to perceptual systems, then, representation or symbol systems involve *cultural* and *historical* as well as individual psychological processes. In humans, the cultural and the individual ('natural') processes are thoroughly mixed, 'mediated apprehension gets *combined* and *fused* with direct apprehension' (Gibson, 1976?, 5–75). We use words to guide our perception and we use perception to guide our sharing of knowledge. 'Look at the——'is a fundamental fact of human childhood, and it conveniently illustrates how thoroughly intermingled is our tacit knowledge of the world and our explicit knowledge about it. The more explicit the knowledge is made, the more it requires a process of socialisation or acculturation to be learned:

> The various affordances of surfaces, substances, layouts, and events get perceived in the course of development of the young animal by maturation and learning taken together, by *encountering* the surfaces in the habitat, without schooling. On the other hand, the referential meanings of marks on a surface get apprehended by children in ways that differ from the preceding, and also differ from one another. They are different for

pictures, drawings, plots, signs, and letters of the alphabet. At one extreme, photographs are independent of cultural conventions. Drawings and diagrams are at least somewhat conventional. Alphabetic writing is wholly conventional. But however different the learning of pictorial reference may be from the learning of linguistic reference (and they *are* very different), they are even more radically different from the learning of what surfaces afford. Encountering these marks is not enough, and the more they vary with the culture to which the growing child belongs, the more this holds true. (Gibson, 1980, p. xiii)

Whereas picture perception requires a process of *perceptual* learning—and in addition a socialised process in the case of diagrams, maps, X-rays and other pictorial material—language learning inherently involves more than a perceptual learning process, a process of explicit interpersonal teaching. Perceptual learning can (though it need not) occur 'out of school', but the scribe, accountant or writer must be taught.

The human self is *both* a natural individual and a member of a culture. In directly perceiving the environment there is always a co-perception of the self (EAVP, p. 182 f.). In mediated awareness there is an awareness of the self as part of the symbolising community, a group that shares knowledge, techniques and taboos. In addition to direct knowledge of ourselves through perception, we also know ourselves through sharing representation systems with others. The human discovery of writing combined the capacity for shared predication with permanence, so that the social group involved in sharing knowledge could be expanded: 'Social interaction became possible without a face-to-face meeting. Messages could be sent over great distances. Knowledge could be accumulated in storehouses. The young could be taught by the wisest teachers, living or dead. History and civilization began' (SCAPS, p. 242). As the child grows and develops in her use of language, numbers, pictures and other representations, she is more and more enabled to take advantage of explicit, socially-gathered knowledge, as well as of socially developed customs. Socialisation is not just a channelling of the self into pre-existing social norms, it is also an opportunity to develop and enlarge the self, through the use of explicit knowledge and socially developed techniques. The socialised child not only knows how to act properly, but also knows more about the world and may even make a contribution to civilisation. Representation systems increase the possibilities for self-development almost limitlessly.

THE USE OF REPRESENTATION SYSTEMS

Gibson's theory of indirect cognition as the socialised self's use of historically developed cultural resources may strike some as being quite similar to Vygotsky's (1978) account of how the child becomes socialised through cognitive means. However, Vygotsky did not have the concept of ecological information, and did not believe direct perception of the environment was possible. Like most cognitivists, he believed that the child's apprehension of the meaningful world required a process of 'internalisation' of speech, and of ideas and rules encoded in speech. (Admittedly, Vygotsky thought that these were socially generated ideas and rules, historical customs, unlike Chomsky's essentially mysterious innate rules of grammar, but the process of internalisation in both cases is similar.) Gibson was sceptical of this idea of internalised speech (EAVP, p. 262). Is there also internal drawing? Internal writing? Why should the *planning* of an act be confused with some sort of internal act? If internalisation means that there exists minuscule speech acts, or drawing acts, etc. in the head, surely it is a mistaken concept. However, if internalisation means that the *process* of speaking or picturing can run *without* a successful end-product, this is quite plausible. After all, even the process of pick-up of information in direct perception is *motivated*, and can run without adequate results. We can, after all, *keep on looking* even when we do not find what we are looking for. Gibson argued that such an open-ended process of pick-up is the basis for visualising and other forms of imagining (EAVP, pp. 255-6). The awareness in such cases is not based on the having of a representation or an image, but on the unconstrained activity of the pick-up system (see also Neisser, 1976). (Strictly speaking, however, such forms of activity should be called *non-*cognitive or non-perceptual, because they do not function to keep us in touch with the actual environment.)

Thinking and planning are modes of indirect cognitive

activity running in this unconstrained manner. One can think without images or words, or one can think with their aid, but the calling up of an internal word or image is incidental to the process. Human cognition does not differ from animal cognition because we can 'internalise' ideas, or visualise, or even plan actions. Evidence of these abilities is difficult to evaluate, but animals likely have at least some such 'internalisation' capacities (Ingold, 1983). It is not the *fact* of visualising, imagining or planning that sets us apart cognitively from other animals, but *with what* we can 'internalise' our thoughts. We can use words, alphabets, measuring systems, etc. all of which help both to consolidate and extend our knowledge and planning abilities. For example, the existence of the alphabet helps us to remember or plan events according to a very complex (but conventional) order (Goody, 1983). The alphabet can be used to consolidate memories into retrievable lists of about two dozen categories, hierarchically organising any pattern into a nested grouping of sub-categories, each of which can also be categorised similarly, and so on. Rhyming, metre, assonance-structure, numbering and other linguistic methods work in similar ways to fix and consolidate our cognitive skills. Human memory cannot have a 'fixed capacity' precisely because civilised humans have continued to invent and improve our 'tools of the intellect' (Goody, 1983, p. 84).

Indirect knowledge is 'culturally transmitted knowledge' that is embodied in 'toys, pictures and words' which enable adults to help make their children aware of the environment in addition to their own perception. These mediators

> transmit to the next generation the tricks of the human trade. The labors of the first perceivers are spared their descendants. The extracting and abstracting of invariants that specify the environment are made vastly easier with these aids to comprehension. But they are not themselves knowledge, as we are tempted to think. All they can do is to facilitate knowing by the young. (EAVP, p. 258)

Knowing is the process of using information. It may be guided by words, pictures, models or tools, but the mere having of these aids in no way guarantees that knowing will occur. Further, perceiving and knowing are self-motivating, they are desirable in their own right. Children are inquisitive and will make the effort to know regardless of what information and representations are available. These efforts towards cognition are not cognition themselves, but visualising, daydreaming, planning, and so on are excellent ways of developing and tuning the various processes of cognition. Whatever we know tacitly of the world is based on information. Whatever we know explicitly about the world is based on descriptions, depictions, indices, etc. that help to consolidate the available information and processes of using that information. The re-calling or re-presenting of mediators to our minds may *accompany* the effort to know, but it is not the process itself. The great ballad singers of the world, who can recite Homeric-length epics, do not recall the words but the story: they recreate the words in retelling the story each time (Lord, 1960). In Luria's (1929/1978) study of the development of writing, he found that the three or four year old first discovers that his scribbling on paper can be used as a functional aid to remembering and only then develops the ability to consolidate and retrieve memories. Goody (1977) claims that it is only literate cultures that consider memory to be analogous to the recalling of items from a text or list. The symbols of language are not mere reflections of our mental achievements, they themselves *are* achievements. 'In oral memory the many failures tend to get forgotten in favour of the occasional hits. It is the systematic recording (or even the possibility of so doing) rather than an attitude of mind' that allows for the kind of self-improvement only possible through critical thought. 'Writing renders contradiction and proof explicit—the ideas themselves are certainly present in oral societies—it not only makes possible a particular type of formalised proof (e.g. *modus tollens*), it also accumulates and records these proofs for future generations and for further operations' (Goody, 1983, pp. 91, 96).

CONCLUSION: THE ECOLOGY OF SYMBOLISING

The tendency to separate symbols from their symbolisers, to hypothesise a mental realm that guides our action in the physical environment is an ancient and pervasive fallacy in western thought. However, once one gets stuck in this realm of the ideal, no one has ever figured how to get back out to the real world (Fodor, 1980). The problem of meaning and cognition cannot be solved by considering human behaviour physically, as responses to stimuli. But it is equally true that the hypothesis of an ideal realm of meaningful symbols does not further our understanding of cognition considered as knowledge of the environment. The correct question to be asked is how people come to know the meaningful environment, not how they respond to stimuli, nor how they become aware of inner ideas. No one has stated this better than Gibson (SCAPS, p. 26):

> In the study of anthropology and ecology, the 'natural' environment is often distinguished from the 'cultural' environment. As described here, there is no sharp division between them. Culture evolved out of natural opportunities. The cultural environment, however, is often divided into two parts, 'material' culture and 'non-material' culture. This is a seriously misleading distinction, for it seems to imply that language, tradition, art, music, law, and religion are immaterial, insubstantial, or intangible, whereas tools, shelters, clothing, vehicles, and books are not. Symbols are taken to be profoundly different from things. But let us be clear about this. There have to be modes of stimulation, or ways of conveying information, for any individual to perceive anything, however abstract. He must be sensitive to [stimulus information] no matter how universal or fine-spun the thing he apprehends. No symbol exists except as it is realised in sound,' projected light, mechanical contact, or the like. All knowledge rests on sensitivity.

The process of direct perception has been differentiated and refined in a vast number of ways by human societies and civilisations. A tentative list of some of these peculiarly human modes of indirect cognition is given in Table 10.2. Note that each mode of indirect awareness has its roots in ecological information. Note also that each mode is *standardised* and embodied in culturally developed *representation systems*. These cultural-historical entities are preserved, modified and used in communication and teaching. They are the fundamental tools of cognition. It is about time that cognitive science broke out from the stale metaphors of computerese into the rich field of human history and comparative culture, so that we can begin to investigate these marvellous and diverse ways of apprehending reality, and of sharing our knowledge with others. True,

Table 10.2: Human Modes of Indirect Cognition

Ecological Information		*Cultural Institutions*
For objects and events	Picture-making	Drawing systems
For orientation	Body-scaled measure	Standardised measuring
For paths through the environment	Maps	Cartography
For speech	Pre-alphabetic scripts	Alphabetic writing
For affordances for oneself and others	Exchange of goods	Systems of exchange and storage of values (money)
For events	Time measurement	Clocks and calendars

Notes

Each representation system is a cultural institution that has evolved from a basis in direct perception, through a process of mediated perception. On the left is listed the information basis of the systems in direct perception. In the middle is the kind of non-systematic, individualistic mediated perception that evolved from the direct form. On the right are the culturally specific institutions that evolved from the direct and indirect modes of awareness to their left.

Sources of material for the study of representation systems are as follows: Pictures (Hagen, 1986), measurement (Kuala, 1985); mapping (Crone, 1966); the alphabet (Diringer, 1962; Gelb, 1963, Schmandt-Besserat, 1980); exchange and money (Marx, 1973; Polanyi, 1957); time (Landes, 1983; Zerubavel, 1985).

One further system, the number system, is not illustrated. This is because it apparently evolved from a consolidation of several modes of indirect perception, or even from *all* other modes (see Menninger, 1969). For what is known about the evolution of language (also not listed here) see Lieberman (1984).

cognition can and does proceed without materially produced writing, pictures, etc., but without these it is seriously curtailed, and education becomes exceedingly awkward and ritualised, instead of facile and available to individuals on their own. These aids to cognition, these tools of the intellect, have now become cultural institutions, in which all participate. The study of these institutions is the province of sociology, anthropology and history. But to understand the basic function of these modes of cognition is the job of psychologists. What enables these systems to be used for sharing awarenesses? How is the information coded, the tacit knowledge made explicit? What about historical and cultural variation and the cultural specificity of representation systems? These are important questions that cognitive psychology can ignore only at the peril of becoming irrelevant to human concerns.

REFERENCES

Arnheim, R., *Visual Thinking* (Berkeley: University of California Press, 1969).

Bassett, M.F. and Warne, C.J., 'On lapse of verbal meaning with repetition', *American Journal of Psychology*, 1919, *30*, 415–18.

Brown, R., *A first language: The early stage* (Cambridge, MA: Harvard University Press, 1973).

Chomsky, N., Review of B.F. Skinner's *Verbal Behaviour, Language*, 1959, *35*, 26–58.

Chomsky, N., *Rules and Representations* (New York: Columbia University Press, 1980).

Crone, G.R., *Maps and their Makers: An introduction to the history of cartography* (London: Hutchinson, 1966, 3rd edn).

Daanje, A., 'On the locomotory movements in birds and the intention movements derived from them', *Behaviour*, 1950, *3*, 48–98.

Darwin, C., *The Expressions of the Emotions in Man and Animals* (London: John Murray, 1872).

De Villiers, J. and De Villiers, P.A., *Language Acquisition* (Cambridge, MA: Harvard Univeristy Press, 1978).

Diringer, D., *Writing* (London: Thames & Hudson, 1962).

Don, V.J. and Weld, H.P., 'Lapse of meaning with visual fixation' *American Journal of Psychology*, 1924, *35*, 446–50.

Fodor, J.A., *The Language of Thought* (New York: Crowell, 1975).

Fodor, J.A., 'Methodological solipsism considered as a research strategy in cognitive psychology', *The Behavioral and Brain Sciences*, 1980, *3*, 63–109.

Fodor, J.A., Precis of *The Modularity of Mind, The Behavioral and Brain Sciences*, 1985, *8*, 1–5.

Gallistel, C.R., *The Organization of Action* (Hillsdale, NJ: Erlbaum, 1980).

Gelb, I.J., *The Study of Writing* (Chicago: University of Chicago Press, 1963).

Gibson, E.J., 'Improvement in perceptual judgements as a function of controlled practice or training', *Psychological Bulletin*, 1953, *50*, 401–31.

Gibson, E.J., *Principles of Perceptual Learning and Development* (New York: Appleton–Century–Crofts, 1969).

Gibson, E.J., 'The concept of affordances in development: The renascence of functionalism', in W.A. Collins (ed.), *The Concept of Development* (Hillsdale, NJ: Lawrence Erlbaum, 1982).

Gibson, E.J., 'Perceptual development from the ecological approach', in M. Lamb, A. Brown and B. Rogoff (eds.), *Advances in Developmental Psychology*, Vol. 3 (Hillsdale, NJ: Erlbaum, 1984).

Gibson, E.J., Owsley, C.J. and Johnston, J., 'Perception of invariants by 5-month-old infants: Differentiation of two types of motion', *Developmental Psychology*, 1978, *14*, 407–15.

Gibson, J.J., 'Adaptation, after-effect and contrast in the perception of curved lines', *Journal of Experimental Psychology*, 1933, *16*, 1–31.

Gibson, J.J., 'Adaptation with negative after-effect', *Psychological Review*, 1937, *44*, 222–44.

Gibson, J.J., 'The Aryan myth', *Journal of Educational Sociology*, 1939, *13*, 164–71.

Gibson, J.J., *The Perception of the Visual World* (Boston: Houghton-Mifflin, 1950).

Gibson, J.J., 'The registering of objective facts: An interpretation of Woodworth's theory of perceiving', in G. Seward and J. Seward (eds.), *Current Psychological Issues: Essays in honour of Robert S. Woodworth* (New York: Holt, Rhinehart and Winston, 1958).

Gibson, J.J., *The Senses Considered as Perceptual Systems* (Boston: Houghton-Mifflin, 1966).

Gibson, J.J., *The Ecological Approach to Visual Perception* (Boston: Mifflin, 1979).

Gibson, J.J., 'Foreword. A prefatory essay on the perception of surfaces versus the perception of markings on a surface', in M.A. Hagen (ed.), *The Perception of Pictures*, Vol. 1 (New York: Academic Press, 1980).

Gibson, J.J., *Reasons for Realism: Selected essays of James J. Gibson*, E. Reed and R. Jones (eds.) (Hillsdale, NJ: Lawrence Erlbaum, 1982).

Gibson, J.J. and Pick, A.D., 'Perception of another person's looking behavior', *American Journal of Psychology*, 1963, *76*, 386–94.

Gibson, J.J., Smith, O.W., Steinshneider, A. and Johnson, C.W., 'The relative accuracy of visual perception of motion during fixation and pursuit', *American Journal of Psychology*, 1957, *70*, 64–8.

Goody, J., *The Domestication of the Savage Mind* (Cambridge: Cambridge University Press, 1977).

Goody, J., 'Literacy and achievement in the ancient world', in F. Coulmas and K. Ehrlich (eds.), *Writing in Focus* (New York: Mouton, 1983).

Hagen, M.A., *Varieties of Realism: Geometries of representational art* (Cambridge: Cambridge University Press, 1986).

Heil, J., 'The gap in the ecological approach', *Journal for the Theory of Social Behaviour*, 1979, *9*, 265–96.

Holt, E.B., *The Freudian Wish and its Place in Ethics* (New York: Holt, 1915).

Ingold, T., 'The architect and the bee: Reflections on the work of animals and men', *Man* (N.S.), 1983, *18*, 1–20.

Johnson-Laird, P.N., *Mental Models* (Cambridge: Cambridge University Press, 1983).

Kula, W., *Measures and Men* (Princeton: Princeton University Press, 1985).

Landes, D.S., *Revolution in Time: Clocks and the making of the modern world* (Harvard University Press, 1983; paperback edition, 1985).

Lieberman, P., *The Biology and Evolution of Language* (Cambridge, MA: Harvard University Press, 1984).

Lord, A.B., *The Singers of Tales* (Cambridge, MA: Harvard University Press, 1960).

Luria, A.R., *Working Brain* (New York: Basic Books, 1973).

Luria, A.R., 'The development of writing', in M. Cole (ed.), *The Selected Writings of A.R. Luria* (New York: M.E. Sharpe, 1978; first published 1929).

Marr, D., *Vision: A computational investigation into the human representation and processing of visual information* (San Fransisco: W.H. Freeman, 1982).

Marx, K., *Grundrisse* (Harmondsworth, Middlesex: Penguin Books, 1973).

Mayr, E., *Population, Species and Evolution* (Cambridge, MA: Harvard University Press, 1972).

Menninger, K., *Number Words and Number Symbols: A cultural history of numbers* (Cambridge, MA: MIT, 1969).

Michaels, C.F. and Carello, C., *Direct Perception* (Englewood Cliffs, NJ: Prentice-Hall, 1981).

Miller, G.A., Galanter, E. and Pribram, K., *Plans and the Structure of Behavior* (New York: Holt, Rinehart and Winston, 1960).

Niesser, U., *Cognitive Psychology* (New York: Appleton–Century–Crofts, 1967).

Neisser, U., *Cognition and Reality* (San Francisco: W.H. Freeman, 1976).

Pinker, S. (ed.), *Visual Cognition* (Cambridge: MA: MIT, 1985).

Polanyi, K., *The Great Transformation* (Boston: Beacon Press, 1967).

Pylyshyn, Z.W., *Computation and Cognition* (Cambridge, MA: MIT, 1984).

Reed, E.S, 'An ecological approach to the evolution of behavior', in T.D. Johnston and A.T. Pietrewitcz (eds.), *Issues in the Ecological Study of Learning* (Hillsdale, NJ: Lawrence Erlbaum, 1985).

Reed, E.S., 'James J. Gibson's revolution in perceptual psychology: A case study of the transformation of scientific ideas', *Studies in the History and Philosophy of Science, 17*, 65–98.

Reed, E.S. and Jones, R.K., 'Is perception blind? A reply to Heil', *Journal for the Theory of Social Behaviour*, 1981, *11*, 87–91.

Requin, J., Semjen, A. and Bonnet, M., 'Bernstein's purposeful brain', in H.T.A. Whiting (ed.), *Human Motor Actions: Bernstein reassessed* (North-Holland: Elsevier, 1984).

Schlesigner, I.M., 'Relational concepts underlying language', in R.L. Schiefelbusche and L.L. Lloyd (eds.), *Language Perspectives: Acquisition, retardation and intervention* (Baltimore: University Park Press, 1974).

Schmandt-Besserat, D., 'The envelopes that bear the first writing', *Technology and Culture*, 1980, *21*, 357–85.

Severance, E. and Washburn, M.F., 'The loss of associative power in words after long fixation', *American Journal of Psychology*, 1907, *18*, 182–6.

Skinner, B.F., *Verbal Behavior* (New York: Appleton–Century–Crofts, 1957).

Turvey, M.T., Shaw, R.E., Reed, E.S. and Mace, W.M., 'Ecological laws of perceiving and acting: A reply to Fodor and Pylyshyn', *Cognition*, 1981, *9*, 237–304.

Ullman, S., 'Against direct perception', *The Behavioral and Brain Sciences,* 1980, *3*, 373–415.

Vygotsky, L.S., *Mind in Society: The development of the higher psychological processes,* ed. M. Cole, V. John-Steiner, S.Scribner and E. Souberman (Cambridge, MA: Harvard University Press, 1978).

Woodworth, R.S., 'Reinforcement of perception', *American Journal of Psychology*, 1947, *60*, 119–24.

Zerubavel, E., *Hidden Rhythms: Schedules and calendars in social life* (Berkeley, CA: University of California Press, 1985).

NOTE

1. All material in the archives is Accession #14/23/1832 of the Department of Manuscripts and Archives, Cornell University Libraries and is cited with their kind permission.

ACKNOWLEDGEMENTS

Some of the material in this chapter was presented in talks to the International Society for Ecological Psychology in October 1983 at Trinity College, Hartford (US) and December 1984 at University College London. Parts of this chapter will appear, in substantially altered form, in a forthcoming book, *Revolution in Perception: James Gibson's Ecological Psychology*. The research and writing of this chapter was supported by grants to the author from the National Science Foundation SES-8204853 and the National Endowment for the Humanities FA-24240-84. I thank Geri Solomon, Thomas Hickerson, Julia Crepeau and all the staff at the Manuscript Department of Olin Library, Cornell University for their kind assistance with my research in the James J. Gibson Archives housed there. I thank Eleanor Gibson for her kind permission to let me see James Gibson's personal papers and books, as well as her many hours of patient help. Discussions with Carol Fowler, Rebecca Jones, Bill Mace, and the editors of the present volume helped to sharpen the argument. All remaining mistakes and opinions, however, are my own.

Section IIB:

The Radical Tradition

Gibson's revolutionary new approach, discussed in the previous section, nevertheless has its precursors and parallels. It was preceded, and is accompanied, by many other attempts to find an alternative to the dualism inherited as part of scientific thought since Descartes, and currently established within cognitive science. This radical tradition of anti-dualism is no narrow thread, but a complex network of thinking which includes Hegel (Chapter 13 by Marková), and modern phenomenology (Chapter 14 by Bolton), as well as the functionalism/pragmatism of James, Dewey and Mead.

Whilst behaviourism emerged from the American tradition of anti-dualism, this movement lapsed easily into the mechanistic form which reverts naturally to cognitivism. However, within behaviourism, there was always the potential for genuine alternatives (Chapters 11 and 12). Much depends on what is meant by 'behaviour'. If behaviour is viewed as the product of a stimulus-response automaton, then any behaviourism will eventually need to be supplemented by internal 'mental' mechanisms in order to do justice to observed complexities; thus dualism will be restored. But if behaviour is taken to be meaningful or intentional from the beginning, then the way is open to a comprehensive theory which avoids the mistakes of dualism.

11

Tolman's Perception

Arthur Still

INTRODUCTION

> For 50 years theory in hard-core areas of Anglo-American psychology
> remained frozen into behaviourist and neo-behaviourist paradigms. In the
> thaw of the last 10 to 15 years the explanation of the existence and
> properties of consciousness has reemerged as an acceptable and important
> problem for cognitive theory. (Shallice, 1978, p. 117)

Thus the imagery of Nordic mythology serves the rhetoric of
modern cognitivism, and we may add that those versions of the
myth requiring a guardian of the treasure during the barren
years usually nominate Edward Chace Tolman. Admittedly
Tolman was a self-styled behaviourist and a dedicated rat-
runner who once wrote:

> I believe that everything important in psychology (except perhaps such
> matters as the building up of a superego, that is everything save such
> matters as involve society and words) can be investigated in essence
> through the continued experimental and theoretical analysis of the
> determiners of rat behavior at a choice point in a maze. (Tolman, 1938;
> quoted from Tolman, 1951, p. 172)

Nevertheless Tolman's learning theory is labelled cognitive, as
opposed to the S-R systems of Thorndike, Hull, Guthrie and
Skinner (Hilgard, 1956), and it was under the protection of this
theory that the torch of mind was kept burning—or so the story
goes. Such narratives play a legitimate part in the development
of science, whose protagonists are seen to enact a drama
culminating in the triumph of the present orthodoxy. But
history is never quite so stark. The heroes and heroines, and the

villains, are very much of their time, while their ideas are complex and changing, and expressed in words that are open to interpretation. So counter-myths can be constructed, designed to overthrow the status quo and to establish an alternative. This is the purpose of the present chapter.

Tolman obtained his PhD from Harvard in 1915, having been educated into the revolt against dualism (Lovejoy, 1929) by Holt and Perry, both ex-students of William James. In the new theory, mind was a naturally functioning process, evolved like any other, and its origin was therefore to be discovered in animals. Since animals cannot speak, this origin can only be traced by comparative psychologists if it is immanent in behaviour, and behaviourism spelt out this consequence and put it into practice in a variety of ways. Tolman was in the vanguard of this movement, and amongst the first to struggle with its problems. The foremost of these was how to give mind its place in nature, without reverting to dualism by treating behaviour merely as a source of inference to underlying mental activities. A few behaviourists, most notably J.B. Watson, were prepared to give up mind and the mental altogether, but Tolman, following Perry, was convinced that his rats showed purposefulness, and that a language of mechanical reflexes, or what he was to call a molecular behaviourism, could not do justice to what he saw when he watched them. He therefore developed a more appropriate language, that of molar behaviourism, which assumes from the beginning that behaviour is intentional, or directed meaningfully towards the environment.

Watching rats, even in laboratory mazes, one may indeed be convinced that the molar language is the proper one to use, but what is it about what is seen that leads to this conviction? Faced with this question, and encouraged or goaded by strict anti-mentalists such as Kuo (Kuo, 1928; Tolman, 1928), Tolman tried to spell out those features of behaviour that characterise purpose and goal-directedness. To satisfy his critics, it was necessary to ground such molar concepts in mechanical terms, using a language of mere movement, with no mentalistic overtones. But movements, and therefore apparently purpose, can potentially be simulated by real or imagined mechanical devices. Accordingly Hull (1930; 1931) showed how defining features of behaviour, of the kind picked out by Tolman, could be generated by stimulus-response mechanisms. Such demonstrations seemed to prove that there was no need to appeal to purpose, except as a convenient but unscientific label for certain classes of behaviour. In reply Tolman devised ingenious experiments to show that stimulus-response mechanisms are not sufficient, and instead invented, amongst other original concepts, the term 'cognitive map' (Tolman, 1948). But Hull and his followers displayed equal ingenuity by inventing more complex stimulus-response structures to meet the new empirical demands. The resolution of this debate remains unclear. Did cybernetic machines and computers arrive and vindicate Tolman by showing that 'purposes' are just as mechanistic and unmysterious as reflexes, and hence scientifically respectable? Or did they vindicate Hull by showing that a mechanistic account was possible, albeit in a more versatile language than that of traditional stimulus-response theory? How we answer such questions probably depends less on 'facts' than on the myth to which we happen to be attached. So first, it is necessary to spell out our own version of the narrative.

The present myth, or counter-myth, takes Tolman's central problem to be that of articulating what he saw when he watched rats in mazes. There were two traditions upon which he might have drawn, that of reflex automata, and that of a conscious controlling mind, twin poles of the Cartesian psychological universe. But there existed another, less focused tradition, which had struggled to find a way between these extremes by postulating a level of living activity and experience which is neither that of an automaton nor of a consciousness. It never succeeded in establishing itself as a distinct discipline in the nineteenth century, unlike mental philosophy on the one hand, reflexology on the other, and as Vitalism it fell into disrepute in the twentieth. But Danziger (1983) has shown how powerful an influence it was on the development of physiological psychology (cf. also Cassirer, 1950), and William James, while aware of the problems, became clear as his work developed that this is where the proper ontology for psychology would be found. So he developed a language of pure experience (James, 1912), belonging neither to a physical nor a mental world, but forming the basis for our construction of both. Tibbetts (1975) has traced the influence of this doctrine of pure experience on Tolman, and it is plausible to understand Tolman's perception of his rats in terms of this alternative to the traditional dualisms. He was not unique in this endeavour. Behaviourism popularised the break from mentalism, but for the majority of psychologists of this school, this did not signal a reversion to the other pole of dualism—reflex automatism. A warning against such a retrograde step had come years before from John Dewey, who had written, in his classic articulation of the alternative to mentalism and automatism,

> ... the older dualism of body and soul finds a distinct echo in the current dualism of stimulus and response. Instead of interpreting the character of sensation, idea and action from their place and function in the sensori-motor circuit, we still incline to interpret the latter from our preconceived and preformulated ideas of rigid distinctions between sensations, thoughts and acts. ... As a consequence, the reflex arc is not a comprehensive or organic unity, but a patchwork of disjointed parts, a mechanical conjunction of unallied processes. (Dewey, 1896, 357–8)

TOLMAN'S ATTEMPTS TO DEVELOP EXPLICIT CRITERIA FOR ASCRIBING MENTAL PREDICATES

In his effort to do justice to his perception of rats' behaviour, especially of its manifest purposiveness, Tolman set out to develop a behaviourism that would match, in its subtlety and allowance for complexities, the mentalism of William McDougall. He wrote:

> Purpose, adequately conceived, ... is itself but an objective aspect of behavior. When an animal is learning a maze, or escaping from a puzzle box, or merely going about his daily business of eating, nest building, sleeping, and the like, it will be noted that in all such performances a certain *persistence until* character is to be found. Now it is just this *persistence until* character which we will define as purpose. (Tolman, 1925; quoted from Tolman, 1951, p. 33)

He continued by quoting, with approval, the more detailed account of purposive behaviour given by McDougall, and commented,

> But the fundamental difference between him and us arises in that he, being a 'mentalist', merely *infers* purpose from these aspects of behavior; whereas we, being behaviorists, *identify* purpose with such aspects. When one observes an animal performing, one knows nothing concerning possible 'contents' in the latter's mind and to assume such contents seems to us to add nothing to one's description. One does, however, see certain aspects of the behavior itself which are important and for which the term 'purpose' seems a good name. (ibid.)

Thus Tolman tried to distance himself from McDougall's mentalism, but not far enough to please the stricter behaviourist, Kuo (1928). Kuo's objection, as explained by Tolman (1928), was that

> . . . purpose is something which we objective teleologists have to infer from behaviour and not something we can directly observe in it. And, when we have inferred it, it seems to him that we describe it in the same terms as a mentalist uses although we deny that we use introspection. (Tolman, 1928, p. 524).

To this he replied that

> the mere fact that the variable which we have called drive, tendency, purpose, has to be inferred from its effects and cannot be directly sensed need not mitigate against it. For most . . . of the concepts . . . which figure in the equations of the natural sciences are so inferred . . . Space, time, number, velocity, heat, force, energy, electricity as used in physics are never immediately given in perception.
>   Further . . . our concept of purpose, . . . is not, even though inferred, therefore mentalistic . . . We do not describe or define these purposes in terms of their introspected feels.
>   . . . The essential character and definition of a behavior-purpose or drive for us purposivists is the fact of the *contingency* of an act upon its tendency to reach (or get from) a specific type of *end-object*. Where such a contingency exists the act in question is the fact of the learnability . . . of the act with respect to its end. Whenever upon successive occasions, a given act will repeat itself, only if the getting to (or getting from) such and such a type of end-object is achieved by it, this act can be said to be contingent upon such an end. And it can be said to 'purpose' that end.
>   A purpose is a condition in the organism . . . (ibid., pp. 524–5)

In these statements by Tolman, written during the period which culminated in his major work, *Purposive Behavior in Animals and Men* (1932), there is at least one glaring contradiction; in his comments on McDougall he was very clear that purposes are not inferred, while in responding later to Kuo he agreed that they *are* inferred, nevertheless arguing that this is scientifically respectable, and not a reversion to mentalism. In the earlier paper purpose was said to be perceived directly, an idea which forms part of a tradition which was later to include Heider (1939) and Gibson (1979). But later, as an inferred 'condition in the organism' to which introspection has no privileged access, and which is therefore not 'mentalistic', a purpose became the kind of real entity searched for by modern cognitivists (e.g. Johnson-Laird, 1983; cf. Smith, 1982; Amundson, 1983, whose arguments for Tolman as cognitivist are discussed later in this chapter). What Tolman really meant is, as predicted earlier, open to interpretation, but here my claim or conjecture is that his central insight was that purpose is perceived directly. This makes sense historically and in Tolman's own development. For, given his audience, there was an inevitability in the progression of his thought, and one that parallels a recurring theme in the dialectic of psychological thinking. The movement of this dialectic is from tentative and speculative attempts to do justice to *observations*, towards a shaping of observations to fit the demands of mechanistic theorising. In Tolman's case, his insights owed much to a blend of empiricism and phenomenology in the tradition of James, Holt and Perry, but to stay afloat in the mainstream he was eventually obliged to express them in a language akin to that of the more mechanistic psychology that became dominant during the 1930s. Expressed in this way, they conformed to the new mood, became less distinct, and eventually changed. Thus Tolman started with a theory of direct perception of purposes, as an alternative to mentalism and reflex automatism. But when challenged to justify this scientifically he fell back upon an ontology of cues or measurable aspects of behaviour, and then had no option but to conclude that that is all there is, or that these are the basis for inference to unobservable entities.

Why was Tolman unable to stand his middle ground between mentalism and reflex mechanism, and meet the challenge to his theory of direct perception of purposes? He was far from being a weakling, to be swayed this way and that by fashion and the opinions of others; on the contrary, he was following the logic of his own strongly-held beliefs. For Tolman, like nearly everybody else, accepted the scientific observer as (a) detached from the subject matter, and therefore (b) relying upon signs or cues to construct models of reality. The problem with this well-tried and sometimes excellent conception, which is expressed in the language and the best practices of all laboratory psychologists, is that it is part and parcel of the dualist conceptual framework that Tolman was trying to replace. For this framework takes the traditional scientific observer, detached from his or her subject matter, and relying upon cues and inference, as paradigmatic of all perception. Thus, in learning to be 'scientific', trainee experimentalists take on board, through practices and methodologies as well as abstract ideas, a firm grounding in dualism as a potential source of theoretical insight. Naturally then, struggling under pressure to find expression for his insights, Tolman was inclined to fall back upon the language of his apprenticeship, and stifle them. Fortunately for those of us looking to the past for alternatives to cognitivism, they remained alive for long enough to reappear in the theory he developed as an account of his animals' perception. There he found a new voice and invented a language that was a genuine and for a time successful attempt to break away from dualism. But he failed to apply this theory to his own perceptions as scientist, and later neglected it in favour of an attempt to shore up the perceptual dualism of a traditional scientific observer. Thus he eventually reverted to the very mentalism that in his early behaviourism he was trying to avoid. But not before showing us the possibility of a real advance in our understanding of animal behaviour.

TOLMAN'S THEORY OF ANIMAL PERCEPTION

Like many other psychologists in the 1920s (e.g. Thurstone, 1924; Kantor, see Chapter 12 of this book) Tolman rejected a simple S-R account of behaviour, where S is described in terms of physical energies impinging upon the organism, and substituted an account where the environment, as determinant of behaviour, is not absolute but is itself structured by the activities of the organism:

> The intent or noetic aspect of an object adjustment we will define as the object structure (i.e. that behavior possibility) which the animal's behavior can be observed quite definitely to *impute* (whether correctly or incorrectly) to such and such a particular part of the maze. . . . Given . . . that the animal is dominated by the food-seeking impulse, his various behaviors in the successive parts of the maze can be said, at any stage of learning, quite objectively to express his thereunto acquired object adjustments (cognitions) with respect to the "getting-on-toward-food" possibilities of such maze parts. It must be emphasised that these object adjustments to the maze structure have meaning only with reference to the task of *getting to the food and getting there as quickly, both spatially and temporally, as possible.* What the animal's behaviour exhibits in the way of object adjustments to (cognitions of) the maze structure are not, of course, comparable to what the physicist would tell us about the maze, but are merely (cognitions of) adjustments to the maze from the one point of view of getting to the food box. (Tolman, 1925; quoted from Tolman, 1951, p. 44)

Thus the animal's behaviour *imputes* an object structure, appropriate to its goals, to the maze. When the behaviour is successful it is presumably supported by such structures, which are not therefore constructed by the animal, but which exist as 'possibilities' for an appropriately equipped and motivated animal. As such they are not 'comparable to what the physicist would tell us about the maze'. Later Tolman attempted to describe these structures more precisely in terms of discriminanda and discriminanda expectations, manipulanda and manipulanda expectations. This work is contained in his book, *Purposive Behavior in Animals and Men* (Tolman, 1932), and received its final and perhaps definitive statement in Tolman (1933), where his struggles to reach a scientific audience and the beginnings of a move towards dualism and cognitivism are apparent. In this transitional paper, he began as usual by trying to define his terms:

> discriminanda and discriminanda expectations are my names for and understanding of, sense qualities and sensations *when these are defined objectively and in the same way for both men and the lower animals.* . . . I prefer the concept of discriminanda expectations to that of sensations . . . because the former includes openly and avowedly the implication of

'objective reference'—an implication explicitly denied to 'sensations' . . . the discriminanda expectations have as part of their very warp and woof this point-outwardness. When a rat or a human being has the discriminanda expectation of 'dark' he then and there 'expects' that this expectation is going to continue to be confirmed and supported by an actually present environmental situation—that, to wit, he can continue to 'enjoy' and have commerce with such a darkness. Such a darkness is not reacted to by him as to a mere fantasy of his own creation. It is responded to as an in-some-way-objectively-caused darkness . . . (Tolman, 1933; quoted from Tolman, 1951, p. 82)

By his choice of terms Tolman showed that his starting point was the novel and fashionable discrimination experiment, in which discriminanda correspond to stimuli, and can be defined in terms from physics. But discrimanda expectations are not subjectively constructed in any simple way out of these discriminanda, and we surmise that for Tolman they correspond to the 'object structures' ('the intent or noetic aspect of an object adjustment') of the earlier quotation. Clearly Tolman was on the verge of a middle way here, by developing an ontology of object structures that are neither in the mind nor in the world described by physics. He went further in this direction with his concepts of manipulanda and manipulanda expectations:

By manipulanda I would understand those properties of objects which actually support (i.e. make possible) *motor manipulations* . . . just as its sense organs will determine what discriminanda a species is capable of, the motor organs of a species will determine what manipulanda it will be capable of. One and the same environmental object will afford quite different manipulanda to an animal which possesses only a mouth, or only a bill, or only claws. Grasp-ableness, pick-up-ableness, throw-ableness, heaviness (i.e., 'heave-ableness') and the like—these are manipulanda. And it is obvious that they will be present in different measure and in different fashion for species which possess different equipments in the way of prehensile and locomotor organs . . . the same environment will present quite different ranges and orders of solidity,—i.e. stand-on-ableness, rest-in-ableness, and the like—to a species with the muscles and the general form of a gorilla from what it will to puny man or to a mere finned fish. (pp. 82–3)

But just as one must distinguish between discriminanda and discriminanda expectations,

... so one must distinguish between the manipulation possibilities, i.e., the manipulanda, actually presented by such an environmental set-up and the momentary manipulanda expectations (which may be more or less veridical) arising in the organism as a result of that set up. Manipulanda expectations, like discriminanda expectations, are sets or preparations aroused in the organism, which may or may not be confirmed and supported by the actual entities truly present then and there in the environment. (ibid., p. 83)

Tolman identified manipulanda with the 'configurating properties' of Gestalt psychology, and compared them with the traditional 'primary qualities' of solidity, extension, figure, motion, number and situation.

But are not these, I would ask, almost identical with the grasp-ableness, the run-after-ableness, the heave-ableness, the run-after-ableness, the sit-on-ableness, etc., which have just been defined as manipulanda? (ibid., p. 85)

And the environment as so envisaged is

... a means-end field in which the various component objects and situations appear ineluctably in their roles of possible, or impossible, good, or bad, better or worse, means to, or from, such and such other objects or situations. (ibid., p. 86)

Thus spelt out, the 'object structures' became 'means–end fields', which again are not to be identified with the structures of physics, and yet make up the animal's environment and are not merely mental constructs. As 'manipulanda' they are linked indissolubly with possibilities for action, and in this middle way Tolman was close to the mutualism of Dewey as expressed in the paper quoted from above (Dewey, 1896). And yet a potential gap between organism and environment remained, which Tolman never succeeded in bridging without recourse to cognitive mechanisms, whereby he effectively jettisoned the hard-won mutualism. The other possibility (and it should be very apparent to the hindsightful reader of Tolman's work) would have been to anticipate Gibson by declaring that the manipulanda and what they 'afford' are the important structures for a theory of perception, and that they are perceived directly. But to do this, information in the ambient array must *specify* these structures, and it was left to

J.J. Gibson to work out the implications of this conjecture (see Section IIA, on Gibson's ecological approach to psychology). Tolman, meanwhile, edged towards cognitivism, by his failure to consolidate the following assertion of his anti-dualist credentials.

> The so-called primary qualities and the so-called secondary qualities are, of course, in the first instance, both mere discriminanda—i.e. mere stimulus qualities to be differentiated so and so. They are nevertheless different from one another in that the primary qualities do, I believe, tend to exhibit a more consistent and persistent set of correlations with manipulanda than do the secondary qualities. . . . The difference between the primary and the secondary qualities is thus, in the last analysis, due merely to the fact that it was easier for God, or the devil, to smear on and off colors, odors, tastes, temperatures without upsetting the underlying manipulanda than it was to smear on and off different visual and tactual and kinesthetic shapes and sizes and resistances. (ibid., p. 85)

A similar argument had appeared in his book (Tolman, 1932, p. 85), and it is clear that Tolman thus dispensed with one of the marks of Cartesian (or Lockean) dualism, the distinction between primary qualities, which exist independently, and secondary qualities which are added by the observer (Burtt, 1932). For Tolman both qualities had the same ontological status, and the distinction only arises because the 'primary' qualities are more intimately related, via the concept of manipulanda, to an animal's locomotory activities. But given that they don't differ, what *is* their ontological status? Are they both independent of observers, are they constructs dependent upon observers as Berkeley had argued, or is there an alternative consonant with the mutualism of Dewey and other pragmatists? This is where Tolman hesitated. He gave no clear answer and in the later paper he added a revealing footnote:

> . . . the words, 'shape', 'size', and 'resistance' seem to be used under ordinary circumstances to apply indiscriminately to what I am here specifically keeping separate, viz: to 'size' and 'shape' and 'resistance' as true manipulanda, i.e., as defined in the last analysis in terms of 'stand-on-ableness', 'heave-ableness', and the like; and to size and shape and resistance as but the mere *visual* and *tactual* and *kinesthetic* discriminanda correlates of such manipulanda. (Tolman, 1933; quoted in Tolman, 1951, p. 85)

Thus whatever its ontological status, the world referred to by these words is structured in two distinct ways—one, that of physics which is the same across species (discriminanda correlates defined 'in the same way for both men and the lower animals'), another (the ecological world of manipulanda), that is relative to the sensori-motor capacities of particular organisms. Which has explanatory primacy for psychological science? If the former then the perceived structure in the environment must arise from the constructive activities of physiological or mental mechanisms, and we have cognitivism. If the latter then there must be a perceptual specificity to correspond to the manipulatory specificity that makes manipulanda possible. For if the ecological structures are given explanatory primacy this can only mean (a) that they are not first unpacked into component elements and relationships between elements, and then reconstructed by the brain or mind; hence (b) that there is a direct relationship between these structures and experiences or behaviour, and that the laws of psychology will have to do with the delineation of this relationship. Failing to develop such laws, Tolman equivocated between the alternatives. Then as now, the academic pace allows little time for reflection, and, forced to push ahead, Tolman steered towards the framework that became acceptable as cognitive science.

Tolman did not actually repudiate his earlier work, but his attention moved away from mutualist concepts such as manipulanda, towards cognitive terms which it is now hard to interpret as other than cognitivist, dualist, representations and 'in the head'. Thus in 1935 he defined a *hypothesis* as,

> . . . nothing more nor less than a condition in the organism which, while it lasts, produces . . . a systematic selectivity in behavior. Further, it appears that such a hypothesis or selectivity is equivalent to an intention or assertion of a specific relation as obtaining in the environment. In the above case these assertions are to the effect that it is such and such types of door which lead on and such and such other types which are closed. The rats assert—hypothesize—that it is the right-hand doors or the left-hand doors . . . which, as such, lead on. And when any one such assertion proves incorrect, an animal sooner or later drops it for a new one. (Tolman, 1935; quoted from Tolman, 1951, p. 110)

Here, as in the paper with Brunswik (Tolman and Brunswik, 1935) of the same year, *hypotheses* remain linked to action, and might still have been conjoined with the earlier concepts to give a mutualist account of behaviour. But by 1938, in 'The determiners of behavior at a choice point', *hypotheses* had become firmly established as one amongst several intervening variables, each bounded in Tolman's diagrams by arrows, coming in from the independent variables and going out to the dependent variables. Intervening variables are 'capable of a perfectly objective definition and measurement', and

> . . . each . . . is defined by a standard experiment in which its correlative independent environmental variable is systematically varied. Further, in each such experiment all the other independent variables are held constant while the one in question in systematically changed. (Tolman, 1938; quoted from Tolman, 1951, p. 157)

This promises a rigour to satisfy the most hard-headed operationalist, but with its divisions and isolations, and its logical separation of organisms from environment, it is more an anticipation of the 'functionalism' of modern cognitivism (Johnson-Laird, 1983), than of the mutalist functionalism of James and Dewey, from which Tolman drew his inspiration.

CONCLUSIONS

I have argued that Tolman voiced a tradition in psychological thinking that was ready to break away from dualism. He developed appropriate mutualist concepts to effect this, but was held back by the logic of his scientific practices. By using laboratory rats in mazes he was already abstracting from an ecological niche in dualist fashion, and by detached and relatively remote observation he was entering the dualist role of passive observer. Thus he came to treat his own perceptions as a matter of construction from cues or 'criteria', and this was extended by default to his account of perception in rats, in spite of the non-dualist language he had already developed. The insights embodied in this language, we may conjecture, came not from Tolman the stern traditional scientist, but from the playful human being (and scientist) interacting with another animal. This side of Tolman appears again and again in his writings. It is said of Hull that he felt obliged to steel himself into seeing his rats as S-R automata, rather than as sentient beings; clearly Tolman never felt under that obligation. Not only did Tolman (judging from his writings) treat his rats playfully and kindly, he also wrote playfully, taking delight in neologisms and in unmarked and unappreciated parodies of scientific style.

This is one interpretation of Tolman, and one that has been generally neglected, perhaps because it accords less well than others with the systems that have dominated psychology in the last 40 years. To complete the picture with a contrast, I compare it with the recent interpretations of Smith (1982) and Amundson (1983). They give sophisticated versions of the myth referred to at the beginning of this chapter, of Tolman as guardian of the cognitive treasure during the ice age. Both writers start with Tolman as follower of the neo-realism of Perry and Holt, and both see his work as receiving a posthumous fruition in modern cognitive psychology, but the routes they trace to this point differ.

In Tolman's early claim that purpose is immanent in behaviour, Smith (1982) sees a recapitulation of the neo-realists' assertion of the independence of the immanent. But by 1935, Tolman had, according to Smith, moved from assigning purpose and cognition an ontological status of 'subsistence-in-behaviour' to giving them an instrumental status of 'inter-vening-in-equations'. He was thus able to develop a fully molar psychology, and to 'help preserve and shape the tradition of cognitive psychology during a time when it was nearly eclipsed by the ascendency of classical behaviourism' (Smith, 1982, p. 162). Amundson (1983) sees the neo-realist epistemology of Tolman's teachers and his early writings, not as something he outgrew, but as remaining with him throughout, and colouring his use of an ostensibly operation-alist epistemology. His intervening variables, though disguised in the operational jargon of the time, are actually realist and intentionalist. They thus anticipate developments in cognitive psychology and information processing, which, according to Amundson, have bridged the gap between intentionality and objectivity.

These two commentators agree with each other, and with this chapter, in tracing Tolman's development from early attempts to construe purpose as immanent in behaviour, to purpose as an intervening variable. They seem to differ in the status given to intervening variables; for Smith they are instrumentalist, for Amundson they are realist. However, although instrumentalism is often associated with operationalism, which is incompatible with realism, the link is not necessary. The more general and pragmatic instrumentalism is compatible with realism, and since both Smith and Amundson appeal to modern cognitive psychology as an expression of what Tolman was groping for, it seems reasonable to conclude that the difference between them is superficial. What is clear, however, is that both would disagree with the argument of this chapter, not necessarily in matters of historical detail, nor in seeing the later Tolman as a precursor of modern cognitive psychology, but in the high valuation I put upon Tolman's early attempts (under the influence of New Realism, as both point out) to give a scientifically acceptable account of his perceptions of purpose in rats. For both writers, Tolman progressed from his position, either by shaking off the less desirable aspects of new realism (Smith) or by retaining realism while paying lip service to the more fashionable operationalism (Amundson). For the present writer, however, Tolman's greatest insights were contained in his early writings; later they became blurred as he attempted to shore up his theory against S-R theories within the increasingly rigid and mechanistic ideals of the time. The difference between us reflects, perhaps, a difference in our evaluation of modern cognitive theory, as against a theory such as Gibson's. Smith actually points out that 'The neo-realist view of perception revealed in this passage [by Tolman] finds perhaps its closest contemporary counterpart in the perceptual theory of James J. Gibson' (Smith, 1982, p. 159), but this in no way leads him to revise his negative evaluation of that view.

In a later paper, Amundson (1985) has introduced a useful principle of *epistemological parity*, which is: *Accept only those theory/epistemology pairs in which the epistemology would be appropriate to a psychological being truly described by the theory.* Thus just as Tolman's implicit realist epistemology enables him to talk of purposes and expectations even in the absence of operational definitions, so his subjects have knowledge of their surroundings that is not reducible to responses actually made. Any disparity between epistemology and substantive theory leads to a tension which is presumably reduced by alteration of one or the other until they conform. A similar tension was implicit in the earlier argument of this chapter. The language available to Tolman for articulating his perception of rats in mazes corresponds to an epistemology, while the account of his animals' perception is the substantive theory. The latter is altered or neglected to conform to the former. But there is an additional point. The available language was not adequate to do justice to the insight and the insight became blurred. Languages, however, do not exist in a vacuum. There is another kind of parity, that between the scientific practices (apparatus, methodologies, reporting conventions, etc.) and the epistemology. And it is perhaps this parity requirement that is most significant for the argument of this chapter. For, built into the practices that Tolman inherited and to some extent helped to develop, is the idea of knowledge gained by detached observation and controlled intervention, rather than by active participation. Tolman, we may fancy for the sake of argument, and encouraged by his benevolent turn of phrase, gained his knowledge about his rats, their purposes and their expectations, by playing with them or otherwise interacting with them. But he had no way of reporting this knowledge to the scientific community, except by stories of what rats did in mazes when he, the observer, was out of sight (and mind). And therefore, eventually, in order to accord with the conventions of such stories as they developed during the 1930's, Tolman's theory became more dualist and mechanistic as it moved away from the mutualism advocated by Dewey.

To conclude, I return to a question that was left unanswered earlier in the chapter: Is Tolman or is Hull vindicated by modern cognitive science? The cognitivist answer, given by both Smith and Amundson, is Tolman. But the argument of this chapter implies that cognitivists ought to give the laurel to Hull, who predicted in 1930 that

... a 'psychic' machine, with ample provision in its design for the evolution of pure stimulus acts, could attain a degree of freedom, spontaneity, and power to dominate its environment, inconceivable alike to individuals unfamiliar with the possibilities of automatic mechanisms and to the professional designers of the ordinary rigid-type machines. (Hull, 1930, p. 517)

It was this pressure towards mechanistic explanations, rather than his own original insights, that drew Tolman into his cognitive theorising of the 1930s, expressed in diagrams of 'inputs' organised by intervening variables to converge upon an 'output'. His important insight came earlier, when he provided, with his mutualist account of the activities and world of a rat, a first, tantalising glimpse of the real treasure. But the 'world', being one of laboratory apparatus, was built to constrain both scientific thought and animal behaviour along mechanistic lines, and the treasure slipped from Tolman's grasp as he was carried along by the stream.

REFERENCES

Amundson, R., 'E.C. Tolman and the intervening variable: A study in the epistemological history of psychology', *Philosophy of Science*, 1983, *50*, 268–82.

Amundson, R., 'Psychology and epistemology: The place versus response controversy', *Cognition*, 1985, *20*, 127–53.

Burtt, E.A., *The Metaphysical Foundations of Modern Physical Science* (London: Routledge and Kegan Paul, 1932).

Cassirer, E., *The Problem of Knowledge* (New Haven: Yale University Press, 1950).

Danziger, K., 'Origins of the schema of stimulated motion: Towards a pre-history of modern psychology', *History of Science*, 1983, *21*, 183–210.

Dewey, J., 'The reflex arc concept in psychology', *Psychological Review*, 1896, *3*, 357–70.

Gibson, J.J., *The Ecological Approach to Visual Perception* (Boston: Houghton-Mifflin, 1979).

Heider, F., 'Environmental determinants in psychological theories', *Psychological Review*, 1939, *46*, 383–410.

Hilgard, E.R., *Theories of Learning* (New York: Appleton–Century–Crofts, 1956).

Hull, C.L., 'Knowledge and purpose as habit mechanisms', *Psychological Review*, 1930, *37*, 241–56.

Hull, C.L., 'Goal attraction and directing ideas conceived as habit phenomena', *Psychological Review*, 1931, *38*, 487–506.

James, W., *Essays in Radical Empiricism* (London: Longmans, 1912).

Johnson-Laird, P.N., *Mental Models* (Cambridge: Cambridge University Press, 1983).

Kuo, Z.Y., 'The fundamental error of the concept of purpose and the trial and error fallacy', *Psychological Review*, 1928, *35*, 414–33.

Lovejoy, A.O., *Revolt against Dualism* (La Salle, Ill.: Open Court, 1929).

Shallice, T., 'The dominant action system: An information-processing approach to consciousness', in Pope, K.S. and Singer J.L. (eds.), *The Stream of Consciousness: Scientific Investigations into the Flow of Human Experience* (New York: Plenum, 1978).

Smith, L.D., 'Purpose and cognition: The limits of neorealist influence on Tolman's psychology', *Behaviorism*, 1982, *10*, 35–48.

Thurstone, L.L., *The Nature of Intelligence* (London: Routledge & Kegan Paul, 1924).

Tibbetts, P., 'The doctrine of "pure experience": The evolution of a concept from Mach to James to Tolman', *Journal of the History of the Behavioral Sciences*, 1975, *11*, 55–66.

Tolman, E.C., 'Behaviorism and purpose', *Journal of Philosophy*, 1925, *22*, 36–41.

Tolman, E.C., 'Purpose and cognition: The determiners of animal learning', *Psychological Review*, 1925, *32*, 285–97.

Tolman, E.C., 'Purposive behavior', *Psychological Review*, 1928, *35*, 524–30.

Tolman, E.C., *Purposive Behavior in Animals and Men* (New York: Century, 1932).

Tolman, E.C., 'Sign-Gestalt or conditioned reflex?', *Psychological Review*, 1933, *40*, 391–411.

Tolman, E.C., 'The determiners of behavior at a choice point', *Psychological Review*, 1938, *45*, 1–41.

Tolman, E.C., 'Cognitive maps in rats and men', *Psychological Review*, 1948, *55*, 189–208.

Tolman, E.C., *Behavior and Psychological Man* (Berkeley and Los Angeles: University of California Press, 1951).

Tolman, E.C. and Brunswik, E., 'The organism and the causal texture of the environment', *Psychological Review*, 1935, *42*, 43–77.

12

Cognitive Interbehaviour

Noel W. Smith

HUMANS AS COMPUTER PROCESSORS?

Cognitivism has made strong inroads into current psychology and perhaps has even become a dominant conception. One of its most characteristic features is the invoking of analogies to the most recent advancements in science and technology, such as holograms, neural physiology and computers. This has given it an appearance of objectivity and scientific standing. Computer operations have received the most attention and are usually viewed as providing an insight into neural activity. Neurons are, in turn, assumed to be the locus of mind. Computer models, then, will illuminate the neurology of mind. These models are sometimes viewed as metaphors but more often, literally, as a reflection of the computational status of human cognition.

A long-standing alternative to these assumptions is available in the interbehavioural psychology of J.R. Kantor. (Specific interbehavioural critiques of analogies may be found in Blewitt, 1983; Kantor, 1935; 1936; 1978; Swartz, 1958). This psychology will be delineated in this chapter but a brief background about the man may be appropriate at this point. Kantor studied at the University of Chicago under such luminaries as James Angell, leader of the functionalist school of psychology; George Herbert Mead, sociologist; and John Watson (during summers when Watson returned to Chicago from Johns Hopkins University.) While some of the terminology of these men and traces of their concepts can be found in Kantor's early writings he showed a remarkable degree of independence from both dualistic and mechanistic thinking from the very beginning. His published writings span a period from 1918 to the time of his death in 1984. He saw everything in system rather than in pieces and was always adamant about identifying and rejecting any constructs that were not derived from actual events. This approach led him to emphasise the interbehavioural field (Kantor, 1959; Mountjoy, 1976) as the stage on which all events are played and on which they must be viewed.

IMPLICIT TRADITIONAL POSTULATES

The alternative to cognitivism that is usually cited is behaviourism: There are cognitions *and* behaviours, the former often producing the latter. The latter is not reducible to the former because it is primarily effector action. Therefore studies of behaviour, while legitimate and worthwhile, deal with mechanistic acts and cannot include cognitions. Cognitions are also private and not directly observable as are behaviours. Some cognitivists regard them as unobservable in principle because thoughts, images, beliefs, and other 'private' events do not have shape and other physical features of matter. A few cognitivists (e.g. Boneau, 1974; Bandura, 1978) would combine cognitions and behaviour as complementary.

The foregoing account of some of the commonly stated contrasts between behaviourism and cognitivism imply some of the assumptions that cognitivists make. Sampson (1981), in his critique of cognitivism makes clear an important element in its assumptions:

> The cognitive tradition is usually contrasted with the objectivist tradition of British empiricism, which has also influenced the contemporary forms of psychology but which emphasized the properties of the object more than those of the subject. . . . Cognitive psychology recognizes a disparity between what is 'out there' and its internal representation and argues that behavior is a function of the subjective world as transformed and represented internally. (p. 730)

This is revealing, but the implicit fundamental postulates that run through much if not all of cognitivism need to be explicated. The following are usually involved:

1. Stimuli are inputs that are processed by the brain; this is followed by a response output.
2. The brain directs and regulates behaviour and interprets the world for us.
3. All knowledge comes through the senses to the central nervous system where it is processed and then stored.
4. Experience or mind is different from behaviour.
5. The external world is represented internally.
6. External forces control behaviour *or* internal forces control behaviour *or* internal and external forces control behaviour.

Attneave (1974) illustrates several of these (Postulates 1, 2, 3, 5). He advances the Kantian position (without referring to Kant) that the world as we know it is a pure illusion and states that we only have the information that is taken in through the sense organs and then processed by the brain (in Kant's terms, transformed in the 'transcendental unity of apperception'). To assume that our experience of the world is anything but a representation is naive, he insists. There is no alternative to the illusory world. Further, 'there is really no way [this position] can be wrong' (p. 493). (Mason (1976) makes a very similar claim and includes apes.) An assertion such as this rests on unexamined traditional implicit postulates. Because Attneave cannot even conceive of an alternative he is deprived of an informed choice. By comparing these implicit traditional postulates with the following explicit interbehavioural postulates the reader will have that informed choice. The reader may also find an alternative to Haugeland's (1981) lament that 'explaining behavior *without* invoking mental processes is just too hard' (p. 4).

INTERBEHAVIOURAL POSTULATES

Interbehaviourism steps completely outside the historical dichotomy of mechanism verses mentalism and the more recent uneasy hybrid of cognitive behaviourism. Unlike any other system or approach, it has explicitly and formally stated its postulates on all levels of generality (Kantor, 1959; Kantor and Smith, 1975). It is only when fundamental assumptions are clarified in this manner that one can fruitfully proceed to interpret empirical data or to argue about points of logic.

For the sake of brevity the protopostulates are omitted here and the metapostulates and postulates combined and somewhat abridged:

1. Psychological events are continuous with all other events of the universe and equally objective and naturalistic.
2. Such events consist of occurrences that follow their own principles of organisation and are therefore relatively independent of and irreducible to those of any other domain of events such as culture, biology or chemistry although these fully participate.
3. They involve bio-ecological evolution and biological organisation of species, cultural conditions, and interactional history of the individual as conditions for a level of organisation that constitutes psychological events.
4. They must be dealt with as concrete occurrences from which constructs such as relationships and laws are derived and not have traditional constructs such as mind–body diremptions, a homunculean brain, or analogies from domains at other levels of organisation imposed on them.
5. They consist of multiplex fields of interactions involving stimulating objects with evolved stimulus functions, responding organism with corresponding response functions, setting factors, history of past interactions, and media of contact between the organism and the stimulating object.
6. They have their causality not in putative internal or external forces but in the total interbehavioural field.

While the implicit postulates of cognitivism are construct-based and these constructs are then imposed on data, the interbehavioural constructs are event-based; that is, they begin with observations rather than historical doctrines. Bentley's (1950) statement about postulates seems to represent the type of model they present: ' "science" is . . . a procedure of observation and postulation with all observation recognizing that it takes place under postulation, and with all postulation recognizing that it arises out of observation'. Because of the emphasis on a field of events there is no room for such constructs as mechanistic body or metaphysical mind, nor for the common assertion that mind and body are one. The observable field provides no evidence for 'they' or 'one'. These constructs have no concrete referent either in observation or inference. The attempt to ascribe psychological actions to neurons is equally spurious. No one has ever observed a neuron think, perceive, plan, believe, will or remember, or for that matter, to encode and decode. But investigators have observed that the impairment of neurons impairs various actions, and this indicates their necessary role in all psychological activities rather than their sufficiency. The role of neurons as necessary factors is an observable part of the field. The observed field precludes an 'empty organism' or 'black box' just as it precludes treatment of the entire organism or any component as a determiner of complex events.

The interbehavioural field (Postulate 5) also precludes singling out one factor and making it the determiner of the entire event. Thus the environment does not cause or determine the event nor does the organism's biology or its culture. Culture and individual history as well as the nervous and other physiological systems along with anatomical structure and necessary conditions participate in the field (Postulates 2, 3) but do not determine it. Causality consists of the total integrated field (Postulate 6). This psychological field is a level of organisation that must be studied in its own right and not reduced to or determined by any of its components (Postulate 2). Thus any centrisms of organism, culture, setting or individual history are obviated. There is no internal–external, mind–body, cognition–behaviour distinction. Other diremptions such as private–public, real world–phenomenal world, and experiential–objective are equally spurious (Postulate 4). In as much as all events in the universe are held to be continuous with all others (Postulate 1), thought (better, *thinking*) cannot be unextended or any less physical than the radiation of a star, the fall of a stone, or the bark of a dog; and the subtle or covert activities such as imagining, believing, perceiving and reasoning are directly continuous with more overt behaviours and no different in principle.

There are a number of scientific consequences that follow from the interbehavioural approach. Empirical studies are immediately directed towards observable events involving interrelationships. Interpretive constructs, guided by a field of events, are kept in conformity with observations. Simplistic explanations can be avoided as well as mechanism, mentalism, and reductionism. Analogising from other sciences, and hence treating psychological events as things they are not, can also be avoided. Instead, the full range of human activities such as perceiving, knowing, learning, thinking, imagining, feeling and choosing can be given full recognition. These activities will not be converted to hypothetical engrams, animistic powers, inputs and outputs, drives, instincts, and other imposed verbal creations, which, being unobserved and unobservable, violate the scientific requirement of corrigibility. They will be seen rather as fields of complex interactions, amenable to observation and experimentation or other means of study. The resulting constructs of laws, explanations and relationships can be refined and corrected. Prediction and control can be enhanced and their limitations better understood because of the increased number of factors and interrelationships considered.[1]

SOME ISSUES

The Overt–Covert Continuum

Just as observation rejects mind and body it brings to the fore the continuity of psychological events. The concrete and legitimate *acts* that have been confused with such *constructs* as mind and body or brain and body can be seen as occurring at varying degrees of activation. Consider the fencer who is imagining a bout with his next opponent: At first he sits quietly imagining the opponent's thrusts and his own parries and his own thrusts to out-manoeuvre the opponent's parries. As he continues imagining the scene he becomes slightly more overt, his arms moving minutely, his shoulders and torso twisting slightly, and his legs shifting a bit. As he becomes more involved in bettering the opponent his gestures becomes more and more overt until finally he is making full movements of thrusting, ducking, parrying, sidestepping. One who is imagining a debate with an opponent might go through the same continuum from totally covert to fully overt action involving speech as well as gestures. At what point is the action mental and at another bodily or physical? Is it not a continuity of action involving varying degrees of activation and observability with no fundamental difference in kind?

We need to note that in these imaginative acts the opponent is not present. The fencer or debater is interacting with a substitute stimulus object rather than a direct stimulus object (Kantor, 1924). The substitute may be a calendar or a watch that reminds the individual of the coming event, something heard or read, or any number of other possibilities. It is curious that we have a convention in the English language of referring to *mental* arithmetic but to *silent* reading. Is there any difference in principle between the two? Is not 'mental' arithmetic just silent arithmetic, a concrete activity at the covert end of the continuum? Is not 'silent reading' more concretely meaningful than would be 'mental reading'? Silent arithmetic may involve the use of juxtaposed numerical images which reading does not, but these images or those of reverie or those stimulated by reading are all interactions with substitute stimulation.

Children regularly engage in imaginative acts that are mixtures of varying degrees of covertness and overtness as in the case of one who pretends to drive a car while sitting in a box and making sounds to simulate a motor and moving hands in such a manner as to imitate the back and forth motions of hands controlling a steering wheel. The child does not imagine and then overtly act but engages in a unified act. It makes little sense to try to divide these acts into mental and physical. They are concrete imaginative interactions with substitute stimulus objects. It is not that imagination affects action but that imagination is action.

Privacy as Bogus

The notion of privacy is often invoked in support of private states of consciousness. These are often said to differ from physical events and are unknowable. It is often said, as Haugeland (1981) has noted, that thoughts 'cannot be observed', ' . . . they are somehow essentially subjective', and are only 'inferred or hypothesized intermediates' (p. 4). The perennially favourite example of a private event is the toothache. But what is the basis of this assertion of privacy? It can only be that you are not in a position or situation to observe my toothache. And that is only to say that my toothache is not your toothache.

If we examine the components of the interbehavioural field we observe that in some cases a stimulus object may be observable to only one person and in other cases to many. A motion picture may stimulate many people simultaneously, and they can report on its contents with considerable agreement although their evaluation of it may vary considerably and such reactions are less readily observable. However, knowing something of the individual's past history will increase our probability of correctly inferring that person's evaluative or affective response.

In some cases it is the response that may be available to many or to few. We cannot directly observe a silent chuckle, but we can observe a grin. Thus, the stimulus object or the response phase of the field may vary in observability in different cases and in various circumstances. Probably the entire interaction is unobservable in the case of a toothache, but even here the dentist can observe swelling or inflammation and anticipate a painful reaction. In nearly all situations one or another aspect of the field is observable to someone other than the individual in question and is thereby available to some extent for study.

This does not differ in any fundamental way from the situation that other sciences face. Whether analysing the artefacts and soil samples from an archaeological excavation, attempting to understand a distant star from its radiation spectrum, or writing a biography from scraps of information all investigators are confronted with less than total access to the information they need. Psychology is not in an inferior position in this regard, assumptions about a private mind notwithstanding. In fact, psychology has a special advantage in its opportunity to use self-reports, a striking contrast with the silence of the stone tool from an ancient campsite. This does not overlook the fact that self-reports must be cautiously used and do not themselves constitute complete access, but they are important additional sources of information. Limited access and self-reports provide no basis for special principles that are paraded under the banner of cognitivism. Objective measurements of covert behaviours are available by such means as Stephenson's (1953) Q-Methodology.

The Myth of Brainology
Cognitivism has its roots in the turbulent and socially insecure Hellenistic and Graeco-Roman periods of western develop-

ment. During this period the scholars at Alexandria and other intellectual centres turned increasingly toward abstractions as replacements for the observations that had characterised the Greek approach in the Hellenic period. The psyche known to Aristotle as functioning characteristics of an organism (Kantor, 1963; Smith, 1974) became the immortal soul. It was the soul or psyche that willed, sensed, thought, reasoned and chose salvation or damnation. Cognitivism became an intrinsic part of western theology.

As the science of physiology began to develop in the late eighteenth and in the nineteenth centuries, it became a source of inspiration for converting psychology's theological construct of mind or soul into a body organ. This was usually the brain, but at times has also been endocrine glands, muscles and genes. The doctrine of a homunculean/computer brain became the substitute for the doctrine of theological soul. The terminology has changed to the jargon of technology but the principle remains the same. Note the following definition of soul from *Webster's New Twentieth Century Dictionary* (1968): 'an entity which is regarded as being the immortal or spiritual part of the person and, though having no physical or material reality, is credited with the functions of thinking and willing, and hence determining all behaviour.' In this ordinary dictionary definition, a reflection of a cultural mode of thinking, if we change 'soul' to 'brain' and read only the part beginning 'is credited . . . ' we have the current dogma about the brain that flourishes in scientific circles. The substitution is transparent.

And yet there is no evidence that the brain does any of these homunculean tasks. The claims for it are based on the elementary confusion of necessary versus sufficient conditions (Kantor, 1947; Smith, 1982). And is there any evidence or logic that would support the assumption that anything can be a cause of itself? Can an organism's behaviour be self-caused? Can an organ within the organism cause itself to act and in turn control the rest of the organism? Does not the causal organ require another causal agent and that another, etc? The classical infinity of homunculi are necessarily invoked by the brain doctrine, as they are by any viewpoint that posits an agent within the organism (or even the organism itself) as causative of actions. Cognitivism, brainology and allied doctrines grew out of theology, not science; and this logical impasse is a direct consequence of that origin.

The only way out of this dilemma is to begin not with historical constructs but with observed events. What we observe are organisms in interplay with things around them in which the interplay or interaction changes historically and in different contexts. This total field of relationships constitutes causality and is not reducible to culture, context, individual history, genes, organism or brain. This field of interactions requires no activating agent, for it goes on continuously, each factor changing and being changed by the others. As the field needs no activating agent neither does it require an invisible interpreter, processor, or storage depot. As Kvale and Grenness (1967) have put it,

> The necessity of an 'inner man' to guide behaviour falls away when behavior is conceived as man's relatedness to the world. Behavior is independent of the others. (p. 137)

SOME COGNITIVE BEHAVIOURS

Kantor developed his interbehavioural field psychology in the 1920s, and refined it for the next six decades, but it has received little attention (see Smith and Ray, 1982; Morris, Higgins and Bickel, 1983, for possible reasons). Even in his initial analysis of cognitive acts he provided a thoroughly non-mentalistic and objective approach to them while behaviourists were, for the most part, avoiding them. A reading of these early works (e.g. 1920, 1921, 1923a, 1923b, 1924–26) is still rewarding. (For a complete bibliography of Kantor's work up to 1976 see Smith (1976).) They remain a major and seminal statement about cognitive as well as other interbehaviours (originally called 'organismic'). The following are brief accounts of a few covert interbehaviors.

Perceiving
This type of interaction is semi-covert because the stimulus object is often overt or explicit. It is a discriminating act that

often precedes another action. The sailor notices that his sail does not have the best configuration and then adjusts it accordingly. Perceiving is not something that occurs inside the organism which must involve processing or interpreting but is a joint function of perceptible object and perceiving organism. As a field act it includes (a) the nature of the stimulus object and its meaning to the individual based on past contacts; (b) a medium of contact such as light, sound or flesh (touch); (c) an organism with the appropriate sense organs and biological organization; and (d) a setting. In the example of the sailor this would include a sail with its configuration in the wind; a setting requiring adjustment of the sail (such as having an appreciable distance to go rather than coming into a dock); the organism with eyes, brain, metabolism, circulatory system and other vital anatomical structures and physiological processes; the interactional history of the sailor with various sail configurations as they relate to sailing efficiency; and sufficient light to facilitate the interaction.

As this example illustrates, perceiving is not simply a reaction to the intrinsic properties of a thing but what it means to the individual. Various configurations of the sail mean not just configurations *per se*. They mean more or less efficiency in sailing. Even further removed from intrinsic properties is an object that may mean evil or holiness or special value or use to an individual. The meanings consist of the interaction of the field factors, their joint relationships. (For a recent extensive treatment of perception, including research studies see Smith, 1983.)

Voluntary Acts

These acts are those of choosing. They may be anywhere on the continuum from covert to overt. Choosing is usually approached as an act that is either (a) determined by virtue of its position in a sequence of a cause and effect chain, or (b) free by virtue of an exertion of will power. Varying combinations of freedom and will are also profferred as well as a distinction between determinism and causality for which causality is a motivating force. To the interbehaviourist the issue is spurious, for these powers are metaphysical fictions. Instead of invoking such fictions one must examine the actual factors involved

when individuals make choices. Such an examination leads us
to a quite different approach. By way of example let us consider
the individual who browses in a library and selects a book to
read. We do not observe any series of causal events that
determine the browsing and selecting or that surmounts
determinism by exercise of free will. But when we turn to events
rather than constructs we may learn something of the
individual's interests, the preference for simple or detailed
information, the amount of time available for reading,
recommendations by a teacher or a friend, and other factors.
After describing the various factors such as the individual's
looking at a few books, checking tables of contents, texts and
indexes, and considering these against needs, time available,
previous recommendations and other relevant factors and
perhaps impulsive ones as well, there is no need to add a
metaphysical force of determinism or will that executes the
decision. Rather, the field of ongoing factors as described
constitutes the choosing. These factors are the casual
conditions. There is nothing else to add and no justification to
impose any abstract forces.

This descriptive approach includes the events that can be
correlated with other events—particular sets of conditions
such as examining each book, noting its relevance or other
important features in terms of needs, reading time, etc. These
field factors change continuously with each book examined,
new thoughts about possible uses for it, its comparison with
previous books examined, rejection of one or another of these,
and tentative acceptance of one or more while anticipating
others. Selecting the final book that is most useful is a final field
of events for that series. Noting the time and proceeding to a
checkout station would be another series of fields. The course
of events that involves proceeding to the checkout station
would constitute a volitional rather than a voluntary event, for
it involves no distinct choosing but requires instead a series of
intermediate or auxiliary acts to consummate a goal response.
(See Kantor, 1924–26, for a description and distinction of
each; and Smith and Shaw, 1979, for a further analysis of
volitional acts.)

Knowing

Knowing is a relationship of the knower and the thing known (Kantor, 1924–26; Kantor and Smith, 1975; Parrott, 1983). In this type of conduct the individual does not bring about any change in the thing known but only becomes newly oriented to it. It differs from meaning in that meaning interactions are incomplete and often result in some further action such as manipulation or verbalisation—selecting the ripest apple after discriminating ripeness or correcting the fingering on a violin after hearing an unharmonious note—while knowing is complete and independent. The two may, of course, go hand in hand. Each act of knowing is the establishment of a new relationship. Some of these may be merely perceptual as in coming to newly discriminate subtle differences in the facial features that distinguish one member of a pair of identical twins from the other member. The act of recognising is one of knowing something that has been distinguished earlier. In understanding we are able to relate a thing to other conditions: to one who knows, a piece of rock discloses mineral contents, its origins, and its possible commercial uses. In sum, the joint relationship between a knowing organism and a knowable world constitutes knowing.

Memory and Recollection

Interbehaviourism distinguishes between 'memory' and 're-membering' on the one hand and 'memorisation' and 'recall' or 'recollection', on the other. Perhaps these could be called $memory_1$ and $memory_2$ in as much as the English language has two meanings for the word. $Memory_1$ is the postponing of an action until some later time when we remember to carry it out; it intimately involves substitute stimulation. To illustrate the latter function a little further than that given in a previous section, if I announce to a class that I am about to rake my fingernails across a blackboard and make preliminary movements many students will cringe or shudder. They react to my announcement and gestures as a substitute for the actual raking of fingernails. If I suggest that they imagine that they are eating their favorite icecream many will report that to some extent they can taste it. (This is precisely the principle involved in hypnosis: Smith (1978).) This substitute stimulation makes possible inventions, art, symbolisation, analogies, metaphors, inferences, reminiscences and remembering. It allows us to act in the absence of the original objects and to develop the most complex of human acts and human products. Culture depends heavily upon it. It is of special note that it obviates the abstractions of mental processes and brain storage.

In remembering we project events into the future and complete them at projected times by substitute stimulation. A shoe repairer tells me that my shoes will be ready next Tuesday. If I use a formal reminder I jot it down in an appointment book which, when I turn the page on Tuesday, reminds me to fetch my shoes. If I use an informal reminder I think of something else I will be doing on that day and when that event transpires I am reminded of the shoes. The latter is, of course, more tenuous and unreliable, and I may *forget*. In the latter case when I reach for the pair of shoes to put on but find them missing I have a new substitute stimulus or reminder. We are continually projecting future actions, sometimes weeks or even years ahead, for which the original stimulus will not be present. We remember or forget to carry them out, depending on the adequacy of the substitute stimulus. Despite the great importance this conduct assumes in our daily lives there is apparently no research on it, nor have any psychologists other than Kantor even considered it.

In contrast to memory$_1$, memorisation and recall (memory$_2$) have received an enormous amount of attention. Much of this is patterned after the nineteenth-century work of Ebbinghaus in which association units such as nonsense syllables, lists of words or numbers, and the like are studied. Kvale (1974) and Giorgi (1976) have criticised this for the elimination of meaning when meaning is precisely what we should be studying.

The interbehaviourist notes that recall or recollection is a reperformance. That is, one repeats a previous act with more or less accuracy. The potential for doing so is from one or more contacts or practice sessions with something to be reperformed —a poem, the principal points of a theory, the general contents of a written sentence or passage. It does not involve postponing an action as does memory$_1$ but rather is a reference to the past (Kantor, 1924–26; Kantor and Smith, 1975). In neither case

does interbehaviourism assume that there is any storage depot
or coding and decoding. As Bourne *et al.* (1971) have observed,

> While it is clear that a person does accumulate and remember ways of
> behaving and normally does behave in a way that is consistent with his
> present circumstances, there is no clear evidence in logic or in data that
> these behaviors are really internal physical units that get stored, processed,
> searched for, selected, and invoked by some set of internal storage or
> processing devices. That argument only leads to regressive questions about
> the mechanisms underlying the mechanisms. It is not an accident that the
> description of symbolic processes (the functions of some alleged symbolic
> device) is given in behavioral terms, such as storing, sorting, and
> selecting. That in itself is a strong clue that, rather than being functions of a
> device at all, they are functions of a person, i.e., part and parcel of or,
> better, parameters of his behavior. (p. 13)

One does not retain or store memories$_2$ but rather re-performs
in the presence of the original or a substitute stimulus. Setting
conditions can also facilitate or inhibit recollection. For
example, we may re-perform better in the setting where we
originally practised or in one that is similar than in a very
different one.

Bransford *et al.* (1977) also question the storage notion of
memory$_2$. They suggest that one 're-creates previous experiences' (p. 462). They 'have argued that learning involves the
detection of invariant information from a set of acquisition
experiences' and that 'remembering is assumed to depend on
the organism's state of attunement following acquisition'
(p. 462), attunement being attitude.

By showing how recollection can be retroactive, Kvale
(1974) has demonstrated the untenability of a stored memory$_2$.
As a result of an extensive research programme, Jenkins
(1974) has had to abandon the associationist doctrine of
memory$_2$ and replace it with a contextualist approach. He has
found that people do not recall sentences, linked words that
make up chains of associations according to the association-
ists. Instead they recall meanings of sentences in accordance
with contexts. In these studies it is difficult to see how the
recalled meanings could be stored. Jenkins is explicit about this
same point: 'Regardless of our particular analysis, it is clear
that the phenomena disclosed by these experiments pose
formidable problems for storage theories of memory' (p. 792)

and 'memory is not a box in a flow diagram' (p. 749). Although these experimenters have undertaken their work in complete independence of interbehaviorism, that work converges directly upon it.

Imagery

Our last example concerns imagery. Images have long been the stronghold of the mentalist whose treatment invokes all the historical metaphysical constructs. To the interbehaviourist images are subtle but concrete interactions whether visual, auditory, tactual, olfactory, gustatory, kinesthetic or other sensory-linked acts. Such a list almost declares that images involve vestigial remnants of sensing acts. In the gustatory example used in a previous section concerning imagining the eating of icecream, there is some degree of salivation and probably activation of taste buds and probably a good many other physiological events that would be involved in the actual eating of icecream in addition to the substitute stimulus with which the interaction takes place. Thus gustatory imaging clearly consists of concrete interactions with the world. Skinner (1963) has noted that whilst we are tempted to say that vision *represents* the world, this is less so for hearing, and least of all for touch. Yet is there any reason to expect any difference in principle with visual or auditory images? They too are better regarded as vestigial actions in which the brain is but one necessary condition in a field of interacting factors.

If we attribute the image (better, *imaging*) to the production of a sense organ or the brain, and treat it as a mere representation of an external 'real' object, we end up once again in the logical problem of an infinite regress.

The work of Shepard (1978) and Shepard and Cooper (1982) is an interesting example of the confusion of constructs with events. Despite a thoroughgoing mentalistic interpretive framework, the research actually shows the close relationship between images and covert conduct, as well as the role of substitute stimulation. This suggests, as Kantor has noted, that all research is interbehavioural—even when it is not so interpreted, for all that organisms can do is to interbehave and all that investigators can do is to interbehave with the interbehaving organism. If one starts with descriptions of events rather than traditional constructs that get imposed on the events the interbehavioural programme becomes an inevitability. And this can be effected by examining one's postulates and making them conform to observation. By merely observing a cardinal rule of good science that one's interpretive constructs must be consistent with the events they interpret, the approach would be interbehavioural even if different in terminology. To put it another way, postulational constructs must match operations. That is the message of interbehaviourism.

REFERENCES

Attneave, F., 'How do you know?', *American Psychologist*, 1974, *29*, 493–511.

Bandura, A., 'The self-system in reciprocal determinism', *American Psychologist*, 1978, *33*, 344–58.

Bentley, A.F., 'Kennetic inquiry', *Science*, 1950, *112*, 775–83.

Blewitt, E., 'The computer analogy in psychology: Memory as interbehaviour or information-processing?', in N.W. Smith, P.T. Mountjoy and D.H. Rubin (eds.), *Reassessment in psychology: The interbehavioral alternative* (University Press of America, 1983).

Boneau, C.A., 'Paradigm regained? Cognitive behaviourism restated', *American Psychologist*, 1974, *29*, 297–309.

Bourne, L.E., Lyle, E., Ekstrand, B.R. and Dominowski, R.L., *The Psychology of Thinking* (Prentice-Hall, 1971).

Bransford, J.D., McCarrell, N.S., Franks, J.J. and Nitsch, K.E., 'Toward unexplaining memory', in R. Shaw and J. Bransford (eds.), *Perceiving, Acting, and Knowing: Toward an ecological psychology* (Erlbaum Associates, 1977).

Giorgi, A. 'Phenomenology and the foundations of psychology', in *Nebraska Symposium on Motivation*, Vol. 23 (University of Nebraska Press, 1975).

Haugeland, J., 'Semantic engines: An introduction to mind design', in J. Haugeland (ed.), *Mind Design: Philosophy, psychology, artificial intelligence* (MIT Press, 1981).

Jenkins, J.J., 'Remember that old theory of memory? Well, forget it!', *American Psychologist,* 1924, *29*, 785–95.

Kantor, J.R., 'Suggestions toward a scientific interpretation of perception', *Psychological Review*, 1920, *27*, 191–216.

Kantor, J.R., 'An objective interpretation of meanings', *American*

Journal of Psychology, 1921, *32,* 231–48.

Kantor, J.R., 'An objective analysis of volitional behavior', *Psychological Review,* 1923a, *30,* 116–44.

Kantor, J.R., 'The psychology of feeling or affective reactions', *American Journal of Psychology,* 1923b, *34,* 433–63.

Kantor, J.R., *Principles of Psychology* (Principia Press, 1924–26).

Kantor, J.R., 'Man and machine in science', *Journal of Philosophy,* 1935, *32,* 673–84.

Kantor, J.R., 'Concerning physical analogies in psychology', *American Journal of Psychology,* 1936, *48,* 153–64.

Kantor, J.R., *Interbehavioral Psychology: A sample of scientific system construction* (Principia Press, 1959).

Kantor, J.R., *The Scientific Evolution of Psychology,* Vol. 1 (Chicago: Principia Press, 1963).

Kantor, J.R., 'Man and machines in psychology: Cybernetics and artificial intelligence', *Psychological Record,* 1978, *28,* 575–83.

Kantor, J.R. and Smith, N.W., *The Science of Psychology: An interbehavioral survey* (Principia Press, 1975).

Kuo, Z.-Y. *The Dynamics of Behavior Development: An epigenetic view* (Random House, 1967).

Kvale, S., 'The temporality of memory', *Journal of Phenomenological Psychology,* 1974, *5,* 7–31.

Kvale, S. and Grenness, C.E., 'Skinner and Sartre: Towards a radical phenomenology of behavior', *Review of Existential Psychology and Psychiatry,* 1967, *7,* 128–50.

Mason, W.A., 'Environmental models and mental modes: Representational processes in the great apes', *American Psychologist,* 1976, *31,* 284–94.

Morris, E.K., Higgins, S.T. and Bickel, W.K., 'Contributions of J.R. Kantor to contemporary behaviorism', in N.W. Smith, P.T. Mountjoy and D.H. Ruben (eds.), *Reassessment in Psychology: The interbehavioral alternative* (University Press of America, 1983).

Mountjoy, P.T., 'Science in psychology: J.R. Kantor's field theory', *Revista de Análisis de la Conducta,* 1976, *2,* 3–31.

Murray, G., *Five Stages of Greek Religion* (Doubleday, Doran, 1955).

Parrott, L.J., 'Perspectives on knowing and knowledge', *Psychological Record,* 1983, *33,* 171–84.

Rostovtseff, M.I., 'The mentality of the Hellenistic world and the afterlife', *Divinity School Bulletin,* 1938–39, Harvard University, 5–25.

Rostovtseff, M.I., *The Social and Economic History of the Roman Empire,* 2 vols. (Oxford: Clarendon Press, 2nd rev. edn 1957).

Sampson, E.E., 'Cognitive psychology as ideology', *American Psychologist,* 1981, *36,* 730–43.

Shepard, R.N., 'Externalization of mental images and the act of creation'. in B.S. Randhawa and W.E. Coffman (eds.), *Visual Learning, Thinking, and Communication* (Academic Press, 1978).

Shepard, R.N. and L.A. Cooper, *Mental Images and their Transformations* (MIT Press/Bradford Books, 1982).

Skinner, B.F., 'Behaviorism at fifty', *Science*, 1963, *140*, 951–8.

Smith, N.W., 'The ancient background to Greek psychology and some implications for today', *Psychological Record*, 1974, *24*, 309–24.

Smith, N.W. 'The works of J.R. Kantor: Pioneer in scientific psychology', *Revista Mexicana de Análisis de la Conducta*, 1976, *2*, 137–48.

Smith, N.W., 'Hypnosis de-mystified: Facts and fallacies', State University of New York at Plattsburg, 1978.

Smith, N.W., 'Brain, behavior, and evolution', *Psychological Record*, 1982, *32*, 483–90.

Smith, N.W., 'Sensing is perceiving: An alternative to the doctrine of the double world', in N.W. Smith, P.T. Mountjoy and D.H. Ruben (eds.), *Reassessment in Psychology: The interbehavioral alternatives* (University Press of America, 1983).

Smith, N.W. and Ray, C.E., 'A citation study of the interbehavioral field psychology of J.R. Kantor', *Revista Mexicana de Análisis de la Conducta*, 1981, *7*, 117–34.

Smith, N.W. and Shaw, N.E., 'An analysis of commonplace behaviors: Volitional acts', *Psychological Record*, 1979, *29*, 179–86.

Stephenson, W.S., *The Study of Behavior: Q-technique and its methodology* (University of Chicago Press, 1953).

Stephenson, W.S. Consciousness out—subjectivity in. *Psychological Record*, 1968 *18*, 499–501.

Swartz, P., 'A note on the computing machine analogy in psychology', *Psychological Record*, 1958, *8*, 53–6.

Webster's New Twentieth Century Dictionary of the American Language, unabridged (Publishers Guild, 1968.)

NOTE

1. The last two paragraphs are largely from Smith and Ray (1981).

13

The Concepts of the Universal in the Cartesian and Hegelian Frameworks: Consequences for Psychology

Ivana Marková

In its attempt to establish itself as a science, psychology has long sought to discover so called *psychological universals*, basic principles of behaviour and mental processes. Although such aims may, at least at first sight, appear relatively clearly defined, a number of questions arise if one starts asking what kinds of principle qualify as universals; what is the nature of universals? Are they biological, cognitive or environmental in character? By what kinds of method can they be established? and so on. Answers to these and similar questions depend largely on the conceptions of the universal used within particular theoretical frameworks.

In this chapter I shall contrast the conceptions of universals in the Platonic–Cartesian and Hegelian philosophies. The choice of the two is not fortuitous. The Platonic–Cartesian philosophy is an explicit and dominant point of reference of much of modern cognitivism (cf. for example Chomsky, 1966; Fodor, 1981). References to Hegelian philosophy, on the other hand, are relatively rare in psychology although some of the most important Hegelian ideas have been implicitly adopted by psychologists without realising their original sources (Marková, 1982). Although I do not accept Hegel's philosophy wholesale, there are two basic reasons for my appeal to him. First, there are historical reasons. It was Hegel who, in modern philosophy, formulated the principle of the interactional effect of the two mutually dependent factors involved in the concept of *development*. The latter is fundamental for his concept of the universal. Secondly, Hegel's philosophy has been highly influential in the rise of various forms of evolutionism, dialectics, phenomenology, symbolic interactionism, and so on. It is my conviction that psychology will benefit by returning directly to Hegel's original formulation of the principle of development and human agency. I do not deny that there is a considerable overlap between Hegel and the majority of approaches based on his work. However, a discussion of Hegel's original ideas of development and agency is important if they are to be understood in the historical context in which they evolved and in separation from the biases imposed by later interpretations of and additions to Hegel. In discussing the conceptions of the universal in the two philosophical frameworks I shall emphasise that the Hegelian (i.e. the developmental conception of the universal) has considerable theoretical and methodological advantages over the Cartesian, i.e. the static conception of the universal in psychology.

THE PLATONIC–CARTESIAN CONCEPT OF THE UNIVERSAL

The assumption that if knowledge is at all possible it must be of entities that are immutable and eternal has a long history in western culture. The problem, however, is that since the world is changing, and new inorganic, organic and social objects emerge, exist for a while, and disintegrate after a period of time, how can one identify what is *unchanging* and therefore true, and separate it from the *changing* and ephemeral phenomena? In his attempt to solve this problem, Plato developed a theory of Forms, which are *universals* existing independently of objects of perception and of minds. Forms are apprehended by the intellect, while their particular manifestations in individual objects are apprehended by the senses. Examples of Forms are Man, Fire, Motion or Rest. In contrast, an individual man, an instance of fire, or motion or rest take part in the Form in question. While Forms or universals are immutable and eternal, individual objects change in time. Thus, true knowledge must be of universals only.

If one accepts that knowledge is of entities that are eternal and immutable the question arises as to how knowledge can be acquired by individual human beings who themselves are neither eternal nor immutable. Plato's reponse to this problem was that although people themselves are mortal, the human soul is immortal. It is incarnated again and again, and between incarnations it knows everything there is to know and thus has nothing new to learn. Seeking and learning is nothing but recollection of knowledge from the soul's previous lives (Plato, *Meno*). For example, in Plato's *Meno*, Socrates leads the slave Meno to rediscover for himself what, in fact, he already knows about virtue. In general, if suitably questioned and guided, or if given a proper stimulus, any human being is able to recollect his or her *a priori* knowledge, this being independent of learning and experience.

Plato's notion of the universal was adopted in its essence by the Cartesian philosophy of the seventeenth century. According to Descartes, innate ideas are those which account for universals and make universal knowledge possible. In his letter to Mersenne of 16 June 1641, Descartes says that ideas such as God, Triangle or Mind represent true and eternal essences because they are universals (Descartes, 1641, p. 104). On another occasion Descartes calls universals the primary germs of truth that nature implanted in the human mind (Descartes, 1628, p. 12). Universals are hidden in the human mind like the fire in a flint. Just as the fire is revealed only when triggered off by striking the flint on a stone, so universals are revealed only when triggered off by appropriate environmental stimuli (Descartes, 1647, p. 442).

It is important for our purpose to note that in the Platonic–Cartesian account universals have both ontological and epistemological significance: they refer to the eternal and unchangeable essences of the world, and they also refer to the way these eternal and unchangeable essences are apprehended by the human mind. Thus altogether, in the Platonic–Cartesian conception, universals in their ontological and epistemological guises amount, ultimately, to the same thing, *psychologically* they appear to have a dual nature, being both something *out in the world* and also something *in the mind*.

The conception of the universal in its dual guise has had a tremendous influence on psychology as it has emerged from philosophy. Concerning the ontological guise psychology has taken it for granted that in order to become a science it should search for universals that underlie human behaviour. Unfortunately, if an ontological universal is an attribute of the human mind, it is liable to be conflated with universals in the epistemological sense. The main doctrine of Chomsky's *Cartesian Linguistics* (1966) is that the general principles which determine grammatical structure in particular languages are common to all human languages and are therefore linguistic universals. These principles, which, according to Chomsky, underlie the structure of the human mind, are of biological, rather than of logical necessity (Chomsky, 1977). Similarly, according to Lenneberg (1967), linguistic universals are presumed to be innate and invariant capacities of the mind that are based on uniform neurophysiological structures. Fodor (1981) argues and gives evidence that the most plausible theories of concept formation, both rationalistic and empiricistic, are all based on the assumption of the innateness of primitive concepts. Both kinds of theory assume that *primitive* concepts such as Red, Line or Angle are innate and that their emergence is contingent upon the activation of the sensorium. In full agreement with Descartes, therefore, the essential primitive concepts are hidden in the mind and become available to the knower because of appropriate environmental triggering. Fodor labours the point that rationalists from Descartes to Chomsky all agree that

> the environment of the developing organism actually provides a *poor* inductive basis for the concepts that the organism acquires. . . . All the environment does is provide the triggers that release the information. (Fodor, 1981, p. 280)

The implication of such theorising is that the conceptual base in human beings is to a considerable degree invariant across variation in experiences. Since the mind is structured, *a priori* availability of primitive concepts automatically gives rise to more complex concepts. Although all primitive concepts are triggered, there is nevertheless a hierarchy of triggers and from this hierarchy the order in which the concepts are acquired can be predicted. Fodor concludes his arguments with the claim that 'everybody is a Rationalist in the long run' because everybody accepts that there must be a primitive conceptual base from which logical constructions of complex concepts arise, while primitive concepts are not learned. The only difference between the rationalism of Descartes and that of Locke is how big such a primitive conceptual base is.

CRITICISM OF THE CARTESIAN CONCEPTION OF THE UNIVERSAL

While the clearest expression of the Cartesian conception of the universal in modern psychology is provided by the work of Chomsky and Fodor, the search for cognitive, linguistic and behavioural universals has been prolific in various areas of psychology. At the same time, severe criticism of and objections to the Cartesian conception of the universal have been raised. In considering these I shall draw attention to two issues: first, to the tremendous liberality with which the word 'universal' is used in psychology; and secondly, to the consequent diversity of criticism of the conception of the universal, from attempts to complement the search for universals by the study of individual differences, to the outright rejection of the concept of the universal and efforts to substitute for it a concept of a totally different kind. Since the Cartesian conception of the universal has primarily influenced cognitive psychology and the psychology of language, it is natural that the major attacks have emerged within these subjects.

Concerning the first issue, I would like to point out that the word 'universal' conveys totally different things to different researchers. In consequence, while all criticism is directed against the Cartesian conception of the universal, it does so from positions that have little or nothing in common with each other except perhaps for the very word 'universal'. For Chomsky and Fodor universals are *abstract* principles due to the structure of the mind; Comrie (1981a, b) searches for them through the exploration of some *concrete* concepts, perform-ances or expressions; Gopnik (1983) rejects universals because concepts and knowledge change; Finnegan (1981) argues that it is not clear how 'universal' a universal should be in order to have the claim to be so called; for Dasen (1981) there are weak and strong universals; Bruner (1981) holds that there are process and outcome universals, and Hardy-Brown (1983) that there are innate and environmental universals; and finally Feldman (1980) claims that universals undergo change.

With respect to the second issue, criticism of the concept of the universal can be discerned at several levels. In this respect I shall only present examples of broader levels of such criticism.

At one level, researchers have focused their efforts on finding evidence that language acquisition is not just the triggering-off of pre-programmed universals but that the caretakers' speech has a considerable influence upon the way the child acquires language (Snow, 1977). However, as Hardy-Brown (1983) correctly points out, the identification of environmental effects on the child's language acquisition does not challenge the universals hypothesis since language universals may operate at other levels. Although linguistic variability is now receiving much more attention than previously, the assumptions and associated methodological problems of theories of underlying universals and individual differences have not been sufficiently examined. While both approaches to the study of language acquisition, the genetic and the environmental, are necessary because they provide complementary knowledge, their contributions to language acquisition need to be disentangled. Hardy-Brown suggests that one can represent the dual role of heredity and environment with respect to universals and individual differences in four cells: universals due to heredity, universals due to environment, individual differences due to heredity, and individual differences due to environment. Moreover, she contends, there is also an interaction between genetic and environmental factors affecting variation in language acquisition. In sum, Hardy-Brown argues against the reduction of the role of the environment to that of a triggering-off device, and insists on the importance of both genetic and environmental universals in language acquisition.

Another level of criticism is raised against those who, rather than demonstrate that a phenomenon or relationship is a universal, simply start from the assumption that this is so, and challenge anyone who questions the assumption to offer a plausible and comprehensible alternative. In the field of cross-cultural research, Jahoda (1981) points out that 'psychologists conducting studies in the industrialized cultures where the bulk of such work is done are apt to take it for granted that their results would replicate anywhere else in the world' (Jahoda, 1981, p. 43). For Jahoda, the existence of such a universal could only be accepted on the basis of very powerful evidence. Similarly, Comrie (1981a) argues that in order to identify language universals it is essential to explore the whole range of languages. Comrie focuses on universals as formulated on the basis of concrete analyses, and in addition to innateness he is prepared to consider other kinds of explanations for language universals such as functional or pragmatic explanations. Chomsky (1966), however, bases his search for universals on the study of a single language arguing that language universals should be formulated in terms of abstract structures within the transformational-generative grammars identifiable in any human language.

A third level of criticism attacks the concept of universals itself. Gopnik (1983) argues against immutable conceptual and semantic universals: people's knowledge and concepts change constantly in qualitative ways and cannot be reduced to previous knowledge and concepts. Indeed, no single 'language of thought' (Fodor, 1975) can be identified as underlying natural languages. Using examples from science and child development she argues that neither scientists nor children fit Fodor's idea of a language of thought. For instance, it could be held by a defender of universals that the concepts of Euclidean geometry are innate. Indeed, we have already remarked that Fodor (1981) considers concepts such as Line or Angle to be innate primitive concepts. However, as Gopnik points out, non-Euclidean geometries based on totally different geometrical principles are also conceivable, requiring different 'primitive' concepts. Moreover, evidence from developmental psychology demonstrates that the concepts of young children change dramatically as children obtain more experience, and this evidence contests strongly the supposition that they have a single universal representational system. She concludes her criticism by saying that if we want to claim that there are universal characteristics of representations and of the way language encodes those representations, we will have to leave children and scientists out of our universe ... We might draw an analogy between the study of mental representations and the study of species ... The most important fact about species is that they can change, and the principles that explain this change are the most important principles in biology ...

Similarly, the most important fact about knowledge is that it changes. (Gopnik, 1983, pp. 175, 177)

At yet another level, Feldman (1980) rejects the notion of unchanging universals and offers an alternative in terms of changing universals. Addressing the question of universals in cognitive development, Feldman maintains that Piaget, by his preoccupation with universals, ignores the creative achievements of unique individuals, and thus deprives himself of the chance of making real progress in the theory of cognitive development, in particular in his theory of transition rules governing movement from one developmental stage to the next.

There are two essential features of Feldman's approach to the problem of universals. First, he argues for a dynamic relationship between unique and universal achievements, showing that cognitive development may occur within different developmental domains: universal, cultural, discipline-based, idiosyncratic and unique. These domains form a universal–unique continuum. Only some domains of knowledge are mastered universally, that is, by all mankind; others are acquired by members of particular cultures; still others are achieved by a segment of a culture subject to training; while yet others are acquired by specialists who become masters in their particular disciplines; and finally, there are unique achievements representing an original way of organising knowledge. Unique achievements, if they are truly creative—i.e. when they make a substantial contribution to knowledge, and individuals other than the originator find them significant and important —start their journey towards generality and thus, towards universality. On the other hand, non-creative unique achievements, although they may have similar characteristics to those that are creative, do not become part of universal knowledge and eventually they wane away.

The second essential feature of Feldman's approach, following Flavell (1971), is his appreciation of the role of environmental conditions in catalysing qualitative changes between the domains of development, leading to movement on the universal–unique continuum. In human evolution, he argues, every developmental advancement was once just a unique achievement. However, a unique achievement has the potentiality of becoming a critical environmental condition for the next generation entering the evolutionary and historical journey towards universality.

The above examples of criticism of the Cartesian conception of the universal, and the attempts to modify the meaning of the word 'universal', all represent an effort to resolve certain fundamental theoretical and empirical problems in present-day psychology. These problems stem from the fact that the Cartesian conception of the universal is static while psychological phenomena are constantly changing and developing. As a result no coherent framework with respect to the conception of the universal exists any longer because of the acccumulation of anomalies at both the theoretical and empirical levels. Consequently the word 'universal' itself, by taking on so many meanings, is becoming meaningless.

THE HEGELIAN CONCEPTION OF THE UNIVERSAL

The Hegelian conception of the universal can be understood properly only in the context of *evolutionism* that became the *Zeitgeist* of the second half of the eighteenth century. In philosophy, one of the first major proponents of evolutionism was Leibniz whose idea of self-unfolding monads extended far beyond the static framework of the Cartesian philosophy. Although Leibniz was not an evolutionist in the present sense of the word, he emphasised that nature does not consist of segregated groupings of phenomena such as rocks, plants, animals and humans, but instead that it is full of *transitions* from one kind of phenomenon to another that connect them all together. For Leibniz, just as for the majority of the eighteenth century philosophers and scientists, evolution was based on the ideal of preformation, i.e. on the unfolding of miniatures of

completely developed organisms existing in the wombs of their
mothers right back to the beginning of the world. However,
ideas of a true development involving the emergence of totally
new organisms started to appear in Buffon, de le Mettrie,
Maupertuis, and later in Lamarck and in others. Hegel thus
grew up in an atmosphere in which various types of
evolutionism had gradually undermined the certainty of the
Platonic–Cartesian world of immutable Forms. Moreover,
evidence for evolution was coming from biology, palaeonto-
logy, physiology and other newly-founded scientific disciplines. In accord with this trend, the concept of development
became the essential feature of Hegel's philosophy; stability, in
contrast, was conceived only as an aspect of a constantly
changing and developing world of ideas.

Hegel's concept of the universal, which is also part of the
above general evolutionist way of thinking, has two essential
characteristics. First, universals are not ideas implanted in the
human mind innately or *a priori* but the human mind itself
produces universals through its activity. Secondly, universals
develop through their interaction with particulars.

Let us first turn to Hegel's belief that universals are not
implanted in the human mind *a priori*. Just as for Plato and
Descartes, so for Hegel, too, universals are concepts. In
contrast to Plato and Descartes, however, in Hegel's
philosophy concepts are not produced by the human mind in
any fixed and final form. As the mind actively explores
phenomena, concepts, which are its own products, become
more elaborate or, as Hegel says, more *concrete*. While to start
with a concept is *abstract*, i.e. not yet fully developed, in the
process of the mind's activity it becomes more elaborate or
concrete. Hegel maintains that a true universal takes thousands
of years to develop fully. For example, he argued that the
principle of humanity was not completely recognised until
Christianity became established. The Greeks, so advanced in
many respects, did not believe that the barbarians were
humans in the same sense as they were themselves. The
abolition of slavery in Europe was, according to Hegel, related
to the development of Christianity, and thus to the emergence
of the true universal of humanity. One must add, though, that
the recognition of the universal of humanity did not mean that

all humans were guided by it at once and on all occasions after it had appeared. Hegel himself recognised that progress does not proceed along a straight line but may regress before it enters the consciousness of all human beings.

Hegel's idea that the formation of concepts proceeds from abstract to concrete ideas has been adopted in various forms since. If one takes Vygotsky's (1962) theory of the child's acquisition of concepts, a similar point of view emerges. At first, the child's concepts are fuzzy, overlapping with other concepts. Vygotsky refers to such a stage in concept acquisition as *pseudo-conceptualisation.* With the child's increasing experience and maturation proper concepts are acquired. A similar idea to that of evolution proceeding by concretisation was also expressed by Spencer, according to whom biological evolution is 'an integration of matter and a progressive change from a relatively indefinite, incoherent homogeneity to a relatively definite coherent heterogeneity; and during which the retained motion undergoes a parallel transformation' (Spencer, in Collins, 1901, p. 47).

The second characteristic of Hegel's conception is that universals develop in the process of mutual interaction with particulars. Hegel argued that the traditional problem of philosophy was that universals were concepts in which particular features of objects were neglected as unessential. For example, with respect to the universal 'dog', a particular colour, size or psychological characteristic was not part of the universal. A colour, size or psychological characteristic may distinguish one dog from another but dogs of different colours, sizes and psychological characteristics are still *dogs*; their 'dogginess', i.e. the universal, is unaffected by particulars such as dogs of different colours, sizes or psychological characteristics. Hegel, however, strongly objected to such a conception of the universal, calling it a mere phantom and shadow. He argued that the universal 'is not a mere sum of features common to several things, confronted by a particular which enjoys an existence of its own' (Hegel, 1830, p. 292). The universal, on the contrary, is self-particularising or self-specifying. It means that a universal is real only in so far as it realises itself in a *particular*, which may be this or that object, or this or that person. Although objects belonging to the same category have certain features in common, each of these common or universal features reveals itself in a particular way in an individual object. The particular, therefore, is the *antithesis* of the universal: there is no universal without a particular just as there is no particular without a universal. For example, a certain variety of roses may be yellow. However, the yellowness expresses itself repeatedly in each individual blossom, although in many cases the subtle differences among individual roses may not be noticeable to the naked eye.

Hegel's insistence that there are no universals without particulars, just as there are no particulars without universals, must not be reduced to the triviality that both common and individual characteristics of objects are important in concept formation. The relationship between universals and particulars is not something *given externally*, but the more the mind actively penetrates the characteristics of particulars the more elaborate the concept of the universal becomes. There is no end-stage to this developmental process because one can always acquire more knowledge and consider phenomena from other viewpoints. Hegel's conception of development, however, must be conceived primarily as a thought-process rather than a time-process (Ritchie, 1893). The essence of Hegel's philosophy consists in the criticism of thought, in which process thought self-develops from its less adequate to its more adequate, truer forms. This process of the criticism of thought is a logical rather than a *temporal* process. The logic of this process is based on Hegel's so-called oppositions which enable one to view the relationship between universals and particular from yet another side. What does it mean to have a concept or universal of, say, a dog? It means to be able to identify a particular kind of animal as a dog and to distinguish it from, or *oppose* it to, other animals that are not dogs. In other words, one identifies an object not only by the properties that an object has but also by properties that the object does not have. One learns at the same time both what the dog is and what it is not.

Culler (1976) in his study of Saussure explains this idea very clearly. Consider a teacher wishing to teach someone what 'brown' is. It would not be a good teaching strategy, Culler argues, to attempt to teach the pupil to master all the browns in various kinds of brown objects and then to test such knowledge by asking the pupil to point to all brown objects. The problem with such a strategy is that one does not have a clear criterion for the selection of brown objects. Instead, one should teach the pupil to distinguish brown objects from those that are red, yellow, and so on. 'Brown' is not an independent concept that can be learned separately from others: it can be grasped only in relation to other concepts. Thus, one learns a concept through opposing it to other concepts. Moreover, 'contradiction is the very moving principle of the world' (Hegel, 1830, p. 223). Thought actually *develops* through the critical analysis of concepts in their oppositions. For Hegel, something is dynamic because oppositions keep it moving and acting. If a thing is unable to withstand contradictions it disintegrates. In this sense, he maintained, the world itself is a contradiction, and therefore a constant 'becoming'.

Hegel developed his philosophy of the thought-process some fifty years before Darwin formulated his evolutionary theory. There are a variety of features that are similar in the two theories (Ritchie, 1893), but there is one important difference between the two to which I wish to draw attention. The basis of Hegel's theorising is the *mutuality* in the interaction between oppositions. In other words, oppositions such as variability and stability, universal and particular, identity and difference, have equal status in their complementary relationship. It means that they contribute equally to the process of thought-development and that they transform both themselves and each other as a result of their mutual interaction. One might ask how their mutual changes can be measured, how one knows that both components contribute the same amount to the final product, and so on. To answer these questions, one must bear in mind that one is not dealing with physical, biological, psychological or other kinds of objects or with quantities: one is dealing with *concepts*. Hegel's concern is conceptual, not numerical. Any change in one component, however small, produces a change in the concept as a whole.

It is, of course, possible to consider Hegel's conceptual problem in terms of physical, biological or psychological phenomena. Since Darwinian evolutionary theory has been highly influential not only in biology but in all sciences that adopt an evolutionary perspective, let us explore the problem in this context. In contrast to Hegel's concept of development based on the mutuality of effect of the two complementary components, e.g. universal and particular, the Darwinian concept of development is based on a problem-solving approach: the organism is viewed as solving a problem given to it by the environment, and by solving the problem the organism changes. The environment, in contrast, remains relatively unchanged. In other words, while Hegel's concept of development is based on the mutuality of the interaction between the two components, Darwin views development as based on an asymmetrical relationship of the two components with one changing and the other remaining relatively unchanged. In consequence, following Darwin, most models of evolution are unable to cope with the concept of true interaction.

Recently, however, the idea of a problem-solving relationship between an organism and its environment has been criticised (Gould, 1977; Lewontin, 1982; Goodwin, 1985). Lewontin argues that evolutionary epistemologies wrongly conceptualise the environment as an autonomous something 'out there' that presents a problem which the organism has to solve in order to survive:

> Adaptation is the process of reconstituting the organism to fit the environment. Adaptation may be based on autonomously generated novelties, as in the strict Darwinism of Lorenz and Popper, or it may be a directed pseudo-Lamarckian response as for Piaget, but it is always the organism that responds to the environment and not vice versa. Yet our understanding of the real history of organisms has shown that the asymmetric picture is untrue. Organisms construct and reconstruct their environment, not just in their own heads as Piaget would allow, but in reality, 'out there'. (Lewontin, 1982, pp. 167–8)

Lewontin continues by saying that, of course, this does not mean that an organism in its construction of its environment can go beyond its capacities. However, if genetic epistemology is to explain real invention in nature it must be concerned with more than accommodation of the individual to a fixed reality.

It may seem, however, that a truly mutual relationship between an organism and its environment rarely occurs. In the process of evolution individuals become more and more complex, and the environment seems to lose its importance because the various characteristics of the individual appear to unfold according to a predetermined programme when environmental stimuli trigger them off. Indeed, the environment relating to some traits and capacities has been pretty stable for up to a 100,000 years, a time which appears to be sufficient for the traits and capacities themselves to become highly stable (Schilcher and Tennant, 1984). As information becomes encoded into genes not only do developing organisms appear not to be affected by environmental variability but they possess autoregulatory feedback systems 'that buffer out the effect of environmental variation' (Lewontin, 1982, p. 155). For example, if the wing of the embryo of the Drosophila is damaged the development of the entire organism stops while the wound heals so that the adult Drosophila emerges unhandicapped. One can appreciate that such examples of autoregulation appear to grossly devalue the role of the environment.

However, as Lewontin argues, a different picture emerges if one leaves the macro-level of the process and turns one's attention to the micro-level. Lewontin presents several examples demonstrating minute variations in the development of the organism due to 'developmental noise' or subtle environmental interferences. As he points out, the relationship between genes, environment and organism is highly intricate and diverse and different in various species, organs, tissues or enzymes, with some species developing virtually identically in a different environment while others are exceedingly flexible. One would suppose that these findings have implications for more complex species, in particular for those that have developed self-and-other-awareness with the aid of which they exert effect upon their environment.

IS THERE A VIABLE CONCEPT OF THE UNIVERSAL FOR PSYCHOLOGY?

We have outlined two philosophical theories of the universal: the Platonic–Cartesian theory, according to which universals are immutable ideas abstracted from particulars and implanted innately in the human mind; and the Hegelian, according to which universals develop through the mind's activity in mutual relationships with particulars. In both accounts universals are *concepts* and, as such, they are parts of two different philosophical theories of knowledge. Bearing on the above discussion, in this last section I would like to raise a question concerning the theoretical status of universals in psychology: are psychological universals treated as concepts as they are in philosophy, or as something else? The answer to this question may explain at least some of the problems related to the multiplicity of meanings of the word 'universal' and the occurrences of the diverse levels of criticism of the Platonic–Cartesian conception of the universal discussed earlier.

With respect to the question of the theoretical status of universals in psychology, consider first the claim of the cognitivists that cognitive and linguistic universals are innate. According to Chomsky (1980), this claim implies that universals are biologically predetermined programmes not qualitatively different from what we find in the case of the body. Just as an embryo has a highly specific innate endowment that causes two eyes or two kidneys to develop, so it has a neurophysiological basis for the acquisition of cognitive functions. Thus, according to this account, universals appear to be biological *bases for the acquisition of concepts*, but they are not concepts as such. If one considers Triandis's definition, according to which a universal is 'a "psychological" process or relationship which occurs in all cultures' (Triandis, 1978, quoted by Jahoda, 1981), then again a universal seems to refer to a variety of psychological phenomena but not to knowers' concepts as such. Support for my supposition that for Triandis universals are not concepts is to be found in his claim that if universal psychological relationships or processes are not found it does not mean that the universal in question does not exist; various methodological errors within a culture and across cultures might be responsible for a failure to obtain particular results. However, while Chomsky clearly considers universals to be innate bases for the acquisition of concepts, Triandis is agnostic as to whether psychological phenomena identified as universals are innate, environmental in character, or what have you.

In contrast to Chomsky and Triandis, for whom universals appear to be bases for the acquisition of concepts, other researchers assume that universals *are* concepts. Thus, Fodor (1981), following Descartes, discusses universals in terms of innate primitive concepts invariant across experience. However, when Descartes refers to innate ideas one can well understand that it was his way of expressing certain thoughts which, in the seventeenth century, could not be expressed in terms of biological encoding or genetics. Does Fodor, in the twentieth century, really mean that it is our conceptual equipment (i.e. knowledge) that is innate, rather than biological bases for the acquisition of concepts? If one accepts a truly developmental point of view according to which all concepts and knowledge undergo qualitative changes during the knower's life because of his or her active involvement in the world, then there is no place for Fodor's 'language of thought' based on immutable primitive concepts. In a similar way Feldman's universals are also conceptual in nature, since they refer to actual knowledge rather than to biological or psychological bases for knowledge as in the case of Chomsky and Triandis. In contrast to Fodor, however, for Feldman universals are not immutable but undergo changes during the knower's life or during historical and cultural processes in society.

These two different approaches to universals that we have distinguished above, those of *universals as the bases for concepts* and of *universals as concepts*, require different theoretical treatments. If universals are conceived as the bases for concepts rather than concepts themselves then the question of their relationship with the environment must be raised. If they are conceived as concepts, it is their relationship with the knower's active involvement with the world that must be the subject of concern.

There is, finally, an additional issue that requires clarification. In psychology, the term 'universal' in the philosophical (i.e. ontological or conceptual) sense has tended to be confused with *universality* concerning the number of objects to which the universal applies. Although universals have been confused with numerical universality in both Chomsky's and Triandis's approaches, Feldman's (1980) theory demonstrates the point especially clearly. For Feldman universals are supposedly conceptual or ontological. In his unique–universal continuum a creative novelty sets out on a historical journey by the end of which it transforms into a new universal. However, the difference between creative novelty at the beginning of the journey and the universal at the end of the journey is defined merely by the number of people who adopt the novelty in their own behaviour or mental activities. Thus, while at the beginning the creative novelty was unique because it was the possession of a single individual, at the end it became universal because it was in the possession of others, possibly of all others. This confusion in psychology between universality in the numerical sense and universality in the conceptual or ontological sense appears to result from theoretical naivety. In the Platonic–Cartesian framework, since concepts were supposed to be totally immutable and all people were creatures of God, it was true by definition that everybody who is a human being must be in the possession of universals. So, transparently, all universals in the ontological sense were also universal in the numerical sense. In psychology, in contrast, the starting point of the inquiry has often been a search for *something* that is universal in the numerical sense. When *numerical* universality has been demonstrated—and very often, as Jahoda (1981) has pointed out, when it has only been assumed—the existence of an *ontological* universal has been inferred.

For Hegel, in contrast, the existence of a universal is not dependent on the number of people in possession of it, as was made clear in his example of such a universal as humanity. Using Hegel's position it is conceivable that a universal might be acquired by one person only, as is originally the case with any scientific discovery. Such universals, of course, become more elaborate through the knower's involvement with particulars, leading to more true and more concrete theories.

It is important that psychology should clarify for itself whether it is concerned with universals as the biological and psychological bases for concepts, or with universals as the concepts themselves, i.e. with knowledge itself. In either case it is essential that universals should be reconceptualised in developmental terms. If the focus of psychology is on the bases for concepts, then one should seek to explain relative stability, both in biology and psychology, where it exists, and why some behavioural and mental characteristics have become more stable than others. If the focus of psychology is on universals as concepts, it should seek to explain the relationships between relative stability and variability *with respect to the individual and societal development of knowledge.* The question, however, is whether psychologists can start using the idea of the universal in a truly interactive manner, or whether it would not be easier to dispense with the word 'universal' altogether, since the difficulty of dissociating universals from the static assumptions of the cognitivist may prove unsurmountable.

REFERENCES

Bronowski, J., 'New concepts in the evolution of complexity: stratified stability and unbounded plans', *Zygon*, 1970, *5*, 18–35.
Bruner, J., 'Review and prospectus', in B. Lloyd and J. Gay (eds.), *Universals of Human Thought* (Cambridge and London: Cambridge University Press, 1981).
Chomsky, N., *Cartesian Linguistics* (New York and London: Harper & Row, 1966).
Chomsky, N., 'Conditions on rules of grammar', in Cole, R.W. (ed.), *Current Issues in Linguistic Theory* (Bloomington and London: Indiana University Press, 1977).
Chomsky, N., 'Rules and representations', *The Behavioral and Brain Sciences*, 1980, *3*, 1–116.
Collins, F.H., *The Synthetic Philosophy of Herbert Spencer* (London: Williams and Norgate, 1901).
Comrie, B., *Language Universals and Linguistic Typology* (Oxford: Blackwell, 1981a).
Comrie, B., 'The formation of relative clauses', in B. Lloyd and J. Gay, (eds.), *Universals of Human Thought* (Cambridge and London: Cambridge University Press, 1981b).
Culler, J., *Saussure* (Hassocks: The Harvester Press, 1976).
Dasen, P., ' "Strong" and "weak" universals: sensori-motor intelligence and concrete operations', in B. Lloyd and J. Gay (eds.), *Universals of Human Thought* (Cambridge and London: Cambridge University Press, 1981).

Descartes, R., *Rules for the Direction of the Mind*, in Haldane, E.S. and Ross, G.R.T. (trs. and eds.), *The Philosophical Works of Descartes*, Vol. 1 (London and New York: Cambridge University Press, 1911).

Descartes, R., *Notes Directed Against A Certain Programme*, in Haldane, E.S. and Ross, G.R.T. (trs. and eds.), *The Philosophical Works of Descartes*, Vol. 1 (London and New York: Cambridge University Press, 1911).

Descartes, R., Letter to Mersenne, 16 June 1641, in Kenny, A. (trs. and ed.), *Descartes: Philosophical Letters* (Oxford: Clarendon Press, 1970).

Feldman, D.H., *Beyond Universals in Cognitive Development* (Norwood, N.J.: Ablex, 1980).

Finnegan, R., 'Literacy and literature', in B. Lloyd and J. Gay (eds.), *Universals of Human Thought* (Cambridge and London: Cambridge University Press, 1981).

Flavell, J., Comments on Beilin's 'The development of physical concepts', in T. Mischel (ed.), *Cognitive Development and Epistemology* (New York: Academic Press, 1971).

Fodor, J., *The Language of Thought* (New York: Crowell, 1975).

Fodor, J., *Representations* (Brighton: The Harvester Press, 1981).

Goodwin, B., 'Constructional biology', in G. Butterworth, J. Rutkowska and M. Scaife (eds.) *Evolution and Developmental Psychology* (Brighton: The Harvester Press, 1985).

Gopnik, A., 'Conceptual and semantic change in scientists and children: why there are no semantic universals', *Linguistics*, 1983, *21*, 163–79.

Gould, S.J., *Otogeny and Phylogeny* (Cambridge and London: The Belknap Press of Harvard University Press, 1977).

Hardy-Brown, J., 'Universals and individual differences: disentangling approaches to the study of language acquisition', *Developmental Psychology*, 1983, *19*, 610–24.

Hegel, G.W.F., *The Encyclopedia of the Philosophical Sciences*, Part 1, *The Science of Logic*, in Wallace, W. (trs.), *The Logic of Hegel* (London: Oxford University Press, 1873).

Jahoda, G., 'Pictorial perception and the problem of universals', in B. Lloyd and J. Gay (eds.), *Universals of Human Thought* (Cambridge and London: Cambridge University Press, 1981).

Lenneberg, E.H., *Biological Foundations of Language* (New York: Wiley, 1967).

Lewontin, R.C., 'Organism and environment', in H.C. Plotkin (ed.), *Learning, Development, and Culture* (Chichester: Wiley, 1982).

Marková, I., *Paradigms, Thought, and Language* (Chichester and New York: Wiley, 1982).

Plato, *Meno*, in E. Hamilton and H. Cairns (eds.), *The Collected Dialogues of Plato* (Princeton: Princeton University Press, 1961).

Ritchie, D.G., *Darwin and Hegel* (London: Swan Sonnenschein, 1893).

Schilcher, F. von and Tennant, N., *Philosophy, Evolution, and Human Nature* (London: Routledge & Kegan Paul, 1984).

Simon, H.A., *The Sciences of the Artificial* (Cambridge and London: MIT Press, 1969).

Snow, C.E., 'The development of conversation between mothers and babies', *Journal of Child Language*, 1977, *4*, 1–22.

Triandis, H., 'Some universals of social behavior', *Personality and Social Psychology Bulletin*, 1978, *4*, 1–6.

Vygotsky, L.S., *Thought and Language* (New York: Wiley, 1962).

ACKNOWLEDGEMENTS

I would like to acknowledge most valuable comments and suggestions on previous drafts of this chapter provided by Colin Wright, Arthur Still and Alan Costall.

14

The Programme of Phenomenology

Neil Bolton

THE FALSE PHENOMENOLOGICAL PSYCHOLOGY

The most popular view of phenomenology within psychology is to see it as being essentially concerned with conscious experience, with the subject's perception of the situation and with his feelings and introspections. Only the most extreme of behaviourists reject the necessity to take subjective experience into account; consequently, phenomenology can be safely assimilated into an empirical psychology in the form of an account of subjective experience along the lines of personal construct theory (Kelly, 1955), or as broadly supportive of the doctrine that reality is socially constructed (as individuals learn to pool their subjective viewpoints), or as a possibly useful adjunct to cognitive psychology's emphasis upon the role of hypothesis-testing in the construction of the world. A consensus appears to have emerged within contemporary psychology broad enough to encompass the conflicting armies of behaviourists and humanists: a recent president of the British Psychological Society gave this consensus his blessing in his Presidential Address (Hetherington, 1983).

There not only an agreement about the content of psychology, but about procedure. The construction of reality can be experimentally studied: the development of hypotheses, limitations of memory, and strategies of information-processing can be described and ultimately summarised through a theory which cuts across the old concerns of subjective experience versus actual behaviour. The programme of this empirical-cum-phenomenological psychology thus readily assumes a substantial material form. The intelligent machine becomes the working model for both behaviour and experience, for the development of computer programs enables us to define operationally the imprecise concepts of human psychology. As Mackay (1951) pointed out, it is useless to say in defence, 'Yes, but you will never get a machine to do X', because the exact delineation of what X is, involves an operational specification that could, conceivably, be embodied in a computer program. Thus, notions such as 'intentions', 'perception', 'memory', and so forth, can be rewritten, and we can understand how concepts regarded as relating to subjective states of mind can find their rightful place within a science of human behaviour (Boden, 1977). Moreover, the assumption can be made that this level of description of behaviour will one day be matched in some sense against a description at the level of neurophysiology; the two will be seen, in the language favoured by the Gestalt psychologists (Kohler, 1940) and by Piaget (1950), to be isomorphic or 'structurally equivalent'.

It is easy to understand how this consensus should be so appealing. The everyday language of mentalistic concepts can be retained because it can be transmuted into a powerful programme of experimental investigation, which, in turn, will ultimately be shown to have a basis in the physical world. There is a definite programme to be completed by a recognisable community of scholars. Of course, there are differences of emphasis within the paradigm, but these fade into insignificance in the face of the widespread agreement as to the proper subject matter of psychology and the methods appropriate to that subject matter. In view of this, any criticism of the fundamental assumptions of this cognitive-phenomeno-logical world-view are likely to be rapidly dismissed: the strategies employed in defence would themselves make an interesting PhD study, but the commonest response by far is, not surprisingly, 'But I have not *yet* come across any such fundamental criticism'.

There are, however, some good reasons for not taking these defensive reactions at their face-value. First, what we know of the history of science must make us sceptical about any theoretical framework as comprehensive and coherent as the one which dominates modern psychology; at least, caution should lead us to question our framework because there is no reason to believe that the psychological paradigm, in its development and possible decline, is likely to be different from other such perspectives on reality. Second, the very successes of a perspective depend just as much upon the limitations of the assumptions of the perspective as upon its freedom from assumptions. This is a postulate of cognitive psychology itself—the determination of perception by the interpretive framework—and we have no good reason, again, to exclude cognitive psychology from its own laws. Finally, what psychologists mean by the label, 'phenomenology', is strikingly at variance with what phenomenologists themselves mean by the word. As I hope to show shortly, what has been assimilated into psychology as 'consciousness' is, in certain fundamental respects, a contradiction of what consciousness in essence is. Now, this means that in so far as cognitive psychology claims to be a programme for describing and explaining the functioning of consciousness it rests upon a fundamental epistemological mistake, and this mistake cannot be corrected simply by the development of more sophisticated techniques.

In this chapter, therefore, I wish to examine, not the false phenomenology that has been found more and more acceptable as psychology has moved away from a narrow behaviourism, but the substance of a philosophical phenomenlogy that is just as much 'out of bounds' for the new psychology as for the old. I shall argue, as I and others (Bolton, 1978a, b; 1979; 1982a, b; Giorgi, 1970; Ashworth, 1981) have argued before, that a true assimilation of phenomenology to psychology forces a revision of our basic concepts and of the empirical programme of investigation.

TRUE AND FALSE PHENOMENOLOGY COMPARED

It is the concept of intentionality, developed in the works of Husserl (1911) and Merleau-Ponty (1962),˙ that at first examination appears to support the case for a parallel between phenomenology and cognitive psychology. Intentionality refers to the essential feature of consciousness that it is directed towards an object: all acts of perceiving, thinking, remembering, and so forth, have this feature, and from this we may conclude against any simple empiricist theory of consciousness —the mind is active in the construction of reality, so that what must be studied by psychology are the plans, concepts or schemata, by which reality becomes organised. The basic assumptions are then: perception is a constructive process; the process is to be studied as a series of acts (operations); the construction of reality is a cognitive process—emotion may provide the dynamics (in the form of drive or interference as irrational source of behaviour), but the two systems of cognition and emotion may be analysed independently.

These assumptions viewed from a genuine phenomenological perspective can, at best, be accepted as half-truths. They reflect, precisely, half the truth of the dictum that consciousness is essentially directed towards an object, namely, the half that belongs to the subject.

All the differences between cognitive psychology and phenomenology arise from the former assigning priority to the activity of the subject whereas the latter assigns priority, neither to the subject nor to the object (it is not a form of realism any more than it is a form of subjectivism), but to the 'directedness towards an object'. Subject and object are given equal value, as it were, in the determination of reality, for what is real is the product of an active subject and that which is accepted as transcending the activity of the subject. There would not be any object of consciousness without the activity of consciousness but to talk of it as object implies that it is other than that activity. It is an object of consciousness (an image, a thought, etc.) because it fulfils the intentionality of consciousness, but it fulfils the intentionality of consciousness because it allows that intentionality to be confirmed in something other than its own activity. Put less abstractly, we can and do make the distinction between the activity of cognition and that which confirms it; our very mistakes, as Husserl (1977) pointed out, are interludes within the general certainty of the world as confirmation of our thoughts.

Now, if this is so, it signifies that we perceive the world in a way that is more fundamental than that envisaged by cognitive psychology. Prior to and transcending the object as the outcome of an interpretation, we are capable of experiencing the object as expression of itself. If we could not experience this, intentionality would be unable to fulfil itself as interpetation. Heidegger (1971) gives voice to this conclusion:

> Not only must that in conformity with which a cognition orders itself be already in some way unconcealed. The entire *realm* in which this 'conformity to something' goes on must already occur as a whole in the unconcealed. . . . With all our correct representations we should get nowhere, we could not even pre-suppose that there is already manifest something to which we can conform ourselves, unless the unconcealedness of beings had already exposed us to, placed us in, that lighted realm in which every being stands for us and from which it withdraws. (p. 52)

It is this capacity to perceive 'the world as given' which is absent in the constructivist theory of perception, the theory which Merleau-Ponty (1962) challenged in his *Phenomenology of Perception* with the assertion that 'perception is not an act, but the background against which all our acts take place'. I have argued elsewhere (Bolton, 1982a) that this capacity of consciousness to allow the object to express its meaning constitutes the aesthetic aspect of experience—the aesthetic, then, may be properly conceived as a fundamental part of all knowing; it is the imagination placing us within the world of objects, not through a series of constructions by which a structure is extended and resolved, but by what Polanyi (1967) called a 'dwelling-in' the object. This 'indwelling' is to be understood as personal knowledge in the sense that what is produced is the outcome of my commitment to it as an identity against which my commitment can be measured. This is what we mean when we talk of the 'directedness of consciousness towards an object'.

For the cognitive theorist this directedness flows one way, towards the object which, then, cannot help but become an abstraction: it is created by my mental acts and the condition for its formation is a divorce between the acts and the object; knowing is standing back from something, freeing it from the self's idiosyncracies. What we know is at once created by us and distant from us. But adopt the view that the object is the ground of our acts, not their outcome, and we must admit that the knower is constituted in the act of knowing by the object as much as the object by the act. To talk of the world as constructed is as true (and as false) as talking of the person as constructed by the world, for self and world are jointly revealed to one another. I am defined by the world as I define the world.

Cognitive theory rests upon the mistake of taking one form of knowing—abstraction—as the model for all knowing (Bolton, 1982b). That abstraction is taken as paradigmatic is not surprising in view of the prevalence of the theory of abstraction (in various guises) in psychological theories themselves—in S-R theory, in Piaget's account of reflective abstraction, and in the sequential programs of information-theory (Bolton, 1972; 1977; 1978a). But, however significant the capacity of abstraction is in allowing us to distance self from objects and thus conceptualise them, it is only one form of thought and requires itself to be placed in the perspective of other forms in order that both its power and limitations should be apparent. What phenomenologists refer to as pre-reflective intelligence is the necessary basis for conceptual thought which never succeeds in making do without that openness to the world which is at the heart of our creativity. Cognition as constructive activity occurs within contexts established as the measure of that activity.

The second assumption, that the constructive process may be studied as a series of acts, is designed to delineate the province of psychology. This discipline forms itself by abstracting mental acts from their context—the world given to us by our involvement in it as that which can be known and valued. Modern psychology, for all the objectivism of its methods, condemns itself to be steeped in subjectivity by the very way in which it supposes that the domain of the mental can be isolated (as one might try to isolate a certain type of virus) from its responsibility and care for the truth of things. In this it is thoroughly Cartesian. This dualism is, oddly enough, nowhere more apparent than in physiological psychology, which reduces the body to a series of physical events that parallel the cognitive processes. (The body in phenomenology on the other hand (see especially Merleau-Ponty, 1962) is the condition for our being in the world and the mediator of our dialogue with it.) But dualism is only one consequence of psychologism—the reduction of the relation between knower and known to its subjective aspect. The symptoms of this disorder are everywhere: In the reduction of thinking to its strategies, of morality to social conditioning, of language to communication, of art to a moderate state of excitation. What is produced as a result of this study acquires the style of a technical language merely by the fact that it is divorced from the normal human concerns. Thus do psychologists become experts on the human condition!

The only radical alternative to this spurious science is to return to the phenomena themselves in order to develop a taxonomy for the psychological which relates it essentially to the concern for the truth and value of being. Psychology needs to ground itself, as Husserl (1948) pointed out, on a 'regional ontology'—a description of the different ways in which the world can be understood—in order that the empirical accounts of the development and functioning of the mind can be truthful. I have attempted to show (Bolton, 1982b) the force of a taxonomy whose essential elements are imagination, various kinds of abstraction, and faith. Imagination is the most fundamental of these, because it places us within the world as the field of our actions; abstraction is the most clearly powerful, because it results in the achievements of science and technology; and faith is the most necessary, because it is our quest for the ultimate coherence of our actions with the world.

These foundational concepts are at once technical and moral—the founding concepts of psychology cannot be otherwise, since human nature is neither a physical nor a social fact but exists as concern about its own possibility. This concern is unavoidable but is itself given as possibility and is thus not mechanically accomplished. Man cannot live without truth, Socrates said, but our intellectualism has led us to mistake the meaning of this assertion. It is not an assertion of the power of the rational–cognitive domain over the emotional but a testament to the continuity which exists between them. What we feel most strongly for is the truth of what we do, and in the truth of what we do reason and feeling are one. The third major error of cognitive theory lies in its intellectualism which reduces feeling and motivation to drive or to irrational residue. Thus it can accept as reasonable an account of cognition couched exclusively in terms of information-handling strategies and reinterpret emotional 'states' in terms of those strategies. The relation between learning and value is then seen as a purely extrinsic one, the mechanisms of learning being indifferently true for all value-contexts.

But this is not the case. The true meaning of learning follows from the nature of consciousness as that which is directed towards what can stand as its measure. We can talk interchangeably either of intentionality and transcendence in relation to the objective world or of care and respect in relation to the realm of values. For to know something is to respect it as a reference point for oneself, and it is only known if it is the outcome of our care. Caring *is* the active element in intentionality, respect the submission to reality experienced as transcendent. This is the meaning of learning, not some mechanism of reinforcement or equilibrium, for these are terms which only receive their meaning from our capacity to care and to respect. And we must insist that learning is a social phenomenon, but again not in any reductive sense, because social cooperation demands beings who can present to one another objects which can be cared for. Of course, learning can be mechanical and social forces can determine us without our consent, but to erect these as the cornerstones of a theory of learning is to consent to the aberration and not the norm; in this case the discipline itself becomes symptomatic.

Contemporary psychology represents the triumph of three influences that dominate the western mind: subjectivism, technology and intellectualism. It construes the mind as comprehensible entirely through a study of its subjective aspect; the life of the mind is seen as a series of operations, so that the success of the discipline rests upon our technical capacity to make explicit the structure of these operations; and this structure can be characterised in purely intellectual terms as, say, problem-solving, information-processing, etc. It is difficult to determine how problematic psychology is in the implementation of this programme (it is, of course, impossible to convince such psychologists that they are in error as they are safely ensconced within the paradigm), since it is one which generates a great deal of activity which can be satisfying in itself. The best form of criticism is to show the possibility of an alternative programme which differs systematically from that of cognitive psychology in challenging the three prejudices.

THE PROGRAMME OF PHENOMENOLOGICAL PSYCHOLOGY

It is true to say, I think, that whilst cognitive psychology has profusely materialised in countless empirical investigations, phenomenology has failed to consolidate itself on the empirical level, having had most recognition in psychiatry—there, chiefly as a therapy rather than a form of investigation. This is, indeed, not surprising in view of phenomenology's opposition to the idea of transforming the mind into a series of operational mechanisms, but it does raise the question: Can there be a phenomenological psychology? Granted that there can be a phenomenology determined by the nature of consciousness itself and that there ought to be some connection between this study and the experience and behaviour of persons in a variety of situations, how can theoretical phenomenology lead into an empirical programme if it denies the methodological mechanisms necessary to carry out empirical investigations, namely, the operational definition of variables which permits one to study them as mechanical process? The answer to this question can only be found in a radical reappraisal of the very meaning of empirical investigation in the human sciences.

Whilst the first question of modern psychology is undoubtedly: How do we come to know the world?, phenomenology asks: How is it that there is a world to be known? It may be said that the first question takes for granted that the world exists to be known and thus isolates knowledge and problematic, whereas the second question challenges both the experience of the world as taken-for-granted and our knowing it. But there is a further difference. What is problematic from the psychological perspective is the lack of evidence about the knowing of the world: we do not know how the world is known, but we take for granted not only that the world exists to be known, but also that we can know how it is known—experiments can be carried out and facts accumulated. But what is problematic for phenomenology about the knowing of the world is not to be resolved in *this* empirical sense: it is not a matter of tuning in our concepts more finely to the facts, for it is this very activity which is questionable. Remember that phenomenology seeks to find the context in which abstraction can make sense and cannot find its own justification within the realm of concepts thrown up by abstraction. For phenomenology, in its return 'to the things themselves', is an absolute empiricism and cannot accept the partial empiricism of abstraction. This means that phenomenological truth must be expressed in relation to the whole structure of experience and nothing less.

But how is attentiveness to the whole structure of experience translated into a methodology? I have argued that there are three principle components to this structure: imagination which enables us to enjoy the world as 'lived experience' and which defines the boundary between self and world; abstraction, by which we distance ourselves both from objects and from our actions in order to gain insight into their structures; and faith, which is 'ultimate concern' (Tillich, 1957), and which seeks the concordance of what is most meaningfully lived with what can be ultimately known. The difference between conventional empiricism and phenomenological empiricism is, therefore, that the former defines its methodology exclusively in terms of what can be known through abstraction, whereas the latter extends the idea of what can be known to include the other ways in which man exists in the world, chiefly, I believe, through imagination and through faith. Whilst normal science, with all its emphasis upon abstraction, is itself dependent upon imagination for its effectiveness and faith for its motivation, it rarely wishes to acknowledge this. In the physical sciences themselves this refusal is not methodologically damaging, but in the human sciences it results in an abbreviated perspective on the nature of experience and behaviour. To abide by Husserl's dictum that 'a true science follows the nature of what has to be investigated', the phenomenologically-minded human scientist must admit imagination, abstraction and faith as methodological criteria in his or her investigation.

Now, it is easy to see that a methodology is a set of rules for allowing the investigator to proceed with an investigation and that imagination and faith do not fall within this description. We use our imaginations and rely upon faith only when the customary rules fail us! And thus to insist that they should be present in an investigation is to subvert the customary meaning of a methodology. But there is no alternative but to insist upon this: in a genuinely phenomenological investigation, they must be present as expressions of concern that unite the investigator with the investigated. Against the isolation of investigator and investigated necessary to the success of abstraction alone, phenomenology sets the two together in their shared concern; against the partial perspective of abstraction, phenomenology sets the whole structure of experience as imagination, abstraction and faith. A shared concern for the coherence of experience and its ultimate meaningfulness is the only possible ideal for phenomenological methodology.

In normal perception, we see the figure but not the ground; in the methodology of cognitive science we see the force of abstraction, but not the ground from which it eternally arises and returns. Phenomenology asks of us that we see both ground and figure; it demands, in a sense, a reversal of conventional seeing. Similarly, whilst conventional human science assigns priority to pure research, and treats applied fields such as educational and clinical psychology as subservient to the principles established there (roughly following the methodology possible in the laboratory), phenomenology reverses this order of priority. Pure research must be understood within the parameters defined in the applied field. Let us now look at this spectrum of applied to pure.

PHENOMENOLOGY AS THERAPY

One very common way of viewing therapy is to take it as the necessary outcome of pure research into the normal functioning of the mind. Psychoanalysis and behaviour therapy provide good examples of such an approach: in both we start from a supposedly sound theoretical basis, which accounts for psychological functioning generally and in mechanical terms, to apply the discovered principles to disturbed cases. And whether we speak of conditioning or of defence mechanisms, it is assumed that both normal and abnormal states follow the same psychological laws. Individual cases can thus be treated by reference to a standard set of prescriptions—a particular kind of behaviour therapy on the one hand, reference to a dictionary of symbolic meanings on the other. For phenomenology, too, there is a continuity between behaviour we call normal and that which we judge abnormal. But it is a continuity born of the fact that we all share the problems of being human and the therapist succeeds because he or she is more aware of those problems, not because of superior working knowledge of the mechanics of the mind. Success will not depend upon knowledge of specific techniques or of specific and standard symbolic meanings, but on a capacity to return the individual to a condition in which the world as lived is in accord with consciousness of it.

For, as Habermas (1972) and Heaton (1972) have pointed out, disturbed conditions arise when some important part of conscious experience is 'split off' from the normal, direct involvement in the things of the world. Because of this, the person can no longer talk about this experience in a way that combines the rationality of consciousness with the immediacy of lived experience. Imagination and abstraction are no longer united so that there is no possibility of faith in the potential unity of one's own experience with the nature of the world. The part of experience that is split off has, of course, symbolic significance. All true symbols point in two ways at the same time; they point outwards to transcendent objects and inwards to the subject who constitutes those objects as meaningful. In this sense, they mark the boundary between subjectivity and objectivity. Our sanity depends upon our success in establishing the balance between the two, and we should remember as academics that there is a madness of objectivity as well as of subjectivity (Kierkegaard, 1941). The important point here, I think, is that the meaning of symbols is not determined in any straightforward way by either biological or social programming but arises within the whole context of human being as biological-cum-cultural phenomenon. Vygotsky (1978) has pointed out that beyond a certain stage of development, the child recognises that 'anything can stand for anything else' and this insight needs to be passed on to therapists who believe that the meanings of symbols are absolutely fixed. This has clear implications for therapy. It means that the therapist must discover with the client the meaning of the symbol, the place where the borderline has failed to hold, in such a way as to restore the balance between life and thought. This will not be accomplished through consultation with a theoretical diction- ary, it will only arise out of respect for the individual bestowal of meaning and out of concern for its integration within the rational activity of consciousness. Habermas refers to this as a process of enlightenment through self-reflection and defines this an 'act through which the subject frees itself from a state in which it had become an object for itself' (1972, p. 247).

There are two major dangers when psychologists discuss therapy and mental illness. The one is to romanticise such illness, to see the intensity of experience as an ideal when set against the drab routine of everyday life. The other is to see it simply as aberration, as an extreme departure, and this view tacitly romanticises everyday life with its lack of extremes and intense feelings. We avoid both dangers if we state that the significance of mental illness is to show the difficulty of being human, the constant need to balance thought against feeling and inner against outer reality, if faith in one's purpose is to be retained. The therapeutic process reveals, not the treatment of pathological conditions or a poetic ideal, but the nature of human existence with its essential, creative tensions—tensions which are lost through both mental illness and conventional, everyday life. Because therapy shows us this, it shows the condition to which research must be ultimately referred. This condition can only be described as the context in which research can make sense, since research is formalisation which is always partial, for it can never dispense with the human need for faith: it succeeds only in so far as it leaves that untouched.

PHENOMENOLOGY AS APPLIED RESEARCH

This is why, of course, there is an inevitable tension within applied research. It is not because of any difficulty of translating the pure into the applied, but because the applied researcher wishes to qualify shared concern by an appeal to 'things as they are'. The method of participant observation, in which the researcher is both at one with the investigated and an observer of them, shows the borderline which is crossed when one passes from 'fellow human being' to researcher. There is a reversal of the natural order of social life, for now he participates in order to observe, and he seeks to isolate a realm of facts which can function independently of the ontological and existential concerns of both the investigated and the investigator. But there is now agreement on policy in applied research; the qualitative researcher tries to explore the land from which he came, the quantitative researcher does not wish to abandon the marvellous gadgetry of objective investigation.

MacMurray (1961) has shown the necessary relation between these two forms of knowledge, which he calls personal and impersonal. He concludes that personal knowledge is shared concern and requires no external justification, but that impersonal knowledge, which seeks to establish the facts and has to keep its distance from ordinary human involvement, always requires to be justified through reference to shared concern. One might say: the advances in understanding that come about through the application of operational techniques must always relate to human concerns for the value of life which themselves transcend all such techniques. And is this not a formula for the continuation of applied research in its present form, for we can be as impersonal as we wish as long as there is some reference, at the end of the day, to the higher ideals? I think not. We will not justify a science of human beings if our programme presupposes an opposition between the activity of being a scientist and that of a human being. Kelly (1955) saw this, but erred in believing the answer lay in human beings being treated as scientists, for there is far more to human being than being a scientist. Human science must be founded upon human being. It must take as its focus that which is central to human being, and in doing this it will be an applied science, for that which is central to human being develops human being.

To say that what characterises human being is shared concern has several implications for an applied phenomenology. Sharing signifies that we define together what is true and of value. Just as the survival of the species involved the sharing of food and defence (Leakey, 1981), so man's survival as a truthful and moral being depends upon individuals sharing with one another and thus constituting what they hold to be the truths and principles transcendent to them. These truths are not a matter of indifference to us, but the means by which we define our hold on reality; they have existential and ontological status because they are expressions of the way we live in the world. There is no separation of the intellect and of the emotions in these truths. We are, after Freud, familiar with the idea that the various expressions of a man's personality are part of a coherent structure (even with its conflicts), so that there are correspondences between emotional and intellectual life. Phenomenological truths are of this order except that they have reference, not to an 'inner man', but to man in his philosophical dimension of 'being-in-the-world'. And, finally, there is no validation of shared concern other than shared concern; there can be no reference to independent criteria or to methodological sophistication as the ultimate course of appeal for the worth of an investigation. There is no methodological alternative to reflection.

What matters, then, in applied research is not a particular set of practices on the part of the investigator or a particular set of conditions of the investigated that must be put right, but the furtherance of the activity of self-reflection, in which participants question and then define the truths and values which they take as their reference points. All fact-gathering is subsidiary to this philosophical purpose. And all methodologies fail unless they culminate in the kind of thought which kindles the imagination and restores faith. We are familiar with Hume's dictum that works which contain no quantitative analysis or causal reasoning should be cast upon the fire, but equally we are all too familiar with that kind of research which contains nothing else. Let us then counter Hume with a challenge to the drabness of mechanical research: if we take in our hand any research report, let us ask, 'Does it contain any metaphor or idea which reveals a reality deeper than the conventional one? No. Does it excite you to a moral involvement in the affairs with which it deals? No.' Commit it then to the flames, for it is nothing but information that will soon be superseded by more information.

We can say that applied human science is necessarily a moral science because it permits us to develop ourselves as human beings. Now, many applied scientists who do not subscribe to the views outlined above would concur with this view. But they would see the enlargement of the moral realm made possible by the accumulation of evidence through the application of appropriate methodology by impartial researchers (see, for example, Broadbent, 1961). They see no need for the therapeutic statement in which truth is not a matter of intellect alone but of the whole person seeking a course to steer by. Indeed, the very prejudices of these scientists—their subjectivism, intellectualism and faith in technology—lead them to judge therapeutic statements as outside the boundary of science, belonging perhaps to literature. And, of course, so they are, if human science is defined by these prejudices. It is important at this point to note the interdependence of statements of proper methodology and statements of the true content of a discipline. At any stage in the development of a science the two go hand in hand. The way in which psychology has defined perception or learning or thinking is related to assumptions about the proper way to study such phenomena—as interior cognitive mechanisms. Therefore, if phenomenological psychology is going to offer an alternative programme of investigation, it will be based upon quite different notions of the nature of psychological phenomena.

PHENOMENOLOGY AS CRITICAL SCIENCE

In fact, the major phenomenological concepts themselves present a coherent challenge to psychological concepts. Merleau-Ponty's (1962) understanding of perception, Heidegger's (1971) view of language, the idea of play for Gadamer (1975), Marcel's (1950) 'intersubjectivity', reject totally the psychologism and intellectualism of the equivalent concepts in cognitive psychology. The most serious error that psychologists make about phenomenology is to see it as an illumination of the conventional psychological concepts through introspection, as though there were certain minor faults only with these concepts and nothing amiss with their essential nature. However, the illumination phenomenology offers does not leave these concepts intact. Phenomenology is a rethinking of psychological concepts, a disturbance of all that we have unfortunately inherited from both Cartesianism and British empiricism. When Merleau-Ponty defines perception as the background to our acts of interpretation or when Heidegger speaks of language as the revelation of being, what is rejected is the dualism of subject and object, or rather the way of formulating this which the two philosophical movements have in common. For the phenomenologist no priority can be accorded to the Cartesian 'I' or the brute reality of empiricism; self and world are jointly articulated. What a dry statement that appears to be! But it formulates the condition of revelation of being through language and perception.

Consider, as a particular example, the concept of play. This has been defined in psychology in various ways, as the means by which inner conflicts are expressed, as fantasy, as a means of adaptation. No one of these definitions captures the whole of play, because play can be all of these and no doubt more. Gadamer finds the essence of play to be the 'to-and-fro', the experience of movement, as when we talk of the play of light, a play on words, and so forth. I have argued elsewhere that the movement of play that is significant from the point of view of the development of the individual is that which occurs around the boundary-line between self and world, that play helps to maintain this line, and that transitional objects and the symbolic function arise out of this activity of boundary maintenance (Bolton, 1983). The phenomenological notion of play refers, then, not to a psychological mechanism but to the way in which the person exists in the world. And all phenomenological concepts have this feature: they refer to the original experience in which self and world are constituted and from which the polarities of abstract thought themselves emerge. There is no psychologism in these concepts, no intellectualism either, because there is no false separation of thought from feeling, and there is no mechanism, no operational specification, for them, for they establish the possibility of there being a world within which we can operate.

For the cognitive psychologists this last assertion amounts to an admission of failure; if phenomenology is not reducible to or isomorphic with a set of mechanical operations, they will conclude either that it should be excluded from serious consideration or that it need not be considered because it does not really exist. I think that phenomenologists need not be as brusque as this in dismissing empirical methodology, which, after all, can bring to clarity significant phenomena. However, they must be as robust in rejecting the idea that methodological sophistication provides the means of judging the significance (or existence) of phenomena. But this returns us to our original question: can there be a phenomenological psychology, an empirical study of man based upon a true understanding of the phenomenon of being human? My own answer to this question is to say that there can be no other true psychology than a phenomenologically-guided psychology. However, I hold that phenomenology guides, not by providing a methodology for collecting data, but through developing a form of reflection by which the conceptual and existential significance of these data can be realised.

Empirical psychology sees itself as a natural science and it has become, in a variety of ways, the study of the mind's contingency, abstraction showing how the mind can be construed as subordinate to this or that class of events. There is no doubt that human beings *are* constrained by any number of such events, which can be traced ultimately to biological or social structures, and that useful information can be gathered. For the phenomenologist, on the other hand, abstraction is only one form of thought, and it is preceded by imagination with its metaphors and transcended by concepts which place us as being in the world. If empirical psychology is the study of the mind's contingency, phenomenology is the study of its freedom, phenomenological reflection showing how abstraction articulates with the 'plunging forward' of the metaphorical imagination and discovers its only possible repose within concepts which return thought to life. Recall what Merleau-Ponty (1962) says of the relationship between the mind's contingencies and its necessary freedom:

Human existence will force us to revise our usual notion of necessity and contingency, because it is the transformation of contingency into necessity by the act of carrying forward. All that we are, we are on the basis of a *de facto* situation which we appropriate to ourselves and which we ceaselessly

transform by a sort of *escape* which is never an unconditioned freedom.
(pp. 17I–1)

The idea that guides contemporary cognitive psychology,
the mind as an intelligent machine, is, of course, a metaphor,
on the basis of which the researcher builds his abstractions.
Necessarily, phenomenology denies the ultimate validity of
this metaphor because, as we have seen, abstraction itself
requires to be placed within the broader context supplied by
other forms of thought. But we know that a metaphor is not
invalidated because it is partial or even because people do not
have an explicit recognition of it as metaphor; the cognitive
psychologist is akin to the lover who believes his lady to be 'like
a rose'—that she is, implicitly, *not* a rose is just what is valued.
Thus, the mistake the cognitive psychologist is likely to fall into
is not that of acting on the basis of a metaphor but theorising
his metaphor away, by making the rose an abstraction, as it
were. It is in this way that the vision of cognitive psychology is
perversely narrow, phenomena being defined and investigated
only to the extent that they are abstractions. The difference or
contrast, so essential to the life of the metaphor, is lost.

To conclude, phenomenological inquiry is not a technique
aimed at particular aspects of experience, at individuals, or
even the life-world; it is the discipline concerned with the
necessary structure that our thinking about experience must
take if it is to make conceptual and existential sense. The
exercise of phenomenological thinking should guide an
empirical psychology by reshaping psychological theory in the
only radical way that such theory can be reshaped—by
showing how its limits coincide with the task of developing
human sensitivity and concern.

REFERENCES

Ashworth, P.D., 'Equivocal alliances of phenomenological psycho-
  logists', *Journal of Phenomenological Psychology*, 1981, *12*, 1–31.
Boden, M.A., *Artificial Intelligence and Natural Man* (Sussex:
  Harvester Press, 1977).
Bolton, N., *The Psychology of Thinking* (London: Metheun, 1972).

Bolton, N., *Concept Formation* (Oxford: Pergamon Press, 1977).

Bolton, N., 'The phenomenology of thinking', in A. Burton and J. Radford (eds.), *Thinking in Perspective* (London: Methuen, 1978a).

Bolton, N., 'Piaget and pre-reflective experience', in B. Curtis and W. Mays (eds.), *Phenomenology and Education* (London: Methuen, 1978b).

Bolton, N., 'Being objective about the mind', in N. Bolton (ed.), *Philosophical Problems in Psychology* (London: Methuen, 1979).

Bolton, N., 'The lived world: imagination and the development of experience', *Journal of Phenomenological Psychology*, 1982a, *13*, 1–18.

Bolton, N., 'Forms of thought', in G. Underwood (ed.), *Aspects of Consciousness*, Vol. 3 (London: Academic Press, 1982b).

Bolton, N., *Forms of Thought: A study in phenomenology and education* (forthcoming).

Broadbent, D.E., *Behaviour* (London: Methuen, 1961).

Gadamer, H.G., *Truth and Method* (London: Sheen and Ward, 1975).

Giorgi, A., *Psychology as a Human Science: A phenomenologically-based approach* (New York: Harper & Row, 1970).

Habermas, J., *Knowledge and Human Interests* (London: Heinemann, 1972).

Heaton, J.M., 'Symposium on saying and showing in Heidegger and Wittgenstein', *Journal, British Society for Phenomenology*, 1972, *3*, 42–5.

Heidegger, M., *Poetry, Language, Thought* (New York: Harper & Row, 1971).

Hetherington, J., 'Sacred cows and white elephants', *Bulletin of British Psychological Society*, 1983, *36*, 273–80.

Husserl, E., *Philosophy as Rigorous Science*, Logos, 1 (1910–11), 289–341. (New York: Harper Torchbooks, 1965.)

Husserl, E., *Experience and Judgement* (London: Routledge & kegan Paul, 1948).

Husserl, E., *Phenomenological Psychology* (The Hague: M. Nijhoff, 1977).

Kelly, G.A., *The Psychology of Personal Constructs* (New York: Norton, 1955).

Kohler, W., *Dynamics in Psychology* (New York: Liveright, 1940).

Leakey, R.E., *The Making of Mankind* (London: Michael Joseph, 1981).

MacKay, D.M., 'Mindlike behaviour in artefacts', *British Journal of Philosophical Science*, 1981, *2*, 105–21.

MacMurray, J., *Persons in Relation* (London: Faber & Faber, 1961).

Marcel, G., *The Mystery of Being* (London: Harvill Press, 1980).

Merleau-Ponty, M., *The Phenomenology of Perception* (London:

Routledge & Kegan Paul, 1962).

Piaget, J., *The Psychology of Intelligence* (London: Routledge & Kegan Paul, 1950).

Polanyi, M., *The Tacit Dimension* (London: Routledge & Kegan Paul, 1967).

Tillich, P., *Dynamics of Faith* (London: Allen & Unwin, 1957).

Index